ST. [
SCH[
1[
YOU[

D0947018

WILLIAM F. MAAG LIBRARY
YOUNGSTOWN STATE UNIVERSITY

ST. ELIZABETH HOSPITAL
SCHOOL OF NURSING LIBRARY
1044 BELMONT AVENUE
YOUNGSTOWN, OHIO....44505

# MORAL TREATMENT
## in Community Mental Health

ST. ELIZABETH HOSPITAL
SCHOOL OF NURSING LIBRARY
1044 BELMONT AVENUE
YOUNGSTOWN, OHIO....44505

# MORAL TREATMENT
## in Community Mental Health

By **J. Sanbourne Bockoven, M.D.**
*Superintendent, Solomon Mental Health Center,*
*Lowell, Massachusetts*

SPRINGER PUBLISHING COMPANY, INC.
NEW YORK

Copyright, © 1972

Springer Publishing Company, Inc.
200 Park Avenue South, New York City, 10003

Library of Congress Catalog Card Number: 70-189446
International Standard Book Number: 0-8261-1280-3
Printed in USA

RC
480.5
.B6
1972

In appreciation of

Robert W. Hyde, M.D. and Harry C. Solomon, M.D.,
without whose tutelage and encouragement
this work would not have been written.

WILLIAM F. MAAG LIBRARY
YOUNGSTOWN STATE UNIVERSITY
11152

# Acknowledgments

In both parts of this volume there is much that developed out of discussions with Dr. Robert W. Hyde, now director of research at the Vermont State Hospital in Waterbury. The material on Butler Health Center and the experiences with milieu rehabilitation benefited greatly from discussions with Dr. Richard H. York, currently chief psychologist at Corrigan Mental Health Center in Fall River, Massachusetts. Considerable material on Worcester State Hospital was obtained from Dr. Bardwell Flower's generous loan of his memory. Dr. Flower retired from the superintendency of Worcester State Hospital in 1969, and is presently consultant to mental health programs in the Rutland, Vermont, area. As from the beginning of our association, Dr. Harry C. Solomon remains an enthusiastic consultant to my historical endeavors. He retired as Massachusetts Commissioner of Mental Health in 1967 and is now consultant to state and veterans' mental health services.

The quoted material on pages 161 to 164 in Chapter X is reprinted, with permission, from "The American Psychiatric Association in Relation to American Psychiatry," by Harry C. Solomon, in *The American Journal of Psychiatry, 115*, No. 1, 1958, pp. 7-8. Some of this chapter was adapted from Solomon Mental Health Center's *Annual Reports* for fiscal 1967 and 1968. Both reports were of my authorship.

Chapter XI was partly adapted, with permission, from my

article, "The Moral Mandate of Community Psychiatry in America," printed in *Psychiatric Opinion, 3,* No. 1, 1966.

Pages 217 to 222 of Chapter XII are adapted, with permission, from an article of mine entitled "Challenge of the New Clinical Approaches" in *The American Journal of Occupational Therapy, XXII,* No. 1, pp. 23-25; and pages 222 to 227 of the same chapter are adapted, with permission, from my article in the same journal, *XXV,* No. 5, pp. 223-225, entitled "Legacy of Moral Treatment—1800's to 1910."

Chapter XIII was adapted from "Milieu Rehabilitation" in *Milieu Rehabilitation for Physical and Mental Handicaps,* by Robert W. Hyde, J. Sanbourne Bockoven, Harold W. Pfautz, and Richard H. York, and printed for Butler Mental Health Center in 1962. Investigation and publication were supported by Research and Demonstration Grant No. 182 from the Office of Vocational Rehabilitation, Department of Health, Education, and Welfare, Washington, D.C.

Chapter XIV was adapted, with permission, from "Community Psychiatry: A Growing Source of Social Confusion," an article by me which was printed in *Psychiatry Digest, 29,* March, 1968, pp. 51-60.

Chapter XV was adapted, with permission, from "Community Mental Health: A New Search for Social Orientation," an article by me, published in *Psychiatric Opinion, 6,* No. 2, 1969, and reprinted in *Mental Hygiene, 54,* No. 1, 1970.

The substance of the first nine chapters of this book first appeared in the August and September issues of the *Journal of Nervous and Mental Disease* in 1956 and were reprinted by permission of the Williams & Wilkins Company, Baltimore, Maryland. At that time, moral treatment was not a topic in which psychiatrists had any particular interest. Indeed, were it not for the historical perspectives of Drs. Paul Yakovlev and Nolan D. C. Lewis, the book would not have seen print.

I am grateful to my son, Peter M. Bockoven, for the care he gave in preparing the Bibliography.

I owe much to Dorothy Lewis, my editor at Springer Publishing Company, for her perceptive contributions, which greatly improved the readability of the last six chapters.

J.S.B.

# Preface

Nine years have passed since the initial publication of *Moral Treatment in American Psychiatry* in book form. During that period, the author's long-standing respect for moral treatment has been greatly enhanced through personal experience in developing a community mental health program. From this experience grew a new enthusiasm for moral treatment as a concept whose goals are both recognized and attainable by most of the people of any community. The relevance of moral treatment as a source of encouragement to present-day mental health endeavors compelled me to write the new material in this book.

The original *Moral Treatment in American Psychiatry* appears here in the first nine chapters, and should again prove heartening to those who have kept faith in their fellow men as agents of good will with an earnest desire to alleviate distress. The new material, an examination of issues and goals in a distinctly modern context, appears in Chapters X through XV. It begins with sketches of five different institutional programs that have attempted to apply the moral treatment idea within the framework of twentieth century science (Chapter X). In the following chapter, perspective is shifted to a hidden and hence damaging conflict between scientific elitist values in the training of psychiatrists and the fundamental cultural values of the American people as reflected in their political institutions. In Chapter XII, perspective again changes to establish a link between early moral treatment and modern occupational therapy. The goal here is to prevent further neglect of occupational therapy as a valuable source of attitudes and practices much needed in community work.

The theme of neglect and its correction is then pursued in another context (Chapter XIII), which describes the attitudes and practices of a rehabilitation teamwork project developed at Butler Health Center in Providence, Rhode Island, by Robert W. Hyde, Richard H. York, Harold Pfruty and the Center's staff in the late 1950's.

The last two Chapters (XIV and XV) change focus to examine the mental health movement from a social point of view. Problems arising from program misrepresentation and public misunderstanding are discussed by comparing two sets of expectations: the public's belief that it will benefit from new services provided by technical specialists, and the mental health worker's belief that patients will benefit from changes which education and consultation bring about in public opinion towards deviance. These chapters also seek to reorient perspectives by citing the enormous needs of *local* governments for resources which will enable them to provide assistance at the vitally-important community level.

*Lowell, Massachusetts*                         J. SANBOURNE BOCKOVEN, M.D.
*January, 1972*

# Contents

xi

# MORAL TREATMENT
## in Community Mental Health

# I

## Mental Hospitals:
## The Problem of Fulfilling
## Their Purpose

What is a mental hospital? Is it a permanent home for the insane and no different from what used to be called an insane asylum? Is it a place where people go for operations or medicines which cure certain kinds of illnesses? Or is it a place where people go to talk with psychiatrists about disturbing personal problems? There is today a growing volume of literature, both fiction and non-fiction, which seeks to elucidate the problems of individual failure and unhappiness by presenting them as understandable and solvable in terms of modern dynamic psychiatry. Science news reports, on the other hand, are keeping the citizen up to date on the development of wonder drugs or other medical and surgical treatments which cure mental disorders.

For the average citizen, there are many indications that medical science has already conquered or is very near conquering mental illness, but he also knows that from time to time the press has a great deal to say about bad conditions in mental hospitals. The massive collection of brick buildings, isolated from the rest of the community, several miles from town is still unknown to him. The sheer size and number of the buildings demonstrate that large numbers of people have to be kept locked up. This fact is difficult to reconcile with the indications that modern psychiatry knows how to cure mental illness. It serves

1

to intensify the feeling of dread which has always been associated with the word asylum.

The typical mental hospital as it exists in America today can be better understood if described and discussed in much the same terms that one would use in telling about a place such as a resort hotel, a naval vessel, a military post, or a university where he had lived for a period of time.

The typical mental hospital impresses a visitor approaching its grounds as having something of the appealing quality of a college campus, with the exception that there are almost no people passing to and fro on the walks. The administration building, in particular, differs little from that of a college. Its interior has an appearance of good taste and dignity, but again it is strangely quiet.

It is not until one enters the wards where the patients live that one feels the impact of what it means to be a patient in a typical mental hospital. Contrary to one's expectations, ward after ward may be passed through without witnessing the violent, the grotesque, or the ridiculous. Instead, one absorbs the heavy atmosphere of hundreds of people doing nothing and showing interest in nothing. Endless lines of people sit on benches along the walls. Some have their eyes closed; others gaze fixedly at the floor or the opposite wall. Occasionally, a head is turned to look out a window or to watch someone coming back from the toilet to take his place on a bench. All in all, it is a scene of inertness, listlessness, docility and hopelessness. Not so bad as might have been expected, one may think. Of course, there are worse wards where people lie on the floor naked and attendants are kept busy mopping up human excreta. Then there are intrepid patients who approach the visitor and plead for him to intercede in their behalf to help them get out of the hospital. And then again, someone may pace the floor who mutters to himself and thereby breaks the monotony. Or there may be a sudden chill of excitement when someone breaks into angry shouting for no apparent reason at all.

The visitor may well feel restless and irritated by the apathy of the patients and their willingness to waste these hours of their lives in meaningless tedium. His irritation may lead to his asking questions. If so, he learns that the attendant is proud of the ward because it is quiet and no mishaps have occurred while he was on duty; because the floor is clean; because the patients are prompt and orderly in going to and from meals. The visitor finds that the scene which appalls him with the emptiness and pointlessness of human life is regarded by the attendant as good behavior on the part of the patients. Thus introduced to the outlook of institutional psychiatry as it is practiced today, the visitor may well be puzzled, for there is little indication that it has anything to do with the psychiatry of current popular literature with its accent on hope and its accounts of enriching human life and showing the way to individual happiness. He must strain his imagination to see how the surrender of actually thousands of people to abject despair and inertia could possibly represent an improvement in their mental condition. On the contrary, he can envision himself going out of his mind if forced to spend many days in such a setting.

The more intimately acquainted a visitor becomes with the mental hospital, the sooner he reaches the final realization that it is engaged solely in the business of providing the physical needs and preserving the physical health and safety of rudderless, despairing people. He may come to admire the efficiency with which the basic operations of feeding, clothing, bathing, and laundering are performed. But he will wonder at the absence not only of treatment in the psychiatric sense but of any regimen whatsoever that the average layman would regard as conducive to mental health. He will learn that every patient is examined by a physician and given a psychiatric diagnosis. He will also learn that some newly admitted patients receive electric shock. But he cannot escape the overwhelming fact that patients numbered in the thousands receive no treatment for their mental disorders.

If the visitor talks with the physician and asks questions, he may be told that no treatment has yet been discovered which will cure the vast majority of the patients. Another physician trained in modern dynamic psychiatry may tell him that most of the patients could be treated with psychotherapy but that there are no psychotherapists available. Still another may tell him that one-third to one-half of the patients no longer need to be in the hospital because their illness has subsided. They remain in the hospital, he says, because there is no place for them to go and no one will give them a job. The superintendent will more than likely tell him that the hospital is crowded with more patients than it was built to care for, and that the hospital is badly understaffed and in need of many more attendants, nurses, social workers, and psychiatrists than the State budget provides or can be expected to provide. The visitor is then given to understand from the superintendent that the hospital as it is does not meet the needs of the patients, but the superintendent may also tell him that everything is being done for the patients that can be done in the way of cure of their mental illnesses.

The visitor can see for himself that the patients are dealt with by the hospital personnel on a mass basis and not as individuals. The patients are moved like an army from their sleeping quarters to their sitting places, to their eating places, and back to their sitting places. Movement occurs only in connection with getting out of bed, eating, and going back to bed.

There are some exceptions, for a number of patients do work in the various service centers of the hospitals such as the kitchen and the laundry. Others may work on the hospital farm or on the hospital grounds. There may be other patients who are allowed out of doors to take a walk in the fresh air. And there may be a select few patients who go to the occupational therapy department, where they are taught to make something with their hands. But even those patients, who do more than spend their days sitting, show by their expressionless faces and reluctance to speak that they have become accustomed to loneliness.

From observation of the great mass of patients, the visitor cannot help but be impressed with their obedience and conformity to the wishes of the hospital authorities. "But why," he may ask, "would the authorities wish the patients to lead an inactive, uncommunicative, lonely existence?" The answer he finds is that it is necessary to prevent the patients from exciting

one another and creating a bedlam. The hospital authorities
regard their chief objective to be protection of the patient from
insane acts harmful to himself or others. All hospital personnel
who come into contact with patients are taught to be constantly
on the lookout for impending mishaps. They must also be on
the alert to prevent the patients from getting hold of any article
which might conceivably be used as a tool of destruction. Matches
are not allowed, for a patient might set himself afire. Patients
are not allowed to shave themselves lest they hide razor blades
with which to cut their throats. Belts are not allowed lest
patients hang themselves. Checker games are not allowed lest
the patients attempt to swallow the checkers and choke. Every
effort is made to prevent the recurrence of any dangerous act
committed by any patient at any time in the past, and to
anticipate any new way of committing one which might be
invented in the future. (This might seem to rest on the theory
that removal of all opportunity or occasion for insane acts or
insane talk will eventually break the patient of insane habits
and behavior.) The patients are handled as though their insanity
were entirely due to an internal disorder and had nothing to do
with the effects of external events on their emotions. Abuse of
patients by personnel is strictly forbidden for obvious human
reasons and not because it is thought that abuse has any effect
on their illness.

There is total absence within the domain of the typical
mental hospital of opportunity to participate in or give attention
to any of the activities with which the members of any free
community occupy themselves. Patients have neither the materials
nor the freedom of movement to develop their talents or acquire
skills, nor to have the experiences of ordinary life. They have
nothing in their current lives to exchange with one another,
either in the realm of material objects or of observations, that
is not a tedious repetition of something already known to all.
There is also total absence of application of any of the principles
of mental hygiene in the day to day program of living in the
hospital. There is no work; there is no play; there is no program
of living.

The forced non-participation in human affairs of the mentally ill would necessarily seem to be based on certain knowledge that the mentally ill are wholly lacking in social intelligence, are totally incapable of perceiving the rights of others and are completely unable to learn to be members of society. The extreme caution exercised in the control of patients must be based on some such assumptions. These assumptions are, of course, in accord with the concept that mental illnesses are malignant, ineradicable diseases which totally destroy the capacity of the individual to behave like a human being or to be a person in any sense of the word.

One who visits the typical mental hospital will not find, however, that the hospital staff holds such a concept of mental illness. On the contrary, he will find that small-scale endeavors are made to provide the patients with entertainments and recreational opportunities which recognize their sensibilities as persons. He will learn that the extreme caution and the stringent restrictions placed on the vast majority of the patients are necessities resulting from the limited resources of the hospital in terms of personnel and facilities. The hospital has, in short, barely sufficient resources to discharge the minimal responsibility of preserving the patients from physical injury.

The visitor may detect a serious misunderstanding in the relation of the hospital to its source of financial support—the citizenry at large. The citizen assumes that the medical specialists who operate the public mental hospitals know that the wretched poverty of normal life activities in the hospital is an ineviitable consequence of the diseased mind. The medical director of the hospital, on the other hand, assumes that the citizenry is not interested in giving money or time to provide mentally ill patients with a fuller, busier, more worthwhile life. He regards the public disinterest as inevitable. The result of this impasse is that patients are seriously demoralized by the disrespect they suffer in being compelled to live subhuman lives. Indeed, it is difficult to find an example of members of lower species being compelled to suffer the indignity of functioning so far beneath their own level.

The foregoing account refers to many of the conditions of life in the hospital which prevent patients from taking part in practically all the activities engaged in by other people. Removal of these negative conditions constitutes a first and vitally important step toward raising the mental hospital to a level where it can perform the function for which it exists, namely, that of restoring the capacity of its patients to resume life outside the hospital.

The most damaging negative condition of the mental hospital is that which derives from what may fittingly be called the closed door policy. This policy not only locks patients in, but also locks out the mentally well members of society whose participation in hospital life can bring the interests and healthful breath of normality of the outside community into the hospital. The mingling of outsiders with patients does away with the deteriorating effects of monotony; it raises patients to their rightful status as human beings by demonstrating that they are recognized as worthy of being associates of citizens in good standing.

The mental hospital that welcomes outsiders within its walls and publicizes the need of its patients for normal human contacts has made an important step toward raising its standards of care. Outsiders who become volunteer workers soon recognize the multitudinous needs of patients and communicate them to the rest of the community. Sooner or later there will be a flow of goods into the hospital: books, magazines, playing cards, checkers, pictures, sewing materials, clothing, hot plates, coffee percolators, tea pots, radios, phonographs, and pianos. Besides material goods, outsiders will give time as instructors in such activities as dancing, sewing, and cooking.

As outsiders become better acquainted with the patients, they come to develop a personal interest in particular patients whom they may take on shopping trips and invite to their homes.

As a group, the volunteers may organize as a society which can raise funds for the benefit of patients.

The activities of volunteers greatly increases the traffic in and out of wards. This, in turn, leads to the discovery that locked doors are not only inconvenient but unnecessary. Patients who

WILLIAM F. MAAG LIBRARY
YOUNGSTOWN STATE UNIVERSITY

would ordinarily try to escape become more interested in the new activities than in running away. Along with the unlocking of doors comes a relaxation of other restrictions and rules which become not only too difficult to administer in a setting of activity, but also unnecessary. As patients regain contact with the community through their new friends, they not only learn of opportunities for jobs, but experience the advantage of being introduced to a prospective employer by a volunteer.

Adoption of an open-door policy is the first step toward raising the standards of care in a mental hospital. Equally important is the adoption of a policy of self-examination on the part of the administrative staff of the hospital in the interests of learning how its traditional functioning as a dictatorship impedes the effectiveness of the hospital personnel. Thought must be given to the advantages to be gained from democratic procedures which facilitate communication from below to above and, vice versa, make the knowledge and experience of those in top positions accessible to those dealing directly with patients. Freedom of expression and participation in policy determination by attendants stimulates their initiative and paves the way for the formation of patient organizations. The inclusion of patient organizations as responsible bodies having a role in the administrative affairs of the hospital is a powerful stimulus in motivating patients to acquire the social and political skills which are indispensable to successful living in the community.

The central theme of mental hospital improvement is removal of barriers to the development of all the positive assets of the mentally ill; there must be the maximum possible degree of freedom and access to whatever means help the patients become more useful citizens. The improvement of the mental hospital requires what is essentially a social revolution in the management of the mentally ill. It involves casting off the antiquated asylum methods which were dictated by ignorance and prejudices of the past and are perpetuated by fear and misunderstanding.

Recent developments in the treatment of the mentally ill which impose minimal obstructions to the patient's participation in society are the establishment of clinics for the treatment of psychoses on an out-patient basis, the establishment of psychiatric wards in general hospitals, and the increase in the number of psychiatrists in private practice who treat patients in their offices.

In the following chapters we will give an account of what human endeavor in America has done, and can be expected to do, toward relief of the severe grades of mental illness which require individuals to be in mental hospitals. There are three phases in American psychiatry. The first phase is one of understanding care which our society sought to give the mentally ill when democracy was young and inspired with its mission to mankind. The second phase is one of decline in human understanding which accompanied social changes during the course of the nineteenth century. The third phase is that of the new hope which modern understanding of human thought, feeling, and behavior has for victims of nervous breakdowns.

The American people are faced with the responsibility of learning what psychiatry today has to offer the mentally ill and how to bring its benefits to them. Americans are not as yet fully aware of the most significant aspect of modern scientific knowledge of the hospitalized mentally ill—namely their great need *for psychological aid and moral support which all people in distress need and which our society is able to give if it is motivated to do so.* Scientific controversy within psychiatry over the validity of particular psychological theories and techniques still obscures from public view the great importance of bringing ordinary psychological and material aids to the mentally ill who are deprived of all contacts in our mental hospitals as they are now constituted.

The condition of the institutionalized mentally ill in America today is largely the result of public opinion led astray. The harmful public attitude, formed under the influence of "scientific" authority which pronounced mental illness incurable over three-quarters of a century ago, contradicts the primary value of the individual and harms many people. And it is the people, primarily, who can do something about the enormous number of man-years of wasted living which attends present-day institutional management of the mentally ill.

# II

## Moral Treatment—
## Forgotten Success in the
## History of Psychiatry

Backsliding has time and again followed progress in man's understanding of self and neighbor. Periods of enlightenment at times left an imprint strong enough to survive generations of darkness and inspire progress anew. At other times, the principles on which these periods were based had to be rediscovered. On the whole, progress over the centuries has been substantial. Religion, politics, and science have all made their contributions.

The greatest challenge to the capacity of men (individually and collectively) to understand neighbor and self arises when mental illness disrupts their relationship to one another. Society's reaction to the mentally ill has oscillated throughout recorded history between brutality and benevolence. When neither was extreme, neglect was the rule.

A basis for understanding human behavior was laid by Plato, who wrote: "And indeed it may almost be asserted that all intemperance in any kind of pleasure, *and all disgraceful conduct*, is not properly blamed as the consequence of voluntary guilt. For no one is voluntarily bad; but he who is depraved becomes so through a certain habit of body, and an ill-governed education. All the vicious are vicious through two most involuntary causes, which we shall always ascribe to the planters, than to the things planted, and to the trainers than to those trained." (8)

10

Hippocrates declared the behavior in psychoses to be due to brain disease and decried belief in demon possession.

These elements of understanding were lost to mankind for several hundred years, to reappear in the writings of Coelius Aurelianus and again disappear during the Dark Ages. They were once more brought to light by Paracelsus and John Weyer. These sixteenth century physicians raised their voices against abuses arising from superstition and warped theological interpretation of the symptoms of mental illness. Their influence led to partial acceptance of mental disorder as a province of medicine.

Consistent care and scientific clinical study were not adopted until the eighteenth century when liberal philosophy and political movements contained the hope that science would enable the achievement of humanitarian ends. The possibility that science could solve the riddle of mental illness captured the imagination. In this endeavor, the goals of science and humanitarianism were undistinguishable. There was no clear-cut line indicating where elimination of abuse ended and scientific therapy began.

The method of the humanistic science of the eighteenth century involved clearing the mind of *a priori* bias in order that it might uncover universal laws. The assumption that laws of science as yet undiscovered were universal (in the sense that the "law" of falling bodies was universal) carried with it the connotation that human behavior, too, was the result of laws. Hence, human behavior must be influenced greatly by unknown forces over which the individual could not have complete control. This had the effect of emphasizing those qualities which individuals have in common and the impossibility of an absolute standard of individual responsibility. Logically, then, all men could be looked upon as equal, and their evil actions could be forgiven. Democratic government and humanitarian treatment of criminals, paupers, and psychotics thus appeared to have their foundations in science.

Humanitarianism favored the view that lunatics had undergone stresses which robbed them of their reason. That such stress could result from disappointment as well as inflammation was a basic assumption. Stresses of a psychological nature were referred to as *moral causes*. Treatment was called *moral treatment,* which meant that the patient was made comfortable, his interest aroused, his friendship invited, and discussion of his troubles encouraged. His time was managed and filled with purposeful activity.

The use of the word "moral" in the terms *moral causes* and *moral treatment* has, at first glance, the capacity to arouse animosity in modern man acquainted with that literature of anthropology and social psychology which demonstrates the relativity of moral standards. Knowledge that the early psychiatrist used "moral" as the equivalent of "emotional" or "psychological" serves to allay such animosity. Reflection on the genesis and meaning of the word "moral" discloses the logic of the usage. The term is intimately related to the word "morale" and carries within it emotional connotations of such words as zeal, hope, spirit, and confidence. It also has to do with custom, conduct, way of life, and inner meaning. "Moral" (and "ethics," too) has many shades of meaning with respect to interpersonal relations, besides having to do with abstract ideas, right and wrong and good and evil.

The word "moral" in *moral treatment* and *moral causes* bears within it an implication, too, about moral responsibility, namely, that the mentally ill were not morally responsible for their acts which were assumed to result either from ignorance or incorrect understanding. Indeed, to its founders, moral treatment of the mentally ill was considered to be a moral mandate on those who were more fortunate. Moral treatment was never clearly defined, possibly because its meaning was self-evident during the era in which it was used. It meant compassionate and understanding treatment of innocent sufferers. Even innocence was not a prerequisite to meriting compassion. Compassion was extended to those whose mental illness was thought due to willful and excessive indulgence in the passions.

Moral treatment is of great significance in the history of psychiatry. It was the first practical effort made to provide systematic and responsible care for an appreciable number of the mentally ill, and it was eminently successful in achieving recoveries.

The great step to moral treatment was taken almost simultaneously by a French physician and an English Quaker in the last decade of the eighteenth century. Phillipe Pinel transformed a madhouse into a hospital, and William Tuke built a *retreat* for the mentally ill. Similar reforms were wrought in Italy, Germany, and America by Chiarugi, Reil, and Rush. Pinel has priority on the debt the world owes for moral treatment. The reforms of Benjamin Rush in America, though not as extensive as those of Pinel, were based on inspiration derived from the same source. Both were steeped in the liberal writings of the physician-philosopher John Locke. Rush did much to stimulate the interest of American physicians in mental illness and paved the way for full acceptance of the principles of moral treatment.

Although the mentally ill had for many years been accepted as patients in several hospitals in America (namely, the Pennsylvania Hospital, the New York Hospital, the Eastern State Hospital at Williamsburg, Virginia, and the Maryland Hospital at Baltimore), it was not until 1817, four years after Rush's death, that a hospital was founded in America expressly for the purpose of providing moral treatment. This hospital, patterned after the York Retreat in England, was built by Pennsylvania Quakers and named the Friends' Asylum. Within seven years, three more privately endowed mental hospitals were built: McLean, Bloomingdale, and the Hartford Retreat. Within thirty years, eighteen hospitals had been built for moral treatment of the mentally ill in America.

The high standards of hospitals built by private philanthropy set a good example for the many state-supported institutions which soon came into being. First of these was the Eastern State Hospital at Lexington, Kentucky, built in 1824, the same year as the Hartford Retreat in Connecticut. Within the next ten years, four more state hospitals were built, now known as the Manhattan State Hospital (New York), 1825; the Western State

Hospital (Staunton, Virginia), 1828; the South Carolina State
Hospital (Columbia), 1828; and the Worcester State Hospital
(Massachusetts), 1833.

The Worcester State Hospital merits special attention because
of the role it played in the history of moral treatment. The first
superintendent at Worcester was Dr. Samuel B. Woodward, who,
with Dr. Eli Todd, had persuaded the Connecticut Medical Society to sponsor the founding of the Hartford Retreat. The two
physicians were long-standing friends who, in their practice of
general medicine, shared an abiding interest in the treatment of
mental disorders. Both became "specialists" of their day; patients
with mental diseases were referred to them by other physicians.

These pioneer psychiatrists conducted a survey of mental
illness in Connecticut to determine the size of hospital necessary
to care for the mentally ill of that state. The elder of the two,
Dr. Todd, was appointed superintendent of the Retreat. Nine
years later, Dr. Woodward was chosen superintendent of the
hospital at Worcester, the first state institution for the mentally
ill in New England. This hospital was built largely through the
enthusiastic support of Horace Mann, father of the American
public school. It might be mentioned in passing that the New
Hampshire State Hospital was founded largely through the
efforts of Dr. Luther Bell (who later became superintendent of
McLean Hospital) and the clergymen of New Hampshire. These
are but a few examples of the active support which professional
men—clergymen, educators, physicians—gave in behalf of the
mentally ill in the early history of American psychiatry.

Worcester State Hospital under the direction of Dr. Woodward served as a proving ground for moral treatment and
demonstrated beyond doubt that recovery was the rule. Year
after year Dr. Woodward gave the statistics of recovery in the
Annual Reports of his hospital.

It was Dr. Todd, however, who first called the attention of
the public to the success of moral treatment. He reported recovery in over 90% of patients who had been admitted to the
Hartford Retreat with mental illness of less duration than one
year. This result was based on relatively few admissions, how-

ever, and it remained for Dr. Woodward to demonstrate, on the basis of a large series of cases, that recovery was the rule in recently ill patients.

It is pertinent at this point to present the statistics kept by the Worcester State Hospital during the time moral treatment was still applicable, that is, before crowding and expansion beyond optimum size fully disrupted vital interpersonal relationships among patients, attendants, and physicians.

Table 1 shows the number and per cent discharged as recovered or improved of the total number of patients admitted who had been ill less than one year prior to their admission. During

TABLE 1—Outcome in Patients Admitted to Worcester State Hospital Who Were Ill Less Than One Year Prior to Admission, 1833-1852

(*Data from the Annual Reports of the Hospital*)

| Five-Year Period | Patients Admitted | Patients Discharged | |
|---|---|---|---|
| | | Recovered | Improved |
| 1833–37 | 300 | 211 (70 %) | 39 (8.3%) |
| 1838–42 | 434 | 324 (74.6%) | 14 (3.2%) |
| 1843–47 | 742 | 474 (63.9%) | 34 (4.6%) |
| 1848–52 | 791 | 485 (61.3%) | 37 (4.7%) |

twenty years there were 2,267 such admissions, of whom 1,618 were discharged as recovered or improved, or 71% (66% recovered, 5% improved). During this same period the total of all admissions (including those whose illness had lasted longer than one year prior to admission) was 4,119, of whom 2,439 or 59% were discharged as recovered (45%) or improved (14%).

Such statistical data invite attention to the assumptions on which the idea of moral treatment was based and its cultural setting. America in the 1830's and '40's was rapidly developing a new liberal philosophy of the individual. Leading American thinkers of the period turned to nature in search of truth. Societies were formed for the abolition of slavery. Experiments were made in communal living. A spirit of freedom and self-expression was in the air. New England Puritanism was growing milder. The jealous God of Cotton Mather was becoming the loving God of William Channing, and a new intellectual independence was coming to the fore. Emerson encouraged the individual to self-reliance, and in one of his addresses, "The Scholar," he stated, "The world is nothing, the man is all." Historically, in the United States, this period has been referred to by Fisher as "The Rise of the Common Man, 1820–1850."

American thought was at this time in close communion with the romantic movement in Germany. American psychiatry was influenced by the then current psychobiological trend in German psychiatric literature. In particular, the long forgotten von Feuchtersleben was often referred to by American psychiatrists. Dr. Gregory Zilboorg has credited von Feuchtersleben's view of mental illness in the 1840's as being much the same as that of present-day psychiatry.

One of the leading spokesmen of early American psychiatry was Dr. Isaac Ray, whose psychiatric career began in the 1830's as superintendent of the Augusta State (Maine) Hospital. Dr. Ray subscribed to the view that the mind includes those qualities which make possible the relations among people which have to do with man's greatest welfare. Love and hate were to him as much manifestations of mind as rational processes. He also contended that every appetite and faculty must have its means of gratification and protested that belief to the contrary was wholly repugnant. He believed in the unity of the individual man and referred specifically to the unity of mind and brain. In his book "Mental Hygiene" (1863) he gave particular attention to the influence of passions, emotions, and temperament on mental health. He strongly recommended, after von Feuchtersleben, that ill-humored individuals be regarded as suffering from disease and advised them to seek every means to rid themselves of it to prevent becoming insane. He also held the view that insanity is but an exaggeration of personality traits which in their less extreme form are regarded as merely disagreeable.

Both Dr. Ray and his colleague, Dr. John S. Butler, superintendent of the Hartford Retreat, were impressed with the importance of child rearing to mental health. Dr. Butler categorically stated that he had traced the cause of insanity to the malign influences in childhood in a large proportion of over 3,000 patients he had personally studied. Dr. Butler also voiced a commonly held opinion of the times that all bodily processes are under the influence of the mind.

The psychodynamic and psychosomatic orientation of psychiatry in the early 1800's found its fullest expression in the elaboration of the psychological therapeutic approach known as the moral treatment of insanity. In the language of Dr. Ray, the proper administration of moral treatment required that the physician learn through inquiry and conversation what occupies the minds of his patients. It required further that he investigate the mental make-up of patients' relatives. The greatest requirement of all was that the physician spare no effort in gaining the confidence and good will of his patients and strive to discover their experiences and supply their needs. The recommendation was made that the physician acquire a large fund of knowledge in order to converse with patients on matters interesting to them and thus gain an understanding of their inner life. The physician was strongly reminded that even the most insane patients are sensitive to manifestations of interest and good will. He was warned, however, to limit the number of patients in his care to those he can know personally.

Although much emphasis was placed on the relationship between physician and patient, moral treatment embraced a much larger psychological approach than individual psychotherapy. Indeed, perhaps the greatest asset of moral treatment was the attention it gave to the value of physical setting and social influences of hospital life as curative agents. In his book "Curability of Insanity" (9), published in 1887, Dr. Butler repeatedly points out the importance of scrutinizing the hospital environment to find and remove whatever is depressing or disturbing. He insists that a cheerful, sympathetic atmosphere and esthetic appeal are essential for the cure of many patients. His goal was to make hospital wards as homelike as possible, for he placed

great faith in the value of family-like gatherings in which patients
could discuss their problems among themselves and with the
physician. He also believed that confidential interviews with
patients were essential, but he was convinced that the turning
point in many a patient's illness took place in group discussions.
He also insisted that appropriate social influences could not be
maintained if hospitals were allowed to care for more than 200
patients at one time. He considered monotony to be the greatest
obstacle to be overcome in mental hospitals and believed heartily
in promoting a wide variety of activities for patients.

The theoretical foundation of early American psychiatry and
the success of its therapeutic approach to insane individuals as
persons were a source of inspiration to those who believed in
the dignity of man and sought to improve his condition. Charles
Dickens and Horace Mann were particularly impressed by the
experience of seeing moral treatment in action. In his 1833 report
(21), as chairman of the board of trustees of the Worcester State
Hospital, Horace Mann told a moving story of 32 fellow beings
who had been restored to their reason under the influences of
the hospital, whose loss to their families would otherwise have
been mourned without hope. He told further of the unbelievable
changes which had taken place in those patients who had not
recovered. When the hospital was first opened, there were at
least one hundred patients who would assail any human being
who came near them. In less than a year only 12 of these
patients were still assaultive. Similarly, of 40 patients who would
tear off their clothing in the beginning, only 8 still did so
at the time of the report. He commented on the civility and
kindness which had come to prevail among the patients. Wailing,
raving, and desponding were dispelled, and the facial expression
of patients reflected their improved state of mind. He credited
these heartening results to the efforts "of all those engaged in
administering the daily affairs of the institution to exclude, as
far as in any manner possible, all causes of mental disquietude,
by substituting persuasion by force, by practicing forebearance,
mildness, and all the nameless offices of humanity, by imbuing,
in every practicable way, the minds of the patients with a new

set of pleasing, cheerful, grateful and benevolent emotions." He summed up the idea of moral treatment in the following words: "The whole scheme of moral treatment is embraced in a single idea—humanity—the law of love—that sympathy which appropriates another's consciousness of pain and makes it a personal relief from suffering whenever another's sufferings are relieved."

Charles Dickens' account (12) of his visit to the Boston State Hospital in 1842 brings to light still more facets of hospital life in the moral treatment era. He commented on the wide variety of activities available to patients, including carriage rides in the open air, fishing, gardening, and several kinds of indoor and outdoor games. Patients worked with sharp-edged tools and ate their meals with knives and forks. The patients organized themselves in a sewing circle which held meetings and passed resolutions. They also attended dances which were held weekly. Dickens was particularly surprised with the self-respect which was inculcated and encouraged in the patients by the superintendent's attitude toward them. He made special note that the superintendent and his family dined with the patients and mixed among them as a matter of course.

The psychological orientation of moral treatment and the recoveries from psychosis accompanying its application cannot be lightly dismissed. Modern psychiatry would do well to regard the mental hospitals of the early nineteenth century as pilot hospitals which demonstrated the value of social and psychological factors in treatment. The reason this finding was largely disregarded for nearly one hundred years is a story in itself. The least we can do is borrow a leaf from our psychiatric forefathers and give full attention to the possibilities of treating psychoses by social and psychological means in the many state and federal hospitals which have so long considered psychosis curable *only* by physical or chemical means.

# III

## The Breakdown of Moral Treatment

It is of great importance to the understanding of forces with which modern psychiatry must contend to determine why moral treatment did not become an enduring basic principle of psychiatric care rather than a soon forgotten temporary success. A successful technique in whatever field of endeavor is not ordinarily abandoned unless displaced by a still more effective technique. Moral treatment, however, simply passed out of existence. It was followed by the void of custodial care.

Of the many factors which contributed to the decline and the eventual discard of moral treatment, lack of inspired leadership after the death of its innovators was probably the most important. The founders of moral treatment were shortsighted in not providing for their own successors in numbers adequate to meet the needs of the future. These leaders each trained but one or two physicians, not enough to replace themselves and staff their own growing hospitals, let alone the numerous hospitals soon to be built. By the time of the Civil War, moral treatment was already crippled by the deaths of the leading moral therapists. Dr. Eli Todd died in 1833; Dr. Woodward resigned from the Worcester State Hospital in 1845 and died in 1850. Dr. Amariah Brigham, editor of the Americian Journal of Insanity, superintendent of the Utica State Hospital and one of the most vigorous writers on the subject of moral treatment, died in 1849. In the same year, Dr. Pliny Earle resigned from Bloomingdale (see Chapter

IV) and did not reenter the field of moral treatment until 15 years later. Dr. Stedman resigned from the Boston State Hospital in 1851. Dr. Luther Bell resigned his position as superintendent of McLean Hospital in 1856. Machinations in Ohio State politics forced Dr. William Awl to resign as superintendent of the Ohio State Hospital in 1850. Dr. John Galt died in 1862, and Nehemiah Cutler in 1859. In 1867, Dr. Isaac Ray resigned from the Butler Hospital, and five years later Dr. Butler resigned from the Hartford Retreat. In 1874, Dr. Stribling died.

Only four of the original 13 fathers of Americian psychiatry and founders of moral treatment survived the 1870's, and two of these had retired to private practice: Dr. Isaac Ray and Dr. John S. Butler. Dr. Pliny Earle continued as superintendent of the Northampton (Mass.) State Hospital until 1885, and Dr. Thomas Kirkbridge of the Pennsylvania Hospital until 1883. The former, although an avid proponent of moral treatment, was paradoxically one of the strongest forces in discrediting its results. Unfortunate events in his life in conjunction with a tendency to despondency and pessimism help explain the stand he took. These circumstances will be discussed in connection with statistical studies of treatment results in Chapter IV.

Lack of foresight in training sufficient numbers of moral therapists for the future was matched by failure to plan ahead for the building of a sufficient number of hospitals. It is presumptuous, of course, to imply that such planning should be expected. No one could have had an inkling of the impending rapid growth in population of the eastern seaboard and the accompanying shift from a rural to an urban mode of life which took place during the second half of the nineteenth century. It was not until 1874 that any particular mention was made of the great increase in the number of patients in the mental hospitals of Massachusetts. In the annual report of the State Board of Health of that year, Dr. Edward P. Jarvis, psychiatrist and recognized statistician, pointed out that all the state's mental hospitals had been enlarged to accommodate far more patients than the original plans allowed. Thirteen years later, Dr. John S. Butler (in his book "Curability of Insanity") sought to influence the

American Psychiatric Association to place a limit on the size of mental hospitals. He invoked the resolutions passed by that association in 1844 and 1851 which stated that the preferable maximum size for a mental hospital was two hundred patients. He decried the resolution passed in 1866 which allowed hospitals to have a capacity for six hundred patients and pointed out that it in effect placed no limit since hospitals had already expanded beyond that number. He quoted Drs. Isaac Ray and Thomas Kirkbridge and other surviving pioneers of moral treatment to the effect that large hospitals harmed patients by denying them personal attention and caused them to be treated like a mob in which they lost their human attributes.

Needless to say, Dr. Butler and his colleagues were not heeded. State hospitals reached an average of 1,000 patients many decades ago and now exceed 2,000, with no limit in sight. The Worcester State Hospital is an example of the steady increase in resident population especially since the time of the Civil War (Fig. 1). Recurrent cycles of overcrowding were met by depriving patients of recreational space. With each new construction for sleeping quarters, there was a further relative decrease in the space and means for recreation, which in turn demanded an increase in regimentation of patients. The rapid increase in hospital population included another factor of great importance, that of the immigration beginning in the post-Civil War period. The influx of patients from poverty-stricken immigrant families into the mental hospital put a severe strain on the flexibility and breadth of understanding of the medical officers of the hospitals. Psychiatrists of old American stock who were filled with compassion on beholding mental illness in one of their own were filled with revulsion by what they considered uncouth and ignorant in the insane foreign pauper. As the proportion of immigrant patients in the hospital increased, there was a tendency for hospital living quarters to deteriorate until they were nothing more than barren dormitories adjoining even more barren day-rooms whose furniture consisted of crude benches along the walls. The resulting apathy of the patients led their physicians to express the belief that they were in no way

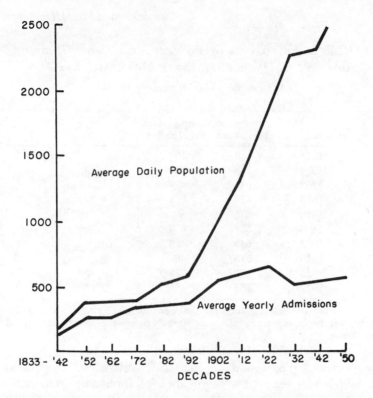

FIG. 1. Resident population and yearly admission rates of Worcester State Hospital, 1833-1950. (*Data from the Annual Reports of the Hospital*)

capable of appreciating anything better. This example of rationalized callousness provides some idea of the degrading effect which compromise can produce when the dignity of the individual is forgotten.

Passages from the Annual Reports of the Worcester State Hospital leave little doubt that racial prejudice played a role in the breakdown not only of moral treatment but of ordinary decent hospital living standards. Mention of foreigners as a problem was first made in the Annual Report of 1854, which laments that the State Hospital was fast becoming a hospital for Irish immigrants rather than for the intelligent Yeomanry of Massachusetts who could pay their board and would not ask

TABLE 2.—Proportion of Foreign-Born among Patients
Admitted to Worcester State Hospital, 1844-1933

(*Data from the Annual Reports of the Hospital*)

| Year | Number of Admissions | Proportion of Foreign-Born | |
|------|------|------|------|
| 1844 | 236 | 10% | |
| 1854 | 288 | 38% | Percentages |
| 1863 | 215 | 47% | based on |
| 1873 | 470 | 38% | total |
| 1883 | 275 | ? | admissions |
| 1893 | 534 | 67% | |
| 1903 | 553 | 45% | Percentages |
| 1913 | 515 | 46% | based on |
| 1923 | 402 | 53% | first |
| 1933 | 484 | 45% | admissions |

*Note*: These particular foreign-born were usually destitute. Mental hospitals were becoming *vast almshouses*—just as today they are becoming "old
folks homes."

for charity. A plea was made for the "classification" of patients,
by which was meant the segregation of foreigners from native
New Englanders. The basis for the plea was that the sensibilities
of patients reared in the proverbially neat and orderly households
of New England were offended by close contact with those who
were accustomed to and satisfied with filthy habitations and
filthier habits.

Yankee physicians found it difficult to identify with the Irish
immigrant. Moral treatment and the "law of love" extolled by
Horace Mann were reserved for those of Yankee stock. Indeed,
in the Annual Report of 1858 (Worcester State Hospital) the
Irish were castigated for a variety of reasons, among which were:
receiving high wages in prosperous times, gratifying vicious in-
dulgences, seeking labor in the most menial capacity, huddling
together in the most objectionable places, neglecting all the rules
of health, and preferring the solace of rum and tobacco to the
quiet, intelligent influences of well-ordered homes.

"Foreign insane pauperism" was the name given to the problem of mental illness in the immigrant population. Its disrupting effects were due not only to racial and religious incompatibilities, but also to economic factors. Patients without settlement in Massachusetts were paid for by the Commonwealth. All other patients' bills were paid either by their families or by the towns in which they resided. The Commonwealth paid so little for its pauper patients that the hospital was forced to charge the towns and families more. In the Annual Report of the State Board of Health of 1874, Dr. Edward Jarvis pointed out that proportionately few of the mentally ill patients of self-sustaining families were sent to state hospitals; most of them were kept at home because they could not pay and were ashamed to "go on the town," whereas the poverty stricken did not hesitate to use the hospitals. Rapid population growth, immigration, and pauperism forced the metamorphosis of mental hospitals from home-like havens of moral treatment to huge custodial asylums. Table 2 shows the proportion of foreign-born in each of the years indicated. If patients of foreign-born parents had been included, the proportion of what the trustees and superintendent of Worcester called foreigners would be much greater in the latter decades of the century.

The phenomenon of the mentally ill from destitute families crowding out and, in effect, preventing the hospitalization of mentally ill from self-sustaining families led to further deterioration of mental hospitals. The attitude that paupers would not appreciate nice things anyway provided a rationalization for not insisting on higher standards. On the other hand, many home recoveries must have occurred among the mentally ill of self-sustaining families who could not afford hospital care. These were probably treated by private practitioners such as Edward P. Jarvis, William Hammond, and Silas Weir Mitchell.

The deterioration in mental hospital living standards through the latter part of the nineteenth century is shown graphically in Fig. 2. For example, in 1869 the weekly per capita income of the United States was $4.00. The weekly cost per patient at Worcester State Hospital was also $4.00. In 1899, the weekly

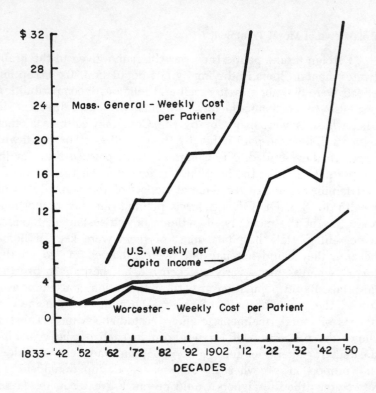

FIG. 2. Worcester State Hospital per capita weekly cost, and Massachusetts General Hospital per capita weekly cost, compared with United States per capita weekly income, 1833-1950. (*Adapted from "The Hospital in Contemporary Life" (Edited by Nathaniel W. Faxon, M.D., Harvard University Press, Cambridge, 1949) and the Annual Reports of the Worcester State Hospital, 1833-1940*)

per capita income of the United States had gone up to $5.00, and the weekly cost per patient at Worcester had *dropped* to $3.50. The Massachusetts General Hospital weekly cost per patient in 1869 was $10.00 and in 1899 was $14.00. Weekly per capita income of the United States by 1929 had gone up to $13.00, or more than tripled since 1869. Massachusetts General's weekly cost per patient had *quadrupled*, while Worcester's had not even *doubled* (from $4.00 to just under $7.00). The general hospital ran ahead of per capita income, while the mental hospital ran behind. To the public, the former was expensive and

26

the latter cheap. Thus mental illness was given, in addition to the universal stigmas, a further one, "cheap," with the peculiar connotation it has in America.

Any criteria adopted for comparing standards of hospital care provided in different eras are fraught with error. Data with respect to the Worcester State Hospital allow construction of indices which may to a certain extent reflect changes in the standards of care during the last century.

The ratio of the number of resident patients per physician for each decade over a period of 100 years is an index of this change. Table 3 shows how the ratio increased over the entire period. The table also shows the ratio of the number of patients per each attendant over the same period. Here a trend in the opposite direction is shown. From decade to decade each attendant had fewer patients in his charge.

In 1904, the 70-hour work week was adopted. From that time on some of the attendants worked night shifts; thus the ratio of patients per attendant at any given time may have been less than indicated in Table 3 after that date. Prior to 1904, the attendants usually had quarters in the wards and were always with the patients, except for a few hours each Saturday.

The relative decrease in the number of physicians and the relative increase in the number of attendants resulted in a large increase in the ratio of the number of attendants to each physician over the 110 years. In the decade 1913-22, the number of attendants to each physician was three times as great as in the decade 1833-42, and 1843-52.

The scale of pay for physicians during the 1890's was more than double that of the 1830's and '40's (from $500 to $1,000 per year for assistant physicians and from $1,200 to $3,000 per year for superintendents), while the scale for attendants only increased about 50% (from $15 a month to $23-$25 a month).

During the 1830's, there were, on the average, two doctors and 15 attendants at the Worcester State Hospital. During the 1930's, there were, on the average, 14 doctors and 336 attendants. The standards of care given the patients in terms of personal relationships suffered in proportion to the increase in social

TABLE 3.—PATIENT-PHYSICIAN-ATTENDANT RATIOS
AT WORCESTER STATE HOSPITAL, 1833-1950

(*Data from the Annual Reports of the Hospital*)

| | Resident Patients | | Attendants |
| Years | Per Physician | Per Attendant | Per Physician |
|---|---|---|---|
| 1833–1842 | 88 | 12 | 8 |
| 1843–1952 | 127 | 15 | 8 |
| 1853–1862 | 128 | — | — |
| 1863–1872 | 156 | — | — |
| 1873–1882 | 146 | — | — |
| 1883–1892 | 132 | 8 | 13 |
| 1893–1902 | 114 | 11 | 11 |
| 1903–1912 | 148 | 10 | 15 |
| 1913–1922 | 205 | 9 | 24 |
| 1923–1932 | 175 | 9 | 20 |
| 1933–1942 | 165 | 7 | 24 |
| 1943–1950 | 230 | 11 | 21 |

distance between physicians and attendants. Opportunities for physicians and attendants to discuss problems of individual patients became fewer.

The retardation of research in mental hospitals and the deterioration of care given patients did not long continue unnoticed. By 1875, members of the rising specialty of neurology had formed their own society—a society which in its early years not only specifically excluded from membership physicians in the employ of mental hospitals, but openly challenged their authority to speak on matters of mental illness. In 1879, the first direct attack on mental hospitals and their medical officers was made by William A. Hammond in a paper, "The Non-Asylum Treatment of the Insane." The first two paragraphs indicate its tenor:

"It is the commonly received opinion among physicians and the public generally that as soon as possible after an individual becomes insane, he or she must be placed under the restraint of a lunatic asylum. No matter what the type of mental aberration, no matter what the facilities for receiving care and attention at home, the asylum is regarded as the necessary destination of the one so unfortunate as to be deprived wholly, or in part, of the light of reason. For this state of affairs, the medical officers of insane asylums are mainly responsible, for they have very diligently inculcated the idea that they alone, by education, by experience and by general aptitude, are qualified to take the medical superintendence of the unfortunate class of patients in question, and that restraint and separation from friends and acquaintances are measures in themselves which are specially curative in their influence.

"It will be among the chief objects of this memoir to show that these views are erroneous; that the medical profession (outside the hospital) is, as a body, fully as capable of treating cases of insanity as cases of any other disease, and that in many instances sequestration is not only unnecessary but positively injurious." ( 27)

In 1894, Dr. Weir Mitchell administered a verbal spanking to the members of the medico-psychological society on its fiftieth anniversary:

"The cloistered lives you lead give rise, we think, to certain mental peculiarities. I could tell you how to mend them. I shall by and by. You hold to and teach certain opinions which we have long learned to lose. One is the superstition (almost is it that) to the effect that an asylum is in itself curative. You hear the regret in every report that patients are not sent soon enough, as if you had ways of curing which we have not. Upon my word, I think asylum life is deadly to the insane. Poverty, risk, fear, send you many patients; many more are sent by people quite able to have their friends treated outside. They are placed in asylums because of the wide-spread belief you have so long, as we think, so unreasonably fostered, to the effect that there is some mysterious therapeutic influence to be found behind your walls and locked doors. We hold the reverse opinion, and think your hospitals are never to be used save as a last resort." ( 30)

Tucker's report on "Lunacy in Many Lands," based on an

extensive inspection tour of mental hospitals of the world, was published in 1887. Unbelievably bad hospital conditions were practically universal. It is a sad comment on the state of psychiatry that Tucker's chief plea was merely for decent standards of living for the mentally ill and elimination of mechanical restraint and enforced baths. Probably the most severe castigation of psychiatry was that by Franklin B. Sanborn, who, as chairman of the Board of State Charities (Massachusetts) for 35 years, had become well acquainted with the medical officers of mental hospitals. In a pamphlet published in 1899, bearing the title "A Remonstrance in the Name of the Insane Poor Against Crowding Them into Hospital Palaces or Asylum Prisons," and intended for the eyes of members of the State Legislature, he made a strong plea. He not only questioned the ability of the medical officers to treat the mentally ill and cited poor recovery rates to prove his point, but he also gave account of an instance in which a capable nurse was obstructed from caring for patients although she had previously been successful in effecting the recovery of apparently hopeless cases. He contrasted this nurse with a hospital physician who, through medical ignorance, had caused the death of many insane women. Nine years later, in 1908, Clifford Beers published "A Mind That Found Itself," in which he described the abuses suffered by patients in mental hospitals. Among the letters received by Beers in response to the manuscript of his book was one from William James, the last paragraph of which is as true today as when it was written in 1907:

"Nowhere is there massed together as much suffering as in the asylums. Nowhere is there so much sodden routine and fatalistic insensibility as in those who have to treat it. Nowhere is an ideal treatment more costly. The officials in charge grow resigned to the conditions under which they have to labor. They cannot plead their cause as an auxiliary organization can plead it for them. Public opinion is too glad to remain ignorant. As mediator between officials, patients, and the public conscience, a society such as you sketch is absolutely required and the sooner it gets under way the better. Sincerely yours, William James." (28)

The sodden routine and fatalistic insensibility to which James refers is the damaging product of the incurability myth within the walls of mental hospitals. The stigma which it places on the mentally ill, in conjunction with exaggeration of the role of heredity, is as effective as the medieval belief in demon possession in denying them their rights not only to the means of recovery but to decent living standards.

Social progress is usually made through the organized efforts of those who themselves are the victims of deprivation. The very essence of mental illness, however, is an incapacity to get along with other people, hence organization behind a leader is impossible. The friends or relatives of the mentally ill are equally immobilized through fear of stigmatizing themselves.

The damaging effect of the incurability myth is a thought provoking revelation of the sensitivity of the mentally ill to the attitudes of those about them. Failure to recognize this factor has inhibited psychiatric progress for over a hundred years and to the present day underlies the low standards of many mental hospitals. It is disturbing to compare the recovery rates of the Worcester State Hospital decade by decade during the Century of Progress 1833-1933 (see Fig. 3 in Chapter V). One may contend that this decline in recovery rates from 45% to 4% is an artefact, but the fact remains that it accompanied not only a diminution in treatment efforts, but also a reduction of the patients' standard of living.

We cannot escape the conclusion that our society had, until very recently, become less and less concerned about the fate of its mentally ill during the very years that its standard of living was increasing at an ever more rapid tempo.

# IV

**Personality and
Scientific Outlook in
Psychiatric Leadership**

The irony of the psychiatric profession today is that it sub-
scribes to the great therapeutic value of dynamic psychiatry in
mental illness yet fails to apply its principles in the care of those
who are in the greatest need: namely psychotic patients legally
confined in our mental hospitals. This failure is largely based on
indecision as to the curability of psychosis. The stigma of hopelessness associated with psychosis in the public mind is, to be
sure, sorely lamented by psychiatrists. Nevertheless by their
own actions they contribute to the stigma by handling psychotic
patients as intractable prisoners, incapable of benefiting from *any*
treatment. The very fact that such a method of handling pre-
dominates throughout the world strongly suggests that psychiatrists themselves harbor belief in the very stigma they would
remove from society by public education. Such a discrepancy
between what is preached and what is practiced does not be-
speak cynicism in the profession but rather a time lag in the
spread of knowledge from research and teaching centers which
do the preaching to the outlying mental hospitals which receive
the vast majority of patients.

As so often happens in science, recently acquired perspectives
turn out to be a more precise form of very old perspectives which
were left undeveloped. Those who have come to rely on certain
habits in giving service, who are not actively engaged in research,
and who no longer preserve an open mind in areas in which their

own habits come into question, naturally resist accepting the new and devaluate it on the grounds that it was "old stuff" long ago and "nothing came of it."

Psychiatrists cannot afford to forget that unprejudiced open-minded effort to discover any and every means for supplying the personal needs and arousing the dormant faculties of psychotic patients was the very purpose which gave birth to psychiatry as a profession in the first place.

With Pinel's twofold discovery, over 150 years ago, that organic lesions could not be found in most instances of insanity, and that recovery could be achieved through effort invested in supplying personal needs and arousing dormant faculties—which he named moral treatment—psychiatry came into existence not solely as a humanitarian reform but also as a successful therapeutic enterprise.

Pinel's report on this discovery, "Treatise On Insanity," was first made available to the English-speaking world in 1806. His account of how he learned of the curability of insanity from a layman is a masterpiece of open-mindedness in psychiatry:

"Of the knowledge to be derived from books on the treatment of insanity I felt the most extreme insufficiency. Desirous of better information, I resolved to examine for myself the facts that were presented to my attention; and forgetting the empty honours of my titular distinction as a physician, I viewed the scene that was opened to me with the eyes of common sense and unprejudiced observation. I saw a great number of maniacs assembled together, and submitted to a regular system of discipline. Their disorders presented an endless variety of character; but their discordant movements were regulated on the part of the governor (lay superintendent) by the greatest possible skill, and even extravagance and disorder were marshalled into order and harmony. I then discovered, that insanity was curable in many instances, by mildness of treatment and attention to the mind exclusively, and when coercion was indispensable, that it might be very effectively applied without corporal indignity. To give all their value to the facts which I had the opportunity of observing, I made it an object of interest to trace their alliance to the functions of the understanding. To assist me in this inquiry, I attentively perused the best writers upon modern pneumatology (defined in Webster as the science of the nature and functions of mind and soul), as well as those authors who have written on the influence of the passions upon the pathology of the human mind. The laws of the human economy considered in reference to insanity as well as other diseases, impressed me with admiration of their uniformity, and I saw, with wonder, the resources of nature when left to herself, or skillfully assisted in her efforts. My faith in pharmaceutic preparations was gradually lessened, and my skepticism went at length so far, as to induce me never to have recourse to them, until moral remedies had completely failed. . . .

"Attention to these principles of moral treatment alone will, frequently, not only lay the foundation of, but complete a cure, while neglect of them may exasperate each succeeding paroxysm, till, at length, the disease becomes established, continued in its form and incurable. The successful application of moral regimen exclusively gives great weight to the supposition, that, in the majority of instances, there is no organic lesion of the brain nor of the cranium." ( 38)

The effectiveness of moral treatment was first made widely known to the medical profession in America by a physician whose open-mindedness also included the capacity to adopt a layman's conception of the treatment of insanity. Dr. Eli Todd, fearing his own susceptibility to insanity from the knowledge that his father and sister died insane, acquainted himself with the philosophy and method of treatment developed by the Quaker layman, William Tuke, at the York Retreat in England. Dr. Todd was not a Quaker but an avowed religious skeptic who subscribed to the philosophies which gave rise to the French Revolution. Nevertheless he expended all his efforts to have a hospital established in Connecticut along the lines of the York Retreat.

Dr. Todd entered the practice of medicine in 1790 at the age of 20. It was in 1812 that he began playing an active role in behalf of obtaining moral treatment for the insane. In that year he was appointed to the Connecticut Medical Society's committee for investigating the condition of the insane. In 1822 he succeeded in organizing a Society for the Relief of the Insane, and in 1824 he was appointed director of the newly founded Hartford Retreat which was sponsored by the Connecticut Medical Society largely because of Dr. Todd's efforts. Thus it happened that at a time when England's physicians scoffed at William Tuke's York Retreat, an American medical society actually sponsored a hospital patterned and named after it.

Dr. Todd had a "profound sympathy for the insane which stamped all his views and conduct." (31) He was acutely aware of the sensitivity and needs of psychotic patients. His view was: "In their whole intercourse with society, their spirits are wounded by a sneer or a jest. . . . The force of their disease is augmented from day to day, and at last suicide or confirmed insanity is the result of accumulated though imaginary insanity." (32) He also commented on the uniqueness of mental suffering: "All other sufferers seek relief from their sufferings and successfully appeal to the kindly feelings of man for sympathy and aid. But unlike all others, the maniac who most needs tenderness and care, is neglected, because he shuns the care and tenderness which he needs, repels the hand stretched out for his relief and would fain bar the door of charity against himself." (50)

Dr. Todd's system of treatment, in the words of Dr. Charles W. Page, "was not a code of rules for subordinates to enforce, no austere, remote, authority, but personal devotion and painstaking labor with his patients—that method of true leadership in a good cause which always commands respect and insures success." (33)

Dr. Samuel B. Woodward, in his report on Dr. Todd's management of the Hartford Retreat, made the following observations: "In respect to the moral and intellectual treatment, the first business of a physician is to gain the patient's entire confidence. With this in view he is treated with the greatest kindness, however violent his conduct may be,—is allowed all the liberty his case admits of, and is made to understand, if he is still capable of reflection, that, so far from having arrived at a

mad-house where he is to be confined, he has come to a pleasant
and cheerful residence where all kindness and attention will be
shown him, and where every means will be used for his recovery
to health. In no case is deception employed or allowed; on the
contrary the greatest frankness as well as kindness form a part
of the moral treatment. His case is explained to him, and he is
made to understand, as far as possible, the reason why the
treatment to which he is being subjected has become necessary."
(34)

In Dr. Todd's own view his method was based on the law of
kindness, mental philosophy, and physiology. He built on the
experience of both Pinel and Tuke and combined medical, die-
tetic, and psychological treatments. Under his direction the
Hartford Retreat became the model after which so many American mental hospitals were patterned during the first half of the
nineteenth century. His personality was also in many of its
qualities the prototype of the moral therapists who followed in
his steps. Qualities ascribed to him such as benevolence, kindli-
ness, cheerfulness, ingenuousness, and magnanimous altruism
were also ascribed to Drs. Samuel B. Woodward, Isaac Ray,
Amariah Brigham, Thomas Kirkbride, Luther Bell, and John S.
Butler. They shared a common interest in patients first and
foremost as *people*. Their writings all contain accounts of their
philosophically minded sympathetic investigations of their patients' state of mind. Indeed they did not seem to even think in
terms of universally applicable disease processes but rather
operated on the general assumption that every patient was a
special case and that their duty as physicians was to use every
possible means to enhance the welfare and self-respect of
patients individually and collectively.

One of the clearest examples of individual psychotherapy as
practiced by the moral therapists is that of Dr. John S. Butler
of the Boston State Hospital (1839-1842) and the Hartford
Retreat (1843-1872), as noted by Charles W. Page: "It was his
common practice to dig deeply into the family and personal
history of his patients, to establish, if possible, a connection between their mental disorder and some accident or error in their

lives. And this he did, not only that he might the more intelligently treat the patient, but that he might be able to give the patient and friends, in case of recovery, such warnings that subsequent attacks might be prevented or at least guarded against." (35)

One of Dr. Butler's principles of psychotherapy was to use positive propositions and never negative ones. It was his claim that all destructive patients responded to persevering efforts in the direction of discovering and respecting their preferences. A specific instance, in the words of Dr. Charles W. Page: "He did not depend upon restraint or seclusion to arrest destructive habits. If a woman tore her dress he aimed to stimulate her self-respect and pride. He would provide her with a new dress conspicuous for its pretty pattern or bright colors. And when he saw her thus clad he would express pride and pleasure, complimenting her on her improved appearance." (36)

Dr. Butler, it is significant to note, was stimulated to enter the field of mental medicine by witnessing, while a general practitioner, the favorable outcome of patients treated by Dr. Woodward at the Worcester State Hospital. He visited the hospital frequently, and as a result of his great interest and avid study of patients he was recommended by Dr. Woodward for directorship of the Boston State Hospital (then Boston City Hospital for the Insane) in 1839. Here Dr. Butler applied the methods of moral treatment in the care of long-term chronically insane patients, the results of which won the acclaim of Charles Dickens as related in Chapter II.

Without benefit of modern psychological discoveries, these pioneer psychiatrists provided a high standard of treatment simply by acting on the philosophical assumption that the healthy mind could understand and influence the sick mind for the better. To them it appeared self-evident that every aspect of hospital life had a bearing on the issue of the patients' mental condition. They believed that success depended on constant vigilance to the needs of patients. At the same time they were aware that disappointment was to be expected in patients with general paresis or other psychoses, accompanied by signs of organic brain disease. Such disappointment did not, nevertheless, undermine their faith in the effectiveness of moral treatment with the majority of patients. It is not unlikely though, that accumulation of patients with undetected brain disease had something to do with the final decline of moral treatment.

From the time of Dr. Todd's demonstration of the success of moral treatment at the Hartford Retreat in the 1820's to the 1840's, a dozen or so small hospitals were founded and a score or so physicians had become proficient in the application of moral treatment.

In 1841 a new personality came into a position of leadership where the care of the insane was concerned. In that year Dorothea Dix discovered that large numbers of insane people were suffering unbelievable abuse in the jails and almshouses of Massachusetts. She also learned of the humane treatment patients were receiving at the three small mental hospitals in that state. From the moment she learned of such suffering and its remedy, her soul would know no rest until every abused insane individual was a patient in a mental hospital. With fanatic singleness of purpose she set out on her amazing career of accomplishing reform by direct appeal to state legislatures. She was rapidly successful in achieving the results she demanded, namely the construction of new, and expansion of already existing, mental hospitals. The Worcester State Hospital was enlarged, as previously noted, in 1843 against Dr. Woodward's wishes by an act of the Massachusetts legislature. Two more hospitals of larger capacity were built in the 1850's. This was only a start. Miss Dix was not content to sit back until every state of the Union, province of Canada, and nation of Europe had provided hospital space sufficient to house all the insane.

Her immense emphasis on eliminating gross abuse of the insane had the most unfortunate effect of driving into the background any serious consideration of the requirements to be met in securing positive treatment. The inundation of mental hospitals with long-standing chronic cases ruined moral treatment. Neither the chronic cases transferred to the hospitals from jails, almshouses, cellars, and attics nor the new cases of recently acquired insanity could benefit from the art and therapeutic know-how which had been learned by moral therapists since the time of Pinel and Tuke.

In the surge of public remorse and·pity aroused by Miss Dix, the reform movement jumped to the conclusion that elimination of abuse *in itself* would result in the recovery of the curable. With adoption of the negative function of preventing abuse, mental hospitals became, in the words of the aforementioned Franklin B. Sanborn ". . . in too many instances . . . centers of intellectual indolence or of semi-political intrigue; to whose busy and well-paid medical men new ideas were irksome, and any forward step in the care of their patients or the guidance of public opinion was the familiar story of goodness going to seed and planting the surrounding fields with a growth which was not goodness, or at least was a degenerate and reverting form thereof." (41)

Dorothea Dix lived to see her goal of placing all insane in mental hospitals largely reached, but, again in the words of Sanborn, "for the needs of the situation *which her own heroic activity had so largely created* she had neither the vital force nor the special knowledge and discrimination required." (41) Nevertheless she functioned as a self-appointed inspector of mental hospitals. Her imperious manner, rigid opinions, and attitude of censorship introduced a new element into hospital psychiatry, namely the element of fault-finding, critical, and punishing authority. Her great political influence with state legislatures gave her considerable voice in the selection of physicians for superintendencies of mental hospitals. It is not unlikely that she was largely responsible for the emphasis which came to be placed on protecting patients against any and all mishaps and the stagnation of hospital life which resulted from it. Dix's goal of moving all patients from almshouses and jails to mental hospitals was never completely accomplished. As late as 1900, there were some 900 patients in the almshouses of Massachusetts, the state in which she began her reform.

In 1904 the State Care Act was passed which completely relieved the towns of paying for their patients' support in state hospitals. This was followed by another large influx of patients into mental hospitals from jails and almshouses.

Thus it happened that the much needed and long venerated social reform, initiated by Dorothea Dix, collided with and brought to a halt a successful approach to the psychological treatment of mental illness.

During the many years this movement was taking place a new type of psychiatrist appeared. He replaced the optimistic, enthusiastic therapeutic orientation of the moral therapist with the prohibitive, restrictive, watchful, mishap-avoiding orientation of the administrative custodian of the insane. Interest in treatment was replaced by interest in diagnosis, legal questions of responsibility, and brain pathology.

A little more than a decade after Dorothea Dix began her campaign for building and enlarging mental hospitals, leadership in American psychiatry passed to the superintendent of the largest state hospital in America—the Utica State Hospital in New York. Dr. John P. Gray was appointed superintendent in 1854, and in 1855 he assumed editorship of the American Journal of Insanity. He held both posts for 30 years. He insisted that insanity was always due to physical lesion, and became the greatest single influence in swinging psychiatry back to the pre-Pinel position.

Dr. Gray was the first to introduce the microscope into American mental hospitals for the study of post-mortem material in the search for the etiology of mental diseases. He also took the role of leadership in changing mental hospital organization to treat the mentally ill patient as *physically* ill. He placed great emphasis on rest, diet, proper room temperature, and ventilation. One of his accomplishments was the invention of a rotary fan for the ventilation of the Utica State Hospital. Dr. Gray was also an authority on legal psychiatry and was in much demand by the courts. He refused to accept deviant behavior such as dypsomania, kleptomania, and moral insanity as psychiatric entities. To consider them as such he deplored as unjustifiable shielding of depravity and crime. He made a sharp distinction between mind and brain, categorically stating that insanity "is simply a bodily disease in which the mind is disturbed more or less profoundly, because the brain is involved in the sickness either primarily or secondarily. The mind is not, itself, ever diseased. It is incapable of disease or of its final consequence, death." (22) He specified in particular that "no moral or intellectual operations of the mind induce insanity apart from physical disease." (23) Dr. Gray was a man of firm religious conviction. He apparently made no distinction between mind and immortal soul and could therefore not accept the idea of mind being susceptible to sickness. Thus his religious belief and his faith in the microscope combined to support a materialistic conception of mental illness.

Dr. Gray's legalistic skill and forceful personality made him the dominant American psychiatrist of the latter half of the nineteenth century. The high point of his career was probably his success as an expert witness in proving to the satisfaction of the jury that Guiteau, President Garfield's assassin, was not insane. All told, he was successful in winning acceptance of his main contentions that insanity is due to physical disease and that "crime and depravity" are not psychiatric conditions. Although in the treatment of the insane he relied on rest and diet to aid nature in the cure of the underlying physical disease assumed to be present, he subscribed to what he termed moral treatment, in the form of amusements, recreation, and occupation as useful adjuncts. This was a complete reversal of the original concept of moral treatment as a direct influence on the patient's mental condition. Dr. Gray's views on the nature of insanity precluded any effort toward psychological understanding of patients. He was "uncompromising, unyielding, and in a certain sense coercive in his views of psychiatry," (29) says his biographer. It is of significance that when the "National Association for the Protection of the Insane and Prevention of Insanity" was organized in the 1880's, it picked Dr. Gray as its first object of attack. He also drew the criticism of the British psychiatrist, Dr. G. A. Tucker, for arguing that the majority of patients at the Utica State Hospital were allowed out of doors, on the basis of the number reported to have gone outdoors on a particular date; Tucker pointed out that this was the very day the members of the Association of Superintendents of Insane Asylums were visiting the hospital.

Dr. Gray, it would appear, aroused a great deal of antagonism with his dogmatic narrow view of mental illness and emphasis on administrative efficiency. Nevertheless he is also remembered for abolishing seclusion and restraint, for increasing the freedom of patients, and for increasing the number of attendants in order to give patients more personal care. He was also mindful of the role of stress—physical stress that is—in the causation of insanity, especially those stresses following childbirth. He admitted that emotional states such as prolonged grief could cause insanity but only by way of producing structural changes secondary to insufficient rest and nourishment. He could not conceive of insanity as a disease unless caused by physical lesion: "If the mind could so contemplate its own operations, its intellectual conceptions, its moral ideas, its emotional states, as to pass into a state of insanity, as it passes into a state of joy or grief, or jealousy, then insanity is no disease." ( 24) Here Dr. Gray revealed the basic dilemma of a psychiatry attempting to hue to the line of materialistic medicine in forming its attitude toward, and hence treatment of, psychosis. The question became one in which the patient's responsibility and culpability hinged on whether his behavior was thought to be the result of physical lesion or not. If his behavior was due to a lesion, then the psychotic patient had a right to be served and waited upon as a sick person. If not, he was deemed responsible for his acts and deserving of punishment. Thus from the point of view of materialistic medicine the medical man should logically disclaim having any role to play with respect to behavior not due to physical disease. Psychiatry could not take this position: if it did so it would be a specialty without patients, for the rising specialty of neurology was preempting the field of organic diseases of the nervous system.

It is curious why the idea of mental illness without physical lesion was so offensive to Dr. Gray and colleagues who entered psychiatry during the latter half of the last century. For it was belief in the psychological origin of mental illness which had originally inspired physicians to specialize in the treatment of mental illness and to found the profession of psychiatry. It would appear that the scientifically oriented psychiatrist of the latter decades of the century felt dutybound to adhere to the neat logic of physical science and to discard the metaphysical theories of the unity of man derived from natural philosophy, upon which moral treatment of the earlier decades was based. Scientific psychiatry eliminated moral treatment as a definitive therapy and retained it in diluted form as a diversionary adjunct to medical treatment persued in the empty climate of custodial care.

Recovery rates decreased steadily with the passage of each decade. Mental hospital directors generally sought to obscure this fact and continued to support the contention that insanity was curable even though they had come to regard it as a physical disease of unknown etiology. They appeared to believe, along with Dr. Gray, that rest, diet, and diversion was a rational program of treatment. Somehow at that time the concept of insanity as a physical disease meant that it was relatively easy to treat and that the special efforts of the pioneer psychiatrists to meet the psychological needs of patients were not necessary. This overly optimistic view was unfortunately accompanied by the low standards of care. Indeed in many instances propagation of such optimism amounted to being a cynical cover-up of culpable neglect and abuse of patients. Mental hospitals had become as reprehensible as the jails and almshouses from which Dorothea Dix had labored so long to remove patients. And fittingly it was an old friend of hers who undertook to reform professional attitudes on the subject of easy curability. He was Dr. Pliny Earle, superintendent of the Northampton State Hospital, Massachusetts.

Dr. Earle's psychiatric career, like that of Butler, Ray, and Kirkbride began in the 1830's and ended in the 1880's. It included both the moral treatment era and the physical disease era. Like Dr. Butler, Earle was inspired to enter the field of psychiatry by Dr. Woodward's work at the Worcester State

Hospital. Dr. Earle took special interest in psychiatry in medical school. His graduating thesis (1837) was "The Causes, Duration, Termination, and Moral Treatment of Insanity." After finishing medical school he went to England and France where he observed the care of patients by Tuke's followers at the York Retreat, and by Pinel's followers at the Bicêtre and the Salpêtrière in Paris. After his return to America he was appointed resident physician to the Friends' Retreat at Frankford, Pennsylvania, in 1840. Here he pursued the methods of moral treatment and eliminated bloodletting and drastic medicinal treatments which had become the practice in that hospital from the influence of Dr. Rush.

Within the framework of moral treatment he included psychological study of his patients' mental state. Like other physicians of that day he was versed in phrenology and familiar with the phenomena of mesmerism. He was impressed with the practical value of the former from personal experience. In 1842 he wrote: "The examination of Stephen Earle's head (Dr. Earle's brother) and of mine by L. N. Fowler did more to convince me of the practical utility of phrenology—not to say of its truth as a science—than anything else that I ever saw, read, or heard. Stephen was told what I believe he might have been rather than what he is. But, for myself, I doubt if any of my nearest relatives or most intimate friends could have given a more accurate synopsis of my character." (42)

Dr. Earle also constructed psychodynamic formulations of the patients' mental conflicts in the anatomic-psychic language of phrenology. The following account of one of his patients at Frankford gives some idea of his effort to understand patients:

"He is unsettled, restless, and constantly worrying about something. His Conscientiousness thinks that the buttons of his vest, which are covered with plain black 'lasting,' are too gay. His Reverence is in an inexplicable quandary in regard to a copy of Scott's Family Bible, which it and Acquisitiveness procured. After the purchase, Reverence, reading the commentary, became dissatisfied, and openly promulgated dissatisfaction. Hereupon Destructiveness advised to burn the book. "That would be a wise expedient for the commentary,' remarked Reverence, 'but for the text it would be sacrilegious, and to separate them is impossible.' Benevolence, hearing the colloquy, proposed to give the book away. 'And contaminate somebody else, eh' cried Reverence, holding up both hands in astonishment. At this point Secretiveness whispered that, if he had the management, he would box the book up, and hide it among the lumber of the garret. 'And thus contaminate posterity,' exclaimed Reverence and Philprogenitiveness, simultaneously. Here the consultation ended, and poor Reverence can see no way out of the dilemma. Acquisitiveness and Conscientiousness have long been in combat. The former came into possession of some notes of hand, and, on the day they were to be renewed, sat down composedly to cast compound interest on the several sums. At this moment Conscientiousness came in, declaring that Acquisitiveness was doing wrong. 'Bigot!' cried Acquisitiveness: 'You are always meddling with other people's affairs.' 'But you outrage justice,' said Conscientiousness in a tone which showed he was spurred on by his neighbor Firmness. 'Grumble and growl away,' retorted Acquisitiveness. 'I shall stick to my text, and pocket the compound interest.' The field was won by the last speaker. Conscientiousness retreated, but has kept up a kind of predatory warfare ever since." (43)

Although Dr. Earle apparently understood the role of conflict in insanity, there is no evidence that he sought to relieve it through direct discussion of mental content and personal history with patients singly or in groups as did Dr. Butler. Quite to the contrary, Dr. Earle relied mostly on lectures on a variety of subjects and demonstrations of scientific experiments to mobilize healthy mental activity. No doubt his experience as a school teacher influenced his choice of method. He also carried out a program of full activity including entertainment, recreation, and work.

In 1844 Dr. Earle was appointed the first medical director of the Bloomingdale Hospital (now Westchester Division of the New York Hospital) which had been under lay management since its founding in 1821. Here Dr. Earle further elaborated his

program of treatment but met with disappointment in attempting
to persuade patients to work. They were of the wealthy classes
and objected to working on the grounds that they paid their
keep. It is not unlikely that his short term of office at Bloomingdale—five years—was the result of disagreements arising over his
efforts to enforce his policy on work for patients. In 1847, while
at Bloomingdale, Dr. Earle discovered the first case of general
paralysis to be diagnosed as such in America. Among the cases
of this disease (established to be incurable by Calmeil), diagnosed by Dr. Earle, one patient recovered who was perfectly
well ten years after his discharge from the hospital.

On leaving Bloomingdale in 1849 Dr. Earle went on an
extended tour of German mental hospitals. In the course of this
tour he came in contact with concepts which held insanity to be
a hopeless physical disease. He also saw many more cases of
general paresis which was regarded by some German psychiatrists
at that time not as a disease entity by itself but as an end stage
of insanity in general. Dr. Earle was greatly impressed with
German administrative efficiency and discipline, especially where
it had put into effect an extensive work-program for patients.

On his return to America, Dr. Earle's expectation of being
appointed superintendent of one of the newly established mental
hospitals did not materialize. He took up residence in his home
village of Leicester, Massachusetts, where he remained in professional inactivity for about three years. He then went to New
York City and opened an office as a consultant on mental disorders. While in New York he was appointed to a committee of
medical visitors to the city asylum on Blackwell's Island where
he saw still more cases of general paralysis and the evil results
of hospital mismanagement. He remained in New York for but
a short time and then travelled in the South and to Cuba. In
1854 he returned to Leicester where he remained in retirement
for 10 years. During this time he studied annual reports from
mental hospitals all over the world. In the words of his biographer: "He bided his time with some impatience and not without
months and days of despondency. He lived at Leicester, in a
small house, and amid humble duties of one sort or another."

(43) The reason for his despondency was presumably his disappointment of seeing physicians less qualified than himself appointed as superintendents of the many mental hospitals built during those years. This is not certain, however, for he was subject to periods of depression throughout his life as were other members of his family. There is some evidence also that his mood swings went in the other direction. His biographer noted: "Punning, indeed, in its many forms was carried by him to an excess. It was one kind of grammatical exercise in which he long delighted."

In 1864 Dr. Earle was finally appointed superintendent of the Northampton State Hospital in Massachusetts. Here, in marked contrast to the wealthy patients at Bloomingdale Hospital, he had charge of 450 patients, practically all of the "pauper classes," nine-tenths of whom were long-standing chronic cases transferred to Northampton to make room for new admissions to the other state hospitals. Nevertheless Dr. Earle pursued the program of moral treatment as developed by him at Bloomingdale. At Northampton he had one advantage at least: there was no objection to his ideas on manual work for patients. He also revamped the administration of the hospital by introducing methods for achieving business efficiency and discipline which he had admired in Germany. Yet in spite of his respect for his patients' love of beauty (he hung over 1,500 pictures in the hospital), in spite of his giving lectures and directing recreational activities more than 300 evenings a year, and in spite of his success in persuading a majority of his patients to work, he found his recovery rates to be much lower than those reported by his contemporaries. He knew that many of his fellow superintendents were political appointees who had no training in psychiatry and no interest in patients. He was also fully aware that none of the other state hospitals had a program of moral treatment remotely approaching his own.

Dr. Earle was a deeply religious Quaker. He was also overly modest, scrupulously honest, and very frugal. He despised ostentation of any kind. He disapproved thoroughly of vindictiveness, but there was one issue which aroused his righteous anger and about which he could not remain silent. He abhorred the current practice of building large "palace hospitals" which he considered to be extravagant shams covering up neglect of patients. From his point of view the rationale for building such hospitals was based on the fallacy of easy curability. He therefore set out to prove through presentation of statistical data that cures were much less frequent than commonly believed at that time. In his own opinion his statistical studies were "an important agent in stimulating the minds of philanthropists to seek—and in several notable instances to adopt—other methods for the custody and care of a large part of the insane than that of collecting them in expensive and unwieldy curative institutions." ( 13)

Unfortunately Dr. Earle's studies had the opposite effect. They promoted extreme pessimism in psychiatry and almost complete cessation of treatment efforts. Yet the very data on which he based his conclusions form a basis for a far more optimistic outlook than is commonly held today. These data are presented and discussed more fully in Chapter V.

In the case of Pliny Earle, to compare him with Dorothea Dix, the "goodness that went to seed" lay in his interpretation of his statistical work to the effect that incurability was an attribute of mental illness itself. His intention was to destroy complacency and bring about sound methods of treatment. He showed that recovery rates were higher in the early decades of the nineteenth century than in the 1870's and '80's. He pointed out that breach of the principle that no more than 200 patients should be cared for in one institution was partly responsible for the poorer results of the later years. Likewise he demonstrated certain fallacies in the statistical reports of the early superintendents which had resulted in some exaggeration of their recovery rates and showed that relapses of recovered cases further reduced the proportion of "true" recoveries. Through his tenacious efforts he was able to convince himself and others that recoveries had been less frequent in the past than had been realized and that they were becoming even less frequent. This insistence on the infrequency of recovery and the statement that the disease itself was becoming more incurable obscured the fact that recoveries were not only possible but had been as frequent as 70% of admissions in well-run institutions.

Dr. Earle was not only successful in changing the outlook of physicians on the curability of insanity, he was also largely responsible for an important change in the attitude of state administrators regarding the functions of superintendents of mental hospitals. His own great frugality, love of arithmetic (he was also the hospital's treasurer), knowledge of farming, and ability to persuade patients to work enabled him not only to operate the hospital more economically than any other superintendent, but to show a profit. The following account by Franklin B. Sanborn portrays in detail Dr. Earle's success as an administrator:

"At the end of Dr. Earle's fourth year (at Northampton) not only had the valuation of the hospital property increased by nearly $30,000 since he came, but the trustees were able to say, 'For the first time since the founding of the hospital we have passed a year without borrowing money,' and they closed the year with a balance of near $10,000 in hand. This balance went on increasing—though often drawn upon for other than current expenses—until when Dr. Earle resigned in 1885, it stood at $34,000; while the valuation figures had gone up from $272,000 in 1864 to more than $440,000 in 1885. This gain came from the high cultivation of the enlarged farm, the better labor of the employed patients, the systematic handling of all expenditure, and for a time the increased income from private patients.

"By the prudent management of the hospital, Dr. Earle disarmed criticism on the economic side, and made his establishment popular with the legislature and the State authorities, who had been accustomed to see it a frequent applicant for appropriations, not only for repairs and new building (as was the case with other hospitals), but for deficiencies in its current expense. To meet the lack of a working capital, which every new hospital feels, the Board of State Charities, in accord with Dr. Earle, procured advance payments for nine-tenths of the State patients there (which was perfectly safe, since they were permanent boarders), and this enabled him to make cash purchases, and

thereby reduce the current cost. This he also reduced materially
by introducing the system of distributing supplies which he had
seen practised in frugal Germany; each person employed being
made accountable for the articles delivered upon his request,
and thus becoming more careful against waste or theft,—the
latter by no means unknown formerly in such establishments.
In this way he became a model for other hospitals to follow, as
they gradually did, but not until some of them had suffered
from extravagance and peculation so as to attract public notice."
(44)

The phenomenon of a mathematically minded, hard-headed
business man with knowledge of agriculture, being at the same
time a wise physician and skilled psychiatrist, was indeed fortunate for the Commonwealth in a financial way. It was unfortunate, however, that his penurious qualities were the ones most
admired by the state administrators and that they helped to
establish a precedent of choosing men for superintendencies who
had these qualities.

Some of Dr. Earle's opinions about insanity provide clues
which suggest why he placed such stress on its incurability. First,
he regarded insanity as a mystery. He said: "The disorder—not
to say 'disease,' inasmuch as disease implies the possibility of
death—in its essential nature, and even in its relation to the
conduct and the practical ability of those who are affected with
it, is an inexplicable mystery to persons who are constantly
surrounded by it, and who are consequently better informed
than any others in regard to it." (45) Second, he discounted the
idea that the insane suffer unhappiness. He even contended that
depressed patients went through the motions of being sad in a
machine-like fashion but did not really feel it. He explained
away the suffering of insanity: "I do not forget, but am most
free to acknowledge, that the worst wards of a hospital of this
kind present a sad spectacle, even to persons familiarized with
it—a very sad spectacle to anyone to whom it is an unaccustomed
sight. But this aspect is the consequence of mental impairment
and bodily deterioration, and is no evidence of unhappiness on
the part of the patients. The observer derives his judgment from

his own feelings and emotions, not from the mental and moral condition of the persons around him, which, particularly if he be a casual visitor, he cannot accurately know." (46)

Yet Dr. Earle was in no way a callous man. Apparently he did not believe insanity to be accompanied by suffering because he, like Dr. Gray, equated mind with immortal soul and did not believe it was susceptible to disease, as indicated in the following statements: "Were the arguments for the hypothesis that in insanity the mind itself is diseased tenfold more numerous than they are, and more weighty, I could not accept them. My ideas of the human mind are such that I cannot hold for a moment that it can be diseased, as we understand disease. That implies death as a final consequence, but Mind is eternal. In its very essence and structure (to use the terms we apply to matter), in its elemental composition and its organization, it was created for immortality. Consequently, it is superior to the bodily structure and beyond the scope of the wear and tear and disorganization and final destruction of the mortal part of our being." (46) "The longer I live, the more I am impressed with a belief in the all-controlling supremacy of mind over matter, of the far-reaching, mysterious power of the divine intelligence within, and of the limited bounds of present knowledge, compared with what is to be known when mind shall have thrown off its fetters of clay. Science is proud, even presumptuous; but how much cause for humility in the fact that it cannot trace one particle of its knowledge upward, through effects, to the original cause and center of all things! Science is lost at once in the mazes of uncertainty and ignorance, whenever it attempts to fathom mind itself." (47)

Apparently Dr. Earle's concept of the incurability of insanity had a special meaning to him in terms of his own philosophy of life. There is little doubt that he felt a great affinity for the insane, for he devoted his life to their care, never married, and was a victim of depression himself. His biographer said: "Consecration is the right word to describe his care for the insane. With all his worldly prudence and common sense, and notwithstanding his broad toleration of theological differences, he was from the first, and essentially, a religious man, governed in all the important actions of life by a sense of religious duty and that regard for the fatherhood of God and the brotherhood of man, which the small sect of his family and forefathers especially cherishes. Of the narrowness of the Quaker church he had nothing; of the profound instinct of divine guidance and the worth of the human soul he had much. In the growing strength of materialism among scientific men and physicians, he still maintained the spiritual and immortal nature of our minds, and could have said with Shakespeare, 'I think more nobly of the soul, and no way approve their opinion', . . It required some courage and firm religious conviction to adhere to this noble opinion during the latter half of the passing century." (46)

Another aspect of Dr. Earle's personality is described by his biographer as follows: "One of the chief qualifications of a superintendent for such a difficult position was as marked in Dr. Earle as in any of the hundred superintendents and directors of hospitals and asylums whom I have personally known in an experience now covering 35 years (written in 1898)—his strictness of discipline, both for patients and attendants. This, which sometimes passed for unkindness, and was really exacting now and then, was the truest kindness when the real interest of all persons was considered. The inflexible justice of a most kindly nature thus displayed itself, often at the cost of much pain to the doctor himself." (48)

There is no doubt that in one sense Dr. Earle took excellent care of his patients. They were not only better fed but had a lower death rate than those of any other hospital in the country. Also they had the busiest and most interesting community life of any hospital at that time. Nevertheless there is some suggestion that there was a connection between the fact of a high proportion of working patients, low discharge rates, and the excellent financial condition of the hospital. Indeed Dr. Earle's biographer makes the following statement: "It was to this steady but not compulsory discipline of labor that the financial success of the hospital was due in great part; and, though the record of recoveries at Northampton showed small numbers, because

the cases were so largely chronic, yet there were many un-
recorded *virtual* recoveries—patients who, while still insane, were
capable of self-support and self-direction under kindly supervision." (49) It might be said that Dr. Earle behaved like an
overprotective father who fostered dependency and could not
countenance patients leaving the family fold.

Dr. Earle's philosophy and methods of patient-care in mental
hospitals are by no means merely an historical curiosity. He was
regarded as the model superintendent by the Massachusetts
Board of State Charities, and through that body he had an
influence on the makeup of mental hospitals which has lasted
up to the present day. Dr. John P. Gray exerted a similar influence on the development of New York state hospitals.

It is over 60· years since Dorothea Dix, Dr. Pliny Earle, and
Dr. John P. Gray died and left behind them the mark of their
particular personalities on the care of the mentally ill. Since
that time revolutionary changes have taken place in the whole
of society, in medicine and in psychiatry itself *as a science*. Yet
in *practice,* psychiatry has had little or no effect on the care
of patients in mental hospitals. Indeed the perspectives and
methods of Dix, Earle, and Gray have become a deeply ingrained
tradition.

As long ago as 1901 Dr. Charles W. Page, superintendent of
the Middletown State Hospital in Connecticut, gently reminded
the psychiatric profession of the need to return to the principles
of the early moral treatment era:

"It is now more than half a century since Butler formulated
in his mind those tenets, or methods, the application, or execution
of which gave him a prominent position as a specialist in mental
disease. This period has been marked not only by great changes
in the social condition of our population, but most surprising
advances have been made in science and the arts.

"Medicine, in some branches at least, has been rewritten
upon a basis of comparatively recent science. In keeping with
the general trend of business affairs, lunatic hospitals have undergone changes. They have rapidly increased in numbers and
vastly expanded in size. In their laudable desire for a scientific

standing they vie with each other in providing laboratory facilities. Medical officers also are burdened with executive obligations, and ambitious ones must devote much time to pathological questions. With the pressure of these new, interesting and important considerations, painstaking personal efforts with individual patients are in danger of being neglected. And yet the power of the mind over the body, and the laws of sympathy which, unfortunately, cannot be stated in scientific terms, have undergone no changes, and will ever respond to right application.

"Is there not an obvious moral to be drawn from a review of Butler's life-work, namely our duty to uphold and utilize as fully as possible in our practice these powerful moral agencies which the fathers of New England psychiatry, Todd, Woodward, Butler, and others found so efficacious in treating the insane?" (37)

# V

## Hospital Statistics and
## Prognosis of Mental Illness

"Figures don't lie but liars can figure" is a saying which expresses an almost universal distrust of statistics. Skepticism mounts even higher when historical statistics are used to support a point of view. Data from historically remote sources can always be said to lack comparability with modern data whatever the subject matter. These difficulties become manifold when one is dealing with recovery and discharge rates from mental hospitals. Comparability of clinical material one hundred years ago and today is not easy to achieve. It is also difficult to achieve comparability between two contemporary hospitals. In neither case can we afford to ignore the quantitative data which are *available*.

Any effort to do a historical statistical study of mental illness is uniquely blessed by the fact that even the most ancient of our mental hospitals were required to submit annual reports to the state legislature. The Annual Reports of the Worcester State Hospital, beginning in 1833, contain a wealth of statistical data in an unbroken series to the present time. They provide us with a panoramic view of the traffic of patients in and out of the hospital. Fig. 3 shows what happened to the recovery rate over that period, a drop from 45% to 4%. The cry can be made that the criteria for recovery became more stringent. And indeed they did. There is also undeniable evidence that standards of treatment declined to a very low level.

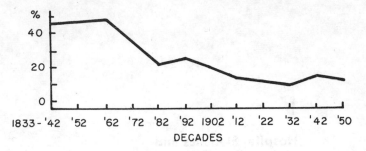

Fig. 3. Per cent of admissions discharged as recovered from Worcester State Hospital by decades for 120 years. (*Data from the Annual Reports of the Hospital*)

The decrease in recovery rates in the post-Civil War period from the level of the early decades of the nineteenth century is by no means a new finding. Attempts to explain the decrease led to one of the most heated controversies in the history of psychiatry, namely, that concerning the curability of insanity. The pessimistic view bluntly thrust on the medical world in the 1870's by Dr. Pliny Earle's statistical studies showing lower recovery rates than those reported in the past, was followed by implications that the statistics of the earlier period had been "cooked." Since Dr. Earle wielded considerable influence and was greatly respected, other superintendents followed his lead. Among them were superintendents of the Worcester State Hospital, first Dr. Barnard Eastman and then Dr. John G. Park who followed him. Stimulated by Dr. Earle's suggestions, they compiled a retroactive report of all admissions and discharges from the day the hospital's doors were opened by Dr. Woodward. They employed their own criteria of recovery and did not distinguish between patients ill for less than one year and those ill for a longer period. The recovery rates shown in Fig. 3 were derived from Dr. Park's table covering the years from 1832 to 1892. When it is remembered that Dr. Park looked on Dr. Woodward's recovery rates with a jaundiced eye and that one of his objectives in doing the study was to demonstrate that Dr. Woodward had exaggerated his recovery rates by juggling his figures, there is little reason to suggest that the number of recoveries was exaggerated. The results of the study, however,

with respect to the years when Dr. Woodward was superintendent did not differ more than two or three per cent from
Dr. Woodward's own figures. This was never commented on
by Dr. Eastman, Dr. Park, or Dr. Earle in the Annual Reports
of the Worcester State Hospital or elsewhere. Not that they
failed to be impressed, for Dr. Park set to work on a follow-up
study (which took 10 years to complete!) of all patients discharged as recovered in the records of the Woodward regime.
It amounted to a follow-up of more than 1,000 patients over a
60-year period.

Follow-up studies of patients discharged from mental hospitals have rarely been made for a longer period than 20 years
after time of discharge. Such studies as have been made seldom
deal with more than one or two hundred patients. A follow-up
study covering a period of 36 to 60 years after discharge involving over a thousand patients is therefore of considerable
interest. Evidence that these patients were discharged from the
Worcester State Hospital during the years 1833 to 1846 not
only adds to the interest, but also provides a unique opportunity
to learn about the treatment results of early American psychiatry.

The study in question was carried out between 1881 and
1892. We have inferred that the patients dealt with were discharged prior to 1847 since the total number of patients followed (1,173) is within 15 of the total number of patients
reported discharged as recovered during the years 1833-1846
(1,188). This was also the period when Dr. Woodward was
head of the hospital. In view of Dr. Pliny Earle's attack on Dr.
Woodward's reports of recovery, it is not inconceivable that Dr.
Earle suggested the follow-up study of Dr. Woodward's recovered patients in order to prove his point that the majority
relapsed. Mention of this study was first made by Dr. Park,
superintendent, in the 49th Annual Report of the Worcester
State Hospital, 1881. The following quotation from this report
discloses that his purpose was to demonstrate the unlikelihood
of recovery.

"A review of insane hospital statistics upon this subject of
recoveries, as tabulated in the annual reports of the institutions,

has brought of late to public notice the fact that a person afflicted with insanity is quite liable to a second and subsequent attacks, and that a relapse, or an attack *de novo*, occurs in this malady more frequently than in any of the other serious forms of disease.

"Now, although it may be a question upon which there may be honest differences of opinion whether each case which recovers may not be fairly called a cure, even if the patient has a second attack within a few months or a year, there can be no doubt that the public have been hitherto widely misled as to the meaning of the word 'recovery,' as used in the hospital reports, and as to the permanency of cures from insanity. Not a small number of patients who were discharged as recovered in the earlier reports of this hospital have many times since become a burden to the public or private purse by reason of a return of their malady.

"In order to obtain definite information on this point the following circular has been prepared, making inquiry about the subsequent mental condition of those patients who were discharged from this institution as recovered on their only admission, and of those who recovered on their last re-admission:

'Dear Sir,—I would esteem it a great favor if you would send me answers to the following questions (obtained either from personal knowledge or as a result of inquiry) relating to . . . . . . . . of . . . . . . , a patient discharged from this institution . . . . . . 18 . . . . .
Did . . . . . . . . . . remain well,
Has . . . . . . . . . . ever been in any hospital for the insane since leaving Worcester? If so, where? How many times? How long a time? and state of health after discharge.
If living, where? and mental condition. If dead, date and cause of death.
Did . . . . . . . . . . die at home, in hospital, or almshouse?
What was . . . . . . . . . . 's mental condition at time of death?
If you are unable to answer these questions, will you be kind enough to give me the address of some member of the family or acquaintance who would be likely to possess the desired information? The object of my inquiry is to perfect the medical history of the hospital.

Very respectfully,
John G. Park
Superintendent

"The above inquiries have, to this date, been made regarding only 211 patients, all of whom were discharges previous to 1840. Owing to the time which has elapsed since their connection with the hospital great difficulty has been experienced in finding anybody who knew or remembered anything about many of them. Satisfactory answers have, however, been received in 94 instances thus far, and as the cases become more recent, a much greater per cent of replies is expected." (3)

Farther on in the report Dr. Park analyzed the returns of the 94 patients about whom replies had been received. Eight were still alive and had remained well since discharge; 40 had died but had remained mentally well all their lives. Of the remaining 46, 7 had committed suicide, 10 had been re-hospitalized, and 29 were considered to be insane at the time of reply, but were not hospitalized.

In the annual report of the next year, Dr. Park revealed the full scope of the study. He also indicated that the source of motivation for doing the study lay in the person of Dr. Pliny Earle, who was at the time arousing considerable attention with his statistical studies designed to prove the incurability of mental illness.

"This subject (i.e., recoveries not permanent cures) has been elaborated at considerable length in the recent reports of Dr. Pliny Earle of the Northampton Lunatic Hospital. From information received upon this point in answer to circulars sent out inquiring about the subsequent mental condition of those persons who were discharged from this hospital as recovered on their *only admission* and of those who were discharged recovered on their *last re*-admission, it appears that of 1,171 circulars sent out, up to September 30, 1882, satisfactory answers have been received from 669. Of this number, 73 men and 80 women remained well and were living at the time of reply, and 83 men and 114 women remained well during life; 19 men and 11 women committed suicide, and the remaining 289 relapsed and had been admitted to other hospitals or had been inmates of almshouses, or had been cared for at home, where they died or are still living. No information could be obtained in 129 cases, 373 circulars remain unanswered. As was stated in my last report, a good deal of difficulty has been experienced in finding any traces of many of these cases. This is especially true of those who were committed from the cities of the state, they represent a roving population, and the records of the overseers of the poor contain no mention of them after leaving the hospital.

"I have been greatly aided by the overseers of the poor of the different towns, and by physicians and others, who have spent much time and shown much interest in obtaining for me the information furnished in table 30." (4)

In the Annual Report of 1883, Dr. Park makes the following remarks: "Information as to the subsequent history of persons who have been discharged from this hospital as recovered on their only admission or last re-admission, as tabulated in table 30, confirms the results shown in the same table last year . . . About 50 per cent suffered no relapse, but as no answers were received to one-third of the circulars sent, and taking into account the liability to relapse of those now reported well, I am inclined to believe that this percentage should be reduced one-half" (5).

This was the last mention of the follow-up study made by Dr. Park. The work of compiling statistics continued, however, until 1893 when 1,157 replies had been received of the 1,173 circulars sent out. Of the replies, 189 provided no record. Information as to the outcome of the remaining 984 patients is presented in Table 4, adapted from table 28 in the Annual Report of the Worcester State Hospital for 1893.

A total of 568 patients had either died without having a relapse or were still living and had never had a relapse. That is, very *nearly one-half (48%) never had a relapse after discharge.* An additional 67 relapsed and were hospitalized, but were again discharged (about 6%). Only 143 relapsed who were re-hospitalized (or sent to almshouses) and not again discharged. Another 142 had relapsed and were either still at home or had died while living at home.

All told, only 210 of the 1,171 patients again became a burden to the Commonwealth—less than 20%.

This unusual follow-up has remained buried in these annual reports for nearly 60 years—a sad comment on psychiatric interest

TABLE 4.—1882-1893 FOLLOW-UP OF RECOVERIES OF
1833-1846, WORCESTFR STATE HOSPITAL

| | |
|---|---|
| Remained well, still alive | 317 ⎫ (568=48%) |
| Remained well through life | 251 ⎭ |
| Relapsed and again discharged | 67 |
| Total well or had died mentally well at 36 to 60 years follow-up point | 635 = 54.13% |
| Relapsed, still living | 100 |
| Relapsed, died in relapse | 239 |
| Relapsed, nothing more known | 10 |
| Total mentally ill, or had died mentally ill at 36 to 60 years follow-up point | 349 = 29.75% |
| No information | 189 = 16.12% |
| Grand total | 1,173 = 100% |

(*Data from the Annual Report of the Hospital, 1893*)

in recovery from mental illness. We suggest here that the results
it contained were so much better than those reported by Dr.
Pliny Earle, the authority on mental health statistics of his day,
that neither Dr. Park nor his successor quite dared to report
those results in their full connotation for fear of arousing unfavorable comment from those who would compare them with
their own results. There is no need for shyness today, however,
for modern treatment results are much superior to those of the
80's and 90's of the last century. There *is* good reason to wonder,
though, if a 50-year follow-up of discharged patients today
would show 50% of them without relapse.

Data available today indicate that the outcome of patients
treated at the Worcester State Hospital was much more favorable
than Dr. Earle contended. It is therefore pertinent to review
Dr. Earle's discussion of the statistical data of that hospital as
presented in his book, "Curability of Insanity." The arguments
he used to prove that repeated recoveries of the same patients
produced falsely large recovery rates, provide a good example
of his one-sided perspective. In his discussion of this matter
he based his arguments on data obtained from the Annual Report

of the Worcester State Hospital of 1878-79 which was written
by Dr. Park.

Dr. Earle first called attention to figures which indicated
that of the 47 patients discharged as recovered that year only
32 were discharged as recovered for the first time. He then made
a big point of the fact that the other 15 patients had been
accredited at some time in the past with a total of 55 recoveries.
In making this point he disregarded his own rule that recovery
figures should not be considered significant unless reported as
a proportion of the number of patients admitted.

He then proceeded to analyze a special study prepared by
Dr. Park of the 11,000 cases admitted to the Worcester State
Hospital from its date of opening in 1833 to 1875. Dr. Earle
began his analysis by pointing out that the 11,000 cases represented only 8,204 *persons*, and that the re-admissions, 2,796,
amounted to one-fourth of the total number of admissions and
one-third the number of persons. He then emphasized that the
number of recoveries on first admissions was only 38.89% of
the *persons* admitted. He also quoted the number of recoveries
of all the re-admissions to be 1,191, and mentioned that the
whole number of recoveries was 4,382 (3,191 plus 1,191). Here
Dr. Earle called a halt to the arithmetic of recovery and failed
to note that the figure for all recoveries, 4,382, was 39.1% of the
total number of admissions, 11,000. He was no doubt embarrassed
by the fact that this proportion is practically identical with the
proportion of first admissions, or of *persons*, who recovered and
were reported by him as 38.89%. Obviously he did not wish to
call the reader's attention to evidence that repeated recovery
of re-admissions made so little difference in the over-all recovery
rate of the Worcester State Hospital. He also made no mention
of the fact that the total number of recoveries of re-admissions
was 1,191 of a total of 2,796 re-admissions, or 40%—which is also
very close to the proportion of *persons* recovered.

After evading evidence which did not support his contentions, Dr. Earle went to the labor of calculating the per cent
recovered for each successive number of admissions from 1 to 23
(which happened to be the greatest number of re-admissions
reported). He tabulated the results of his calculations as follows:

| | | |
|---|---|---|
| 1st −38.89 | 9th−62.92 | 17th −66.00 |
| 2nd−36.78 | 10th−62.50 | 18th −66.66 |
| 3rd −46.66 | 11th−61.11 | 19th −50.00 |
| 4th −45.81 | 12th−71.43 | 20th −100.00 |
| 5th −55.45 | 13th−66.66 | 21st −100.00 |
| 6th −61.29 | 14th−88.88 | 22nd−100.00 |
| 7th −61.36 | 15th−57.14 | 23rd −100.00 |
| 8th −60.60 | 16th−75.00 | |

Regarding the table he then stated: "These gradually swelling percentages are caused by the repeated recoveries of the same persons." (13). It is only too clear that Dr. Earle was going out of his way to convince the reader that repeated recoveries of the same persons caused a falsely large recovery *rate* when in fact they had no such effect. He deliberately reported percentages without giving the actual numbers of patients involved, a device which hid from the reader the information that the number of patients decreased rapidly with each successive re-admission number. Indeed, the 20th, 21st, 22nd, and 23rd re-admissions with recovery rates of 100% were all of a single patient! The data from which Dr. Earle derived his percentages appear in Table 5. Dr. Earle did not present this table because he did not want the reader to perceive that the small number of patients involved could effect the recovery rates, as recorded in annual reports, but very little one way or the other.

Dr. Earle continued his discussion by giving the number of deaths, which was 1,498, and with it the percentage of *persons* admitted which it represented, which was 18.26%. He pointed out that the proportion of deaths was nearly three times as large as was usually reported in the annual statistics of mental hospitals. Here again he sought to convince the reader that hospital reports gave more optimistic figures than was true by neglecting to note that the death rate of 18% referred to the deaths occurring in all admissions over a period of 42 years.

He then went on to quote Dr. Park to the effect that "many" patients who had swollen the number of recoveries in the past had returned to the hospital again and again and finally died there. The actual number of patients who died in the hospital on re-admission status was 318, or less than 4% of the total

TABLE 5.—RECORD OF 11,000 CASES ADMITTED TO
WORCESTER HOSPITAL FROM ITS OPENING TO SEPT. 28, 1875.

(*Data from a table in 1879 Annual Report of the Hospital*)

| Adm. Number | With this Number Adm.'s | Number of Patients | | | | |
|---|---|---|---|---|---|---|
| | | Discharged | | | Died | In Hosp. 9-30-79 |
| | | Recov. | Improv. | Not Impr. | | |
| 1 | 8,204 | 3,191 | 2,218 | 1,524 | 1,180 | 87 |
| 2 | 1,683 | 619 | 471 | 335 | 224 | 34 |
| 3 | 510 | 238 | 137 | 63 | 56 | 6 |
| 4 | 227 | 104 | 74 | 32 | 13 | 4 |
| 5 | 110 | 61 | 25 | 13 | 10 | 1 |
| 6 | 62 | 38 | 15 | 3 | 6 | 0 |
| 7 | 44 | 27 | 9 | 3 | 5 | 0 |
| 8 | 33 | 20 | 10 | 3 | 0 | 0 |
| 9 | 27 | 17 | 7 | 2 | 1 | 0 |
| 10 | 24 | 15 | 8 | 1 | 0 | 0 |
| 11 | 18 | 11 | 6 | 1 | 0 | 0 |
| 12 | 14 | 10 | 2 | 1 | 1 | 0 |
| 13 | 12 | 8 | 2 | 1 | 0 | 1 |
| 14 | 9 | 8 | 1 | 0 | 0 | 0 |
| 15 | 7 | 4 | 2 | 0 | 1 | 0 |
| 16 | 4 | 3 | 1 | 0 | 0 | 0 |
| 17 | 3 | 2 | 0 | 1 | 0 | 0 |
| 18 | 3 | 2 | 0 | 0 | 1 | 0 |
| 19 | 2 | 1 | 1 | 0 | 0 | 0 |
| 20 | 1 | 1 | | | | |
| 21 | 1 | 1 | | | | |
| 22 | 1 | 1 | | | | |
| 23 | 1 | 1 | | | | |

| | | |
|---|---|---|
| Number of persons admitted | | 8,204 |
| Number of re-admissions | 2,664 | |
| Re-admissions without removal from hospital | 132 | |
| Total number of re-admissions | | 2,796 |
| Number of cases | | 11,000 |
| Cases in other hospitals previous to admission here | 996 | |
| Transfers to State Hospitals in this state on 1st admission | 783 | |
| Removal to other institutions in this state on 1st admission | 29 | |
| Sent to hospitals out of state on 1st admission | 15 | |
| Transfers to State Hospitals in this state on re-admission | 282 | |
| Removal to other institutions in this state on re-admission | 11 | |
| Sent to hospitals out of state on re-admission | 8 | |

number of persons admitted. It might also be mentioned that the number of patients re-admitted to the hospital more than twice was 461, or less than 6% of the total number admitted.

Dr. Earle's quotation of Dr. Park continued with the statement that many more patients went to other hospitals and finally died in them. It should be noted that in the follow-up study presented earlier in this chapter this was the fate of less than 6% of the number of patients discharged as recovered. A further statement of Dr. Park quoted by Dr. Earle was that still more patients had had repeated admissions and finally died in almshouses. In the follow-up study, this was the fate of less than 5% of the patients discharged as recovered.

Both Drs. Earle and Park neglect to tell what the total figure was for all patients who either had died in the hospital, were inmates of the hospital at the time of the study, or were inmates of other hospitals or almshouses. Actually it was but 2,759 (assuming that *none* of the 1,261 patients transferred to other hospitals or almshouses had been discharged), or 34%. Thus the significant finding of the entire study was left unstated, namely that 66% of the *persons* admitted had neither died in, nor were patients of, the hospital at the time of the study. He failed to mention also that 65% of the first admissions were discharged as improved and recovered. One can only surmise that Dr. Earle, and with him Dr. Park, refused to see anything in statistical data which did not support the thesis that recovery rates were artificially swollen by the repeated recovery of re-admissions.

Dr. Earle did not make explicit, but rather hid from view, his own puristic criteria of recovery which seemed to preclude the occurrence of an attack of mental illness at any time in the life of the patient. He thus mixed his concept of a recovery rate with that of a follow-up study. By this means he could always defend a pessimistic view with the argument that lifetime follow-ups would inevitably disclose many relapses of mental illness.

Whatever Dr. Earle's underlying purpose was, he succeeded in convincing the psychiatric profession that the prognosis of mental illness was extremely poor and thus exonerated its members for poor recovery rates. The idea that mental illness was incurable became more and more popular. By the turn of the century, recovery rates acceptable even to Earle (approximately 30%) seemed preposterous. By the 1920's few medical officers were inclined to discharge more than 4% or 5% as recovered. Progressive tightening of criteria for recovery and concomitant deterioration in standards of care were equally potent factors underlying this decrease in recoveries. Belief in the incurability of mental illness, which Dr. Earle had sold the medical profession, was a barrier to the adoption of much needed corrective measures which has not yet been torn down.

Not all physicians subscribed to Dr. Earle's thesis of incurability. To be sure there were few who possessed as much experience with the mentally ill as he. But among those equally experienced with Dr. Earle was Dr. Isaac Ray, the American authority on legal psychiatry, a skilled moral therapist and an enlightened hospital administrator.

Dr. Ray had demonstrated to his own satisfaction that the majority of the mentally ill were curable, in his early experience with patients during the 1840's and '50's. He was aware that much had changed in American life during the decades which followed. He could not accept Dr. Earle's devaluation of treatment results reported during the earlier decades. In 1879 he presented to the College of Physicians and Surgeons in Philadelphia a paper, "Recoveries From Mental Illness" (39), which was, in effect, a rebuttal to Dr. Earle's writings.

In this paper Dr. Ray pointed out that Dr. Earle had no basis for contending that statistical reports were more biased in favor of recovery in the early history of mental hospitals than in later years. In Dr. Ray's own view recoveries actually had become less frequent. The factors which underlay decrease in recovery in his experience were: 1) poorer general health of patients from unhygienic urban centers which were increasing in number during the course of the century, 2) the appearance of greater number of patients with cerebral affections such as general paralysis which had been all but unknown in the earlier years, 3) the more frequent hospitalization of patients with the quieter but less recoverable forms of insanity as public use of mental hospitals increased. Dr. Ray contended, furthermore, that a failure to recover was as much the result of a patient's not receiving a fair trial of (moral) treatment as the result of real incurability.

The statistical reports of the Worcester State Hospital provide us today with a working basis for estimating the prognosis of psychosis in general—at least in the earlier decades of the nineteenth century. Dr. Woodward's statistical reports show that he discharged as recovered or improved about 75% of patients ill less than one year before admission. Dr. Park's follow-up study of these recoveries shows that one-half never had a relapse.

Dr. Park's 1879 study of patients who had relapsed and were re-admitted to the Worcester State Hospital from 1833 to 1875 showed that 74% of these patients were again discharged as either recovered or improved on their last re-admission (1,961 out of 2,664). Only 12% had died during their last re-admission (318 out of 2,664).

All told, it is not unreasonable to state that, one hundred years ago, the natural history of psychosis in general (including cases due to organic changes of the central nervous system) was such that a large proportion of patients were able to leave the mental hospital, and only a small proportion, perhaps 20-30%, were destined to die in a mental hospital. Favorable outcome was, of course, even more frequent in the functional psychoses considered alone. Modern discharge rates of even 80 to 90% are of themselves not remarkable in comparison. Indeed, it is not unlikely that modern treatments merely shorten the period of illness and do not produce a greater proportion of discharges than did moral treatment.

Unfortunately there is no satisfactory scientific basis for comparing moral treatment with modern treatment, for there is no way of knowing definitely that patients admitted to mental hospitals 125 years ago were afflicted with mental disorders of the same type and severity as patients of today. It can only be said that case records of that era have many features in common with modern records, the main difference being that patients then were on the average considerably younger. Whatever the differences or similarities between two groups of patients, whether they be separated by one hundred years or one hundred miles, any claims as to their response to a particular treatment can always be challenged on the grounds that criteria for diagnosis and recovery are subjective or that selection of cases favors a particular outcome. Studies of the natural history of untreated mental illnesses are open to the same challenges.

Statistical studies of the outcome of mental illnesses which base their approach solely on the assumption that they are disease entities analogous to those of internal medicine must of necessity exclude all personal and environmental factors as mere incidentals. Thorough search and elimination of such incidentals, however, leave a remarkably small residue of cases which have objective features in common that point to the presence of the same absolute disease entity at work in all the cases. Yet because psychiatry has felt obliged to apply the scientific method, as it is known in the physical sciences, it has had no recourse but to hold to the conclusions arrived at from the study of just such a small selected minority of the patients admitted to mental hospitals: namely that the prognosis of scientifically proven psychosis is very poor and that its course cannot be altered by any known means.

It is possible to criticize the reported good results of both moral treatment and modern psychiatric treatment on the grounds that the majority of the patients treated did not have scientifically proven psychoses. By the same token it may be said that the majority of patients admitted to mental hospitals during the period of therapeutic nihilism of the latter nineteenth century were needlessly deprived of means to recovery which could have been made available to them. An alternative explanation of the low recovery rates of that particular period might be that a far greater proportion of patients had "genuine" psychosis during that period than before or since. Yet in view of the evidence that patients suffered extreme neglect during those years it does not seem a likely explanation.

From both a practical and humane point of view it is essential to learn how over-all discharge rates of mental hospitals are affected by the mode of living which patients experience. The statistics of moral treatment reported here are at least presumptive evidence that efforts to meet the personal needs of patients are well worthwhile.

# VI

## Moral Treatment Defined

We have suggested that moral treatment was in effect comparable to modern therapeutic efforts which include psychotherapy, occupational therapy, and recreational therapy. We have also shown that the founders of American psychiatry had an attitude of hopeful optimism with respect to the curability of insanity by means of moral treatment. We have demonstrated furthermore that their optimism was founded on a practical statistical basis. We have, then, established in some measure the value of moral treatment but have not yet shown specifically and concretely what moral treatment was.

In 1845 Pliny Earle described moral treatment at the Bloomingdale Hospital in the following words:

"In the moral regimen at this institution, every practicable effort is made to pursue that system, at once gentle, philosophical, and practical, which has resulted from the active and strenuous endeavors of many philanthropists, in the course of the last half century, to meliorate the condition of the insane. The primary object is to treat the patients, so far as their condition will possibly admit, as if they were still in the enjoyment of the healthy exercise of their mental faculties. An important desideratum for the attainment of this object is to make their condition as boarders, as comfortable as possible; that they may be the less sensible of the deprivations to which they are subjected by a removal from home. Nor is it less essential to extend them the privilege, or the right, of as much liberty, as much freedom from personal restraint as is compatible with their safety, the safety of others, and the judicious administration of other branches of curative treatment. The courtesies of civilized and social life are not to be forgotten, extending, as they do, to the promotion of the first great object already mentioned, and operating, to no inconsiderable extent, as a means of effecting restoration to mental health." ( 14)

In 1847 Dr. Amariah Brigham, superintendent of the Utica State Hospital, New York, defined moral treatment as follows:

"The removal of the insane from home and former associations, with respectful and kind treatment under all circumstances, and in most cases manual labor, attendance on religious worship on Sundays, the establishment of regular habits of self-control, diversion of the mind from morbid trains of thought, are now generally considered as essential in the moral treatment of the Insane." ( 7)

The means which Dr. Earle went on to describe included manual labor, religious worship, recreative exercise, amusements, restraints, and attendants.

In his discussion of attendants Dr. Earle made clear his concept of moral treatment:

"It requires but little experience, in an Asylum, to convince a person of the identity between a judicious parental government, and that system of management which is best adapted to the insane. The motives, the influences, and, as a general rule, the means necessary for the good government of children, are equally applicable, and equally efficient for the insane. In fact, this system is the great desideratum, at every Asylum; and without it, it is impossible for the management to approximate that degree of perfection which it is desirable to attain.

"The most essential element of success in the establishment and maintenance of such a government, is a corps of intelligent attendants, of kind disposition, and good judgment. Such, and such alone, can sustain a disciplinary code, founded upon kindness and supported with firmness.

"Much pains has been taken, at this institution, to procure attendants of this character, and especially as regards the men's department, the efforts have been rewarded with a good degree of success. Nearly all the young men who have been so employed during the last few years, were from the country, and so well educated that they had been accustomed to teaching school in the winter.

"It is needless to describe, in detail, the numerous advantages of attendants of this kind over those who are ignorant, and whose only ideas of exerting control over others, are measured by the strength of their arms. He who has once tried the former, would greatly deplore the exigency which should render it necessary to return to the latter." (14)

One of Dr. Earle's favorite means of treatment was formal instruction, including lectures and school exercises:

"Soon after the writer of this article first directed his attention to the treatment of the insane, he became convinced that lectures upon scientific and miscellaneous subjects might be made an object of interest, as well as of utility, in the moral treatment of patients in public institutions. Accordingly, being at that time connected with the Frankford Asylum, near Philadelphia, he induced the managers of that institution to purchase an air pump and other philosophical apparatus, and with the aid of these he gave a series of experimental lectures before the patients, in the winter of 1841-42. The results were as favorable as had been anticipated.

"The writer became connected with the Bloomingdale Asylum in the spring of 1844, and in the autumn of the same year, encouraged by the Governors, who made a liberal appropriation for the purchase of apparatus, commenced a course of lectures, which were continued through the winter. The success was sufficient to induce perseverance in the plan, and a similar course has been delivered in each succeeding year since that time. The last commenced on October 12, 1846, and ended on May 3, 1847. It consisted of 38 lectures, as follows:

| | |
|---|---|
| Natural Philosophy | 4 Lectures |
| Chemistry | 6 |
| Animal Physiology | 9 |
| Astronomy | 10 |
| Physical, Intellectual, and Moral Beauty | 2 |
| Recitations of Poetry | 1 |
| History and Description of Malta | 2 |
| Greece as it was in 1838 | 2 |
| Characteristics of the Americans and Europeans | 2 |

"For the suitable illustration of the lectures, the Institution is furnished with the following apparatus:

1st — An air-pump, with its accompaniments.
2nd — A set of mechanical powers.
3rd — A magic lantern.
4th — An orrery.
5th — An electrical machine, with its implements.
6th — Pneumatic trough, receivers, retorts and other articles used in chemistry.
7th — One hundred and forty-six diagrams, painted upon bleached muslin, illustrative of the structure of the human frame, and that of the lower order of animals.
8th — Twenty similar diagrams explanatory of the laws and phenomena of light.
9th — Twenty-five astronomical diagrams.
10th — One hundred diagrams illustrating various subjects.

"The lectures were delivered in the evening and attended by an average number of about 70 patients. Their attention and deportment would compare favorably with that of the audiences ordinarily attendant upon lectures.

"It will be perceived that such subjects were selected as are susceptible of demonstration or illustration, experimentally, or through the medium of diagrams. Such topics are considered as the most suitable, inasmuch as the perceptive faculties are called into action by addressing the eye, as well as the ear. As a general rule, this holds good; but of all the lectures mentioned in the foregoing list, it is believed that none commanded more profound attention, or gave more general satisfaction, than that which consisted of the recitation of poetry, and upon the authors by whom they were written.

"As a simple method of exerting disciplinary restraint, simultaneously, over a large number of patients, a means of fixing the attention and withdrawing the minds of comparatively a multitude from the delusions incident to their disease, we believe there is no other plan, hitherto adopted in the system of moral treatment which will prove more generally and extensively useful than that of judicious and well managed lectures.

"In the autumn of 1845, a school was commenced in the men's department, and continued until the following spring. It was suspended during the winter of 1846-47. It was attended by from twenty to thirty patients, of various ages and in a diversity of conditions, in regard to mental disorder. The ordinary English branches were taught, and in these some of the younger patients made considerable progress. Others reviewed what they had previously studied, and others still, interested or amused themselves by reading from entertaining books and newspapers.

"It is not to be expected that great advancement in valuable knowledge can ever be attained in a school for the insane. The only subject generally within reach, and the only on the acquisition of which needs be expected—and this indeed is much—is the exercise of a moral control over large numbers at once; subduing excitement, rousing the inactive, and giving a new current to the thoughts.

"A miscellaneous library of about one thousand volumes is devoted to the use of the patients, and five daily and eight weekly newspapers, two monthly magazines and four quarterly reviews are also taken for them. Thus an inexhaustible fund of reading is supplied, and a librarian distributes it to such patients as are disposed to make use of it." ( 14)

Dr. Brigham, too, had great faith in the therapeutic value of a teaching program:

"Many cases, we believe, cannot be cured or improved, but by a rousing and calling into exercise the dormant faculties of the mind. Hence schools are beneficial, not merely to the curable class of patients, but to the demented and those approaching this condition.

"In such, the active state of the disease, which originated the mental disturbance, has passed, and left the brain and faculties of the mind in a torpid state. In these cases, medicine is generally of no use, and they cannot often be much improved, but by exercising the faculties of the mind.

"But others also benefitted by devoting a portion of every day to mental improvement. To those who are nearly or quite well, and who remain in an asylum for fear of relapsing at home, or for other reasons, schools afford enjoyment and often means for improvement which are highly valued by the patients themselves.

"The melancholy and despairing, and all those that are uneasy and nervous, that are constantly restless and disposed to find fault and to annoy the attendants and quarrel with all about them, because they had nothing else to occupy their minds, are frequently cured by mental occupation and the exercises of a school, by attending to composition, declamation, the writing and acting of dialogues and plays.

"Various are the methods that may be adopted to awaken into activity the dormant faculties of the mind and to dispel delusions and melancholy trains of thought. A *museum* or collection of minerals, shells, pictures, specimens of ancient and modern art and curiosities of all sorts, should be connected with institutions for the insane. The opportunities are abundant for making interesting and valuable collections of this kind by the aid of the patients that have recovered and their friends.

"By means thus indicated institutions for the care and cure of those affected by mental disorders will be made to resemble those for education, rather than hospitals for the sick, or prisons for criminals, and when we call to mind that the greater part of those committed to such establishments are not actually sick, and do not require medical treatment, but are suffering from deranged intellect, feelings and passions, it is evident that a judicious course of mental and moral discipline is most essential for their comfort and restoration." ( 7)

Dr. Brigham also considered manual labor to be of therapeutic value and recommended that hospitals have a variety of workshops available to the patients.

"Bodily labor as a measure for benefitting and curing the insane is generally recommended and we allude to it now, but to express the hope that better arrangements for this purpose will be made in institutions for the insane, than have hitherto been. Some have an insufficient quantity of land, and are destitute of workshops. We think every such institution should have a good farm attached to it; but still a farm is not sufficient, as it can afford employment but to comparatively few, and only for part of the year. We think several workshops should be connected with every large establishment for the insane, and be so connected, that the patients of each class can go to them without risk or exposure. One or more rooms in connection with each hall for patients, is needed in order to afford employment to all that would benefit by it. In such rooms, dress-making and tailoring, cabinet work, the manufacture of toys, basket-making, shoemaking, painting, printing, bookbinding, and various other employments may be carried on to the advantage of many patients, some of whom cannot be employed on the farm or in shops disconnected with the asylum. In the construction of asylums for the insane, we think there should be more care taken to provide convenient rooms for the purposes mentioned.

"But however useful bodily labor may be to some, we regard it as less so generally as a curative measure, and less applicable in many cases, than mental occupation or the regular and rational employment of the mind.

"In fact, manual labor, we believe, proves more beneficial by producing this result, that is, by engaging the attention and directing the mind to new subjects of thought, than by its direct effect upon the body. Not infrequently manual labor appears to be injurious, especially in recent cases; it accelerates the circulation, and sometimes reproduces excitement of mind in those who have become quiet and convalescent.

"We apprehend many have erroneous views on the subject of manual labor as a remedy for insanity. It is undoubtedly useful of itself in some cases, but it rarely cures. The large majority of patients that recover are restored without it, and most of the work performed by this class in lunatic asylums is after convalescence is well established." (7)

From the writings of Earle, Brigham, Woodward, Butler and Ray it becomes clear that moral treatment was in no sense a *single technique*. Yet it had a definable goal—that of arousing the dormant faculties of the mind. Every available means was employed to achieve this end. The very matrix of moral treatment was the communal life of patients and hospital personnel. Every aspect of daily living was utilized by the physician for its therapeutic effect in awakening feelings of companionship in the patients. The chief modalities used in awakening such feelings were those endeavors which required the patient to invest interest in something outside himself in cooperation with others, namely manual work, intellectual work, recreation, and religious worship.

Psychotherapy, as such, was not mentioned, but it took the form of patients sharing past experiences with each other and discussing these experiences both in groups and privately with their physician. Ray and Butler, in particular, emphasized the need for the physician to know the experiences of each of his patients.

Moral treatment might be defined as organized group-living in which the integration and continuity of work, play and social activities produce a meaningful total life experience in which growth of individual capacity to enjoy life has maximum opportunity.

The moral therapist acted toward his patients as though they were mentally well. He believed that kindness and forebearance were essential in dealing with them. He also believed in firmness and persistence in impressing on patients the idea that a change to more acceptable behavior was expected.

One might say that moral treatment was essentially a teaching program in how to make friends and enjoy outside interests. A hospital managed according to its principles was a going concern as productive as a university in providing individuals with greater capacity to enjoy life and take part in society. Amariah Brigham expresses this thought in the following passage: "When such a system as we have briefly indicated or rather hinted at, is judiciously introduced into asylums, with convenient rooms and suitable books and apparatus, we apprehend that trivial and objectionable amusements will be abandoned by the inmates themselves for more rational enjoyments—enjoyments which, while they serve to dispel the darkness and delusions that effect many, will at the same time have the effect to improve their minds and enable them to leave the institution not only rational, but better qualified by increased intelligence and power of selfcontrol for encountering the troubles and performing the duties of life." (.7)

Moral treatment, in the *modern* technical jargon, is what we mean by resocialization through therapies with prefixes such as recreational, occupational, industrial, music—with physical education thrown in for good measure. These do not add up to moral treatment, however, either in terminology or in application. There is no equivalent to the word *moral* in use today which implies an integrated total treatment program. There is also as yet no such thing as an integrated program of social therapy in force today. And only a few hospitals are making progress in developing such a program.

The modern physician trained in dynamic psychiatry based largely on psychological concepts tends to look upon moral treatment, with its emphasis on work, play, and social activities, as being a rather naive approach to the treatment of mental illness. The most he may grant is perhaps its palliative value. He is not interested in methods not based on finding and removing the cause of illness. He cannot help but feel that the founders of American psychiatry must have been completely lacking in their understanding of mental illness to prosecute with enthusiasm such superficial measures.

It is not quite scientific, however, to judge our psychiatric forefathers as totally ignorant of the nature of mental illness simply because they did not formulate their ideas as we do today and did not use the vernacular of modern psychodynamics. We cannot assume that they were devoid of intuitive understanding of mental illness. There is ample evidence that they thought a great deal about the role of child training and psychological trauma in the causation of mental illness. They took for granted the fact that mental illness was primarily an emotional disturbance, and recognized the need to know each patient's life experience in order to be able to help him.

As therapists they were guided by the philosophical assumption of the totality of personality and were thoroughly familiar with the effect of the emotions on bodily functions. The attitude which they felt must be held toward a mentally ill patient was one which granted him the dignity of expecting him to behave in a normal way but which exercised kindness and forebearance in the face of his abnormal behavior. The inculcation of this attitude in all the hospital personnel was an important part of moral treatment.

Against the background of this attitude, coupled with the

knowledge that physicians and attendants shared the hospital living experience with the patients 24 hours a day, seven days a week, it is not difficult to see how group living could be fashioned into a highly psychotherapeutic experience.

From a psychodynamic point of view it is most significant that the superintendent of the moral treatment era often made reference to "our family" in his annual reports. The family to him included the patients and attendants as well as his own wife and children. It is not remarkable that he should feel like a father to his patients, for he ate, worked, played, and worshipped with them. It would likewise be not surprising that he should acquire a fundamental understanding of personality through prolonged and intimate contacts with his patients in a wide variety of activities and interpersonal relationships.

As we become better acquainted with the family life aspect of moral treatment we realize that, hour by hour, activities within the hospital must have contained events of great psychodynamic importance, which could be turned to therapeutic value by an experienced psychiatrist.

The forebearance of the hospital staff allowed expression of antagonism; opportunity to work at such things as carpentry, toy-making, and gardening gave release to creative urges and satisfaction for recognition. Games of chance and skill provided a setting for giving vent to competitive drives. The writing and acting of drama gave free rein to exhibitionist tendencies. The plastic arts allowed sublimation of pregenital drives. Liberty to handle sharp instruments of steel served to allay fears of impotence and mutilation. In connection with the latter, Dr. Woodward's comment in his Annual Report is of interest: "There is no employment in which they (the patients) so cheerfully engage as in haymaking. From twenty to thirty workmen were often in the field at one time, all busily employed. At one of my daily visits to the hayfield I found *four homicides* mowing together, performing their work in the best manner, and all cheerful and happy." (19)

It might be pointed out that these four homicides each did his mowing with a scythe—a tool with a three foot blade sharpened to a razor's edge.

If we reflect long enough on the attributes of moral treatment, we cannot escape concluding that moral treatment contained much that has been found of value in play therapy with children and group therapy with adults. It not only allowed freedom of expression but provided a variety of means for that expression.

We can also begin to appreciate how great the moral therapist's knowledge of a given patient's behavior must have been and how great the means he had at his command with which to modify behavior. Indeed we might even ask if psychiatrists have ever known psychotic patients so completely or labored so earnestly for their welfare. Outside the moral treatment era few psychiatrists have had opportunity for direct observation of the behavior of their patients in a variety of actual life situations. Only recently has a body of knowledge comparable in content to that of moral treatment been accumulated by workers in the interpersonal relations school of psychiatry. Their findings do not indicate that life experience in a mental hospital is of superficial importance to either patients or hospital personnel. Quite to the contrary they disclose the inadequacy of interview methods by themselves for learning how personality unfolds in the course of actual living.

Personality performance within the circumscribed situation of the interview cannot be assumed to be a representative sample of performance in the open field of society. Those who know full well the complexity of the problem involved in drawing valid conclusions from free associations produced by a patient in a single hour cannot help but feel that any attempt to draw conclusions from the vastly more complex data of social behavior is naive. Psychiatry has not yet reached the stage in which it is recognized that with the same elements there may be many orders of phenomena governed by different laws. In the field of physics, which long ago reached this stage, the researcher in the atomic structure of gases does not feel logically compelled to look upon research in meteorology as naive.

The entry of the social scientists into research in mental illness brings a still broader perspective to bear on the problem. The sociologist can investigate the role and function of a mental hospital with the same methods he would use in studying the relationship of a modern industrial company to society as a whole. The anthropologist can study mentally ill patients with the same approach he uses in studying an Indian tribe.

The absence of social science perspectives explains in part the failure of psychiatrists to apply moral treatment when charged with the care of patients whose ethnic and socio-economic background is unfamiliar to them.

# VII

## "Way of Life" and
## Mental Illness

It is the considered opinion among modern psychiatrists that
mental illness is understandable as a condition in which mental
traits common to all mankind are exaggerated by stressful life
situations to a degree which impairs ability to get along with
one's fellows. In view of this opinion it is pertinent to note the
more obvious differences in the life stresses which obtained in
those periods of American history when the mentally ill fared
the best and the worst in the institutions created for their care.

American life in the early nineteenth century was characterized by a social structure in which the individual could experience a wide range of close human contacts. Families were large,
and communities were small. There was maximum opportunity
for each person to have first-hand knowledge of a large variety
of personalities and behavior. The village school, town meeting
house, and local church were single room structures which
further accelerated getting acquainted among children and adults
alike. The teacher, selectman, overseer of the poor, clergyman,
and physician not only knew individuals well, but knew them
as members of families and groups whose histories were known
to all.

In a setting of such close enduring human relationships the
needs of individuals and their sufferings at the hands of others
were matters of common knowledge. Social responsibility was
based on shared personal experience. Where everyone knew
everyone else's affairs, interactions among individuals were

strongly conditioned by a backlog of knowledge of each other which was so taken for granted that it could remain unspoken and yet be the prime factor underlying mutual understanding and determine the outcome of the interaction.

In this sort of social atmosphere the roots of personality could sink deep and radiate widely. Stability was the natural consequence of growth in the soil of highly interactive community living. Maturity and sense of responsibility came early in life. Self-support, marriage, and child-rearing began in adolescence. Professional men and artisans began their careers in their early twenties, often after serving apprenticeships to their own fathers.

Social stability, early psychosexual maturity, and respect for individuality were as much the consequence of small community life with its reservoir of common experience as of the American ideology of freedom. Indeed the small community was the proving ground of this ideology and, as such, gave it special form—the form of a society whose economic foundation was small-scale subsistence farming and handicraft.

Child-parent-grandparent relationships in this period of high birth rates were such that those past the reproductive period were in a small minority while those not yet biologically mature were in the majority. Those in the reproductive period of life occupied an intermediary position. Grandparents were not only an asset to busy farm households with many grandchildren, but were few enough to be in demand. In the absence of an educational differential between generations in the early nineteenth century, grandparents occupied a revered position as sources of wisdom and knowledge. Their reminiscences of the past were of value to their children and grandchildren since they were still pertinent to current social conditions. Times did not change rapid enough to give the recollections of grandparents a quality of irksome remoteness.

The small community era of American history was attended by stresses to which all were exposed regardless of social or economic status and which all accepted as necessary evils. Morbidity and mortality rates from infectious diseases were high, especially among infants, children, and young adults. The sorrows of sickness and death of loved ones had the effects of strengthening emotional bonds in an already intimate community life.

Richness of human contacts in early American life produced an awareness in community leaders of human needs—an awareness which led state legislatures to support the founding of public schools and state mental hospitals. Motivation underlying the creation of community services for the underprivileged was largely based on first-hand knowledge of the needs of specific individuals.

Unlike Europe, America was in the small community stage of social development when the ideas of the enlightenment became a guiding motif. The humanistic philosophies of Benjamin Franklin, Thomas Jefferson, and Tom Paine which had incubated for several decades found new impetus from men like Ralph Waldo Emerson, William Ellery Channing, Horace Mann, and Samuel Gridley Howe. The early part of the nineteenth century thus witnessed the rise to social leadership of men who were not only imbued with humanistic ideals but who also had personal knowledge of human problems from their intimate contact with small community life. The appearance of moral treatment of insanity was a natural outgrowth of the prevailing spirit of the times. The mentally ill met with the same goodwill, understanding, and sympathy that was extended to all victims of misfortune.

Moral treatment was pursued with the greatest enthusiasm and was most effective during this rather short-lived humanistic, small community phase of American history. This was a period during which mentally ill patients and their physicians both had a backlog of enduring human contacts in their life experience and shared a common cultural heritage. These factors favored understanding of patients by the physician and provided him with clues to their psychological and social needs. Physicians and patients were well versed in group living and endowed their hospitals with the qualities of genuine community life.

Moral treatment was not a specific procedure but rather a general effort to create a favorable environment in which spontaneous recovery could take place. This general effort was supplemented by a more specific effort to give whatever psychological help seemed to be needed. Recovery and discharge rates were not so much statistical representations of the result of a given treatment as they were records of the natural course of mental illnesses in general when not artificially obstructed. Moral treatment was essentially the art of eliminating obstacles and providing aids to the patient as a person. It was little more than a common sense approach to the problem of mental illness which sought, first, to learn the natural course of the illness and, second, to discover what means *already at hand* could assist the recovery process.

During the course of the nineteenth century the familiar pattern of small community life gave way to unfamiliar ever-shifting patterns of big city life in which the individual exchanged enduring contacts with relatively few people for evanescent contacts with a multitude of people. The family became smaller, more dependent on money income, and less secure. The father competed on the open market for work under employers he did not know personally. Except for his immediate family the individual was essentially alone in the midst of many. Remoteness and impersonality in human relations were increased by competition for work and wages.

These changes in the social relations of the individual took place at the same time that public leadership acquired more and more reverence for both property and materialistic science. Political and business leaders acted in accordance with "social laws" which they endowed with the validity of the law of gravitation. The legal system itself became more rigidly mechanistic. Science was not only mechanistic and materialistic but was looked upon as a body of fixed truth, hard cold facts wholly independent and outside man. Science was no longer cherished as man's brain-child or as evidence of the heights to which the human spirit could rise, as it had been in the eighteenth and early nineteenth centuries. It had become the final reality before which man must bow. Idealistic, humanistic social goals had to be abandoned in view of social laws derived from the survival-of-the-fittest version of evolution. Social leadership determined its course of action not on the basis of first-hand human experience but on the basis of reasoning from scientific premises. Impersonality in human relations, carried to the point of scientific detachment, led the educated members of society to look upon human sufferings as consequences of inexorable social laws.

Toward the end of the nineteenth century community life underwent more and more disruptions. Industry expanded immensely. Immigration increased by leaps and bounds, and more than made up for the thousands of Americans who went to take advantage of free land at the frontier. Within a few years the almshouses, hospitals, and public schools of the North Atlantic states were overcrowded with destitute immigrants. The orderly process of building a better society was interrupted. The increased flow of wealth which accompanied the exploitation of natural resources, railroad building, and expansion of factories, found its way to unexpected places. Men became rich who had once received charity. The old ideas of who was underprivileged and who was not no longer held. Many a philanthropist of earlier years found himself poorer than men he had once helped. Such disruption of relations among men left small inclination to benevolence toward mankind as a species.

One of the most vigorous proponents of the thesis that society is subject to immutable laws was William Graham Sumner, professor of Political and Social Science at Yale University from 1872 to 1909. Sumner contended: "The truth is that the social order is fixed by laws of nature precisely analogous to those of the physical order. The most that man can do is by ignorance and self-conceit to mar the operation of social laws." (15) Sumner taught that poverty belonged to the struggle for survival and objected vehemently to legislation for aid to the poor. He wrote: "A law may be passed which shall force somebody to support the hopelessly degenerate members of a society, but such a law can only perpetuate the evil and entail it on future generations with new accumulations of distress." (17) He insisted that poverty was the result of vice and derided the democratic humanitarian ideas of the eighteenth and nineteenth centuries as empty speculation. He predicted that "the mores of the twentieth century will not be tinged by humanitarianism as the last 100 years have been." (18) He urged that competition should be more vigorous and exhorted men to be frugal, sober, and wise. He specifically warned: "Let it be understood that we cannot go outside this alternative: liberty, inequality, survival of the fittest; not—liberty, equality, survival of the unfittest. The former carries society forward and favors all its best members; the latter carries society downwards and favors all its worst members." (19)

During the years that Sumner and other intellectual leaders were preaching against America's traditional democratic ideal, the middle classes were becoming more and more impersonal in their dealings with their fellow men and more careful about the company they kept. They were receptive to the sort of social attitude prescribed by Sumner, for it provided a comfortable and supposedly scientific rationale which absolved them of all guilt for any contributions they might make toward the sufferings of the less fortunate members of society.

Intolerance toward victims of misfortune which had characterized the Calvinism of colonial times reappeared in the latter part of the nineteenth century under the aegis of science. Revelation by way of sermonizing and the Bible was replaced by education as the road to power and survival. Virtue, however, was still a matter of frugality, self-denial and hard work. Its reward was still property. The old severity of Calvinism with its intolerance of the pauper as someone accused also returned. This time the work of heredity rather than the work of the devil was blamed for the pauper's blighted state. The rationalization for accepting poverty as inevitable had one advantage over Calvinism, in that it implied no responsibility whatsoever of the fit rich for the unfit poor.

Science, by the end of the nineteenth century, was no longer a means to a humanistic end. Evolutionary theory had reduced man to the status of a mere subject of physical science.

The great change in American life and thought toward the end of the last century was grimly reflected in the care given the mentally ill. Mental hospitals, as we have seen, became asylums for the hopeless.

Relationships between physicians and patients had changed greatly since the era of moral treatment. Physicians and patients, especially in the large state hospitals, no longer shared a common cultural background. Futhermore, the majority of patients came from a social class which knew no security, while the physician, become alienist, was of a class which blamed the lower stratum of society for its degraded state and prided itself on its remote and impersonal dealings with people. Mental hospitals were mere custodial institutions in which patients were given nothing more than the most meager accommodations and a diagnosis.

The attitudes of physicians toward mental illness had also undergone changes. Social distance between physician and patient, and physician and attendant fostered the development of a habit of mind which dealt with patients as cases. Lack of acquaintanceship with patients as persons and the impossibility of becoming well acquainted with many hundreds of patients were strong forces motivating physicians to seek the answers to mental illness through attempts to discover and identify physical disease entities. The very success of the methods of physical science in pathology, physiology, and bacteriology encouraged psychiatrists to adopt analogous mechanistic concepts of mental ills.

The observation by pathologists of microscopic lesions in the central nervous systems of patients who had been mentally ill made a profound impression on many psychiatrists. Mental illness, they concluded, could no longer be expected to become understandable through study of the patient's behavior. The behavior of the mentally ill could no longer be endowed with meaning having to do with the environment when it was looked upon as a result of mechanical defect in the central control station of the body.

Once the mechanical defect concept of mental illness was adopted, no such thing as true recovery could be accepted. Remissions, to be sure, might occur as in other physical disease such as multiple sclerosis, but the course of the illness could only end in death. The chief psychiatrist of mental hospitals could no longer in good faith discharge a patient as recovered. Indeed, discharge at all seemed ill-advised since relapse was considered inevitable. Also there was the chance that the patient might die at home, and the hospital lose another autopsy. From such a point of view moral treatment no longer made sense, and the cost it involved could not be justified.

The susceptibility of physicians to the dicta of the laboratory rendered them peculiarly harmful as administrators with authority over the movements of people. The mentally ill might have fared better if mental hospitals had been under the direction of lay superintendents with less respect for the findings of the laboratory science of the day.

The decline in recovery rates during the last century might have been due to an increase in the severity of mental illness itself. This does not seem likely, however, in view of the rising incidence of mental illness during the same period. The rising incidence of cancer and diabetes during the past 50 years is usually interpreted to mean that more cases are detected in their earlier and less severe forms as diagnostic ability improves. If the same reasoning be invoked to explain the rising incidence of mental illness, recovery rates should have increased rather than decreased during the nineteenth century. With mental illness, furthermore, early diagnosis was probably aided by the lesser tolerance of urban-industrial civilization for personality deviation.

The shift of psychiatry from an attitude which accepted the challenge of mental illness as a problem to be attacked with every means at hand to one which would not try anything without a guarantee from the clinical laboratory that its labors would not be in vain is a phenomenon worthy of study in itself. Psychiatry apparently did not have the courage to pursue its original course. It, too, accepted the then current notion of science that all phenomena were reducible to simple material units. Mental illness was looked upon as the result of damaged brain material.

The very idea of dead and decomposing brain cells carried with it the connotation of the patient's growing insensibility and unawareness of surroundings. The mental hospital could no longer be a citadel of hope, but had to become an asylum of despair. The psychiatrist became resigned to the task of maintaining order and cleanliness among the victims of progressive dementia. His only recommendation to the families of the mentally ill and to society was to forget these doomed unfortunates and carry on without them. To be pitied for a time and then neglected for the remainder of life became the lot of the mentally ill.

The significant point of interest in the history of American psychiatry is that the highest standards of care of the mentally ill (as gauged by present-day psychiatric criteria), obtained when Americans lived in small communities, were inspired by a humanistic science, and were motivated to go to the rescue of fellow men in distress. Conversely, the lowest standards of care obtained when Americans found themselves living in large industrial-urban communities, were awed by the authority of materialistic science, and were motivated to get to the top in the competitive strife of rugged individualism. It might be said that the Revolutionary War established the precedent of rescuing victims of tyranny and misfortune, and that the Civil War established the precedent of neighbor fighting neighbor for material wealth and power. It is a moot point whether the post-Civil War period was the more damaging to mental health. There is no escaping the facts, however, that the incidence of mental illness increased and that the standards of hospital care deteriorated during that period.

It would appear that the way a society treats its mentally ill is but a manifestation or particular instance of the way the members of that society treat each other.

# VIII

## The Development of
## Scientific Psychiatry
## in America

Scientific psychiatry germinated in American mental hospitals during the last decade of the nineteenth century when the care of mentally ill had sunk to its lowest level of degradation. The plight of patients had become so shamefully distressing that even the belief that they were insensate victims of incurable brain disease could not justify the inhuman mode of life inflicted upon them. It was only after political corruption and medical incompetence reached the point of being a public scandal that progressive superintendents could gain the support necessary to introduce changes. Indeed, the medical officers of mental hospitals, as we have seen, found themselves under fire to "do something," not only by public officials, who protested that state budgets could not indefinitely stand the cost of building ever bigger institutions, but also by their medical colleagues in the specialty of neurology.

The first step toward raising the institutional care of mental patients to the standard of general hospitals was that of introducing nursing schools in mental hospitals. Many superintendents had long been disturbed on a purely humanitarian basis by the effect of ignorant, coarse, and abusive attendants on patients. They entertained the hope that young women trained in the spirit of Florence Nightingale would have a beneficial effect on the morale of patients and also aid physicians in developing a systematic clinical psychiatry. The nursing school movement began at McLean Hospital (Massachusetts) in 1885. In less than a decade, 24 more mental hospitals had opened schools of nursing.

The crucial step toward bringing psychiatry into the fold of scientific medicine was that of adding neuropathologists to the staffs of mental hospitals. This step, first taken in the 1890's, was the earliest recognition, in America at least, of the need for research in psychiatry. Neuropathologists were the physicians most thoroughly trained in the scientific method who dealt with diseases of the nervous system and were consequently the logical choice to direct psychiatric research. The first of the neuropathologists to devote his energies on a full-time basis to research in psychiatry was Dr. Adolf Meyer. His thorough-going organization of case histories, mental and physical examinations, and special laboratory studies, brought to light new findings which led to a completely new concept of mental illness. Data which had been collected to discover relationships between mental symptoms and pathological changes in brain cells or body chemistry disclosed instead an unexpected relationship between the habit-patterns of patients and their mental illness. From his study of patients' lives, Dr. Meyer concluded that mental illnesses were understandable as the particular reactions of the total personality to life stresses. On the basis of this approach, he introduced a new scientific discipline to which he gave the name of *psychobiology*.

Meyer kindled a spirit of research in American psychiatry which drew it out of its state of hopeless stagnation. His psychobiological concept of mental illness attracted workers not only in medicine but in psychology, sociology, and education as well. His prestige in medicine as a neuropathologist and his great learning outside medicine won him the position of spokesman for American psychiatry. Through him, much that was already present in American psychology was incorporated in psychiatry. The ideas of William James, John Dewey, and G. Stanley Hall, it may be noted, had already had a direct influence on at least two psychiatrists before Meyer's time. Edward Cowles, superintendent of McLean Hospital, and William Noyes, the first pathologist at McLean Hospital, both studied under Hall at

Johns Hopkins. The first issue of the American Journal of Psychology contained papers on psychiatric topics, one by Cowles on "Insistent and Fixed Ideas" and one by Noyes, "A Study of the Evolution of Systemized Delusions of Grandeur." It is also significant that Stanley Hall, although not a medical man, was for a time superintendent of a state hospital and a member of the American Psychiatric Association.

Psychological research did not long remain limited to university laboratories. The Pathological Institute of the New York State Hospitals (founded in 1896 under Van Giessen) included a psychologist on its staff, Boris Sidis, as director of research in psychopathology. Dr. Sidis (then a Ph.D. in psychology; he did not receive his M.D. until 1908) carried out research in dissociation in psychoses which demonstrated to his satisfaction that abnormal behavior used the same mechanism as normal behavior and differed only in its social pattern. This research aroused a particular interest in the psychological aspect of mental illness in two physicians, William Alanson White and Richard Henry Hutchings, both of whom later supported the psychoanalytical movement in this country. They were the first superintendents of public mental hospitals to accept psychoanalysis. They were also the first to attempt to apply principles based on scientific psychology in the care of institutionalized patients in the United States. They both received their appointments in their thirties, in the same year, 1903; Dr. White at the Government Hospital in Washington and Dr. Hutchings at the St. Lawrence Hospital in New York.

Dr. White and Dr. Hutchings brought a new optimism into mental hospital work which was reminiscent of the optimism of Dr. Todd and Dr. Woodward in the early days of moral treatment. The actual methods which White and Hutchings employed in the care of their patients were, furthermore, practically identical to those of moral treatment. They concentrated on giving attendants and nurses a psychological understanding of mental illness. They instituted occupational and recreational programs and, despite the large number of patients in their care, sought to bring individualized attention of some sort to every patient.

By the end of the first decade of this century American psychiatry was starting on its way to freedom from the deadlock of the physical disease theory of mental illness. The list of men contributing to the psychological understanding of mental illness was growing steadily. The influence of William James, Stanley Hall, and Boris Sidis had brought a number of psychiatrists and neurologists into the fold of psychology, some of whom like James J. Putnam, Isodore H. Coriat, William Alanson White, and Richard Henry Hutchings had embraced psychoanalysis. Indeed, Freud himself and Jung, too, had, through the efforts of Putnam and Hall, accepted an invitation to come to America in 1909 to express their views. Abraham Brill had begun translating Freud's writings into English in the same year.

During the first two decades of this century American psychiatry began to take on a definite form with the appointment of neuropathologists with broad background in psychology and philosophy to the directorships of mental hospitals. The earliest of these was Albert Barret at the Psychopathic Hospital at Ann Arbor, Michigan, in 1906, followed by Elmer Ernest Southard at the Boston Psychopathic Hospital in 1912, and Adolf Meyer at the Henry Phipps Psychiatric Clinic in Baltimore, in 1913.

The rapid growth of psychiatry in its psychological understanding of mental illness was accompanied by an equally rapid development in neurophysiology and biochemistry which appeared to provide new grounds for questioning the primacy of psychological interpretations. Psychiatrists and neurologists who supported the physical disease theory of mental illness thus acquired research allies. The refined histological techniques of Nissl, Alzheimer, and Ramon Y. Cajal provided new opportunities for finding brain lesions in mental illness. The biochemist provided techniques for demonstrating metabolic disorders, while researchers on the endocrine glands and autonomic nervous system opened up even greater possibilities for finding physical causes.

In New York, Dercum and Van Giessen carried out chemical studies in mental illness as early as the 1890's, and at McLean Hospital, Folin began his chemical studies in 1900. The work of Hughlings Jackson, Sherrington, Brain, and Cannon in the physiology of the nervous system taken together with the findings of experimental physiological psychology seemed to provide a basis for explaining mental illness without the help of the "psychologies of past experience" as represented by Freud and Meyer.

New findings in fields of research pertinent to psychiatry, ranging from psychoanalysis to bacteriology, came in a deluge after 1900. Psychiatry which had been almost devoid of any ideas two decades before became a hot bed of new ideas and controversy. Psychiatrists in general tended to pay most attention to research results which pointed in the direction of metabolic disorders or toxins as causes of mental illness—a proclivity fostered by Emil Kraepelin's writings.

Kraepelin had a curious effect on the course of psychiatry. He brought a semblance of order out of chaos in the field of diagnosis and, at the same time, injected a note of somber pessimism into the whole matter of prognosis. He stimulated a new interest in patients' behavior at the descriptive level, for purposes of differential diagnosis. On the other hand, he succeeded in establishing mental illnesses as disease entities independent of the patient as a person, much as Thomas Sydenham had done in the field of physical ills 200 years before. Kraepelin could invoke, furthermore, all the agents of physical disease which had been discovered since Sydenham's time as causes of mental illnesses. In particular, he favored the view that the cause of dementia praecox was a disorder of metabolism.

From the time of Newton's celestial mechanics, scientists had attributed their progress in uncovering the "laws of nature" to the capacity to arrive at detached, impersonal, dehumanized "objective" abstractions. They abhorred subjective, anthropomorphic interpretations of natural phenomena as false and could not grant validity to concepts which did not have a demonstrable universal applicability. The discovery that night and day were the result of the rotation of the earth and not the rising and setting of the sun had long ago demonstrated that natural phenomena could not be explained by ordinary sense experience. In medicine, Sydenham's concept of the disease entity had proved itself to be such a useful abstraction that all progress in medicine was thought to be purely a matter of isolating more and more disease entities, observing their course, and searching for specific treatments. Kraepelin's delineation of dementia praecox and manic-depressive psychosis through painstaking descriptive studies seemed to indicate that mental ills were amenable to the same methodological approach as physical ills had proved to be. Kraepelin's views of mental ills as fixed disease entities represented a crystallization of the medical thought of the second half of the nineteenth century with respect to mental illness. As such they had a wide appeal and greatly influenced the attitudes of physicians toward mental illness, especially dementia praecox, as incurable.

Psychiatric thought at the beginning of the twentieth century was in a highly confused state of transition from the disease entity concept of mental illness to the concept of mental illnesses as reaction types. Kraepelin's concept of dementia praecox as a disease entity was largely displaced by Eugene Bleuler's concept of schizophrenia, a concept which denoted a psychological process capable of all degrees of gradation rather than a disease entity with an inevitable course. Karl Jung's studies of patients with dementia praecox demonstrated that so-called symptoms had wholly personal meaning to patients in terms of their own past experience. Psychiatry had to contend with two points of view which seemed to be mutually exclusive. Mental illness was either a universal disease entity or a unique reaction to life experience in each patient. Progress toward resolution of these two points of view came with the development of a broader perspective which took greater account of the similarity of personal experiences, feelings, and thoughts among mankind in general as well as among the mentally ill of the world. The very universality of certain behavior patterns which had been the basis for designating a disease entity turned out to be understandable as an example of the universality of supposedly unique and personal inner-life experiences. The concept that psychic experiences could in any sense approach being both personal and universal was a contribution to modern thought which was formulated in a general way by Adolf Meyer, and in a specific and more revolutionary way by Sigmund Freud.

During the first two decades of the present century, psychiatry increased its scope from that of a purely medical discipline to one which included the study of psychological and social factors in mental illness. This trend is well represented in the writings of Elmer E. Southard. From 1901 to 1910, he wrote on histopathology and physical disease entities only. From 1911 to 1920, his writings included many papers on the psychological and sociological aspects of mental illness. One of his chief contributions during the latter decade, while he was director of the Boston Psychopathic Hospital, was the development of the concept of social psychiatry and the founding of psychiatric social work.

Meyer's psychobiology, Freud's psychoanalysis, and Southard's social psychiatry strongly implied or explicity pointed to the role of other people in both the pathogenesis and healing of mental illness. This concept, in some measure, owed its acceptance to a recovered patient by the name of Clifford Beers who told the world of the experiences in mental hospitals which had retarded his recovery. The timing of his story was such that it dovetailed with the concepts emerging in psychiatry, and at the same time caught the public in a receptive mood. His book, "A Mind that Found Itself," published in 1908, was directly instrumental in leading to the founding of the National Committee for Mental Hygiene which chose Beers as its Secretary.

The importance of psychological and social factors in the genesis and recovery of mental illness was largely accepted by leaders in American psychiatry before the first World War. When the United States entered the war, organized American psychiatry was prepared to take psychological factors into account in the care of mental disorders of soldiers. The director of the National Committee for Mental Hygiene, Dr. Thomas Salmon, was appointed chief psychiatrist of the expeditionary forces to Europe. From his experience with war conversion hysteria among soldiers in France, he described (26) the emotional conflict underlying that disorder as the result of "the many demands of the instinct of self preservation stirring deep and strong affective currents against the conscious expectations, desires and requirements of 'soldierly ideals,' imbedded in a matrix of discipline."

French neurologists expressed similar views, placing emphasis on outside stresses rather than on individual susceptibility. Babinski stated in his book (with Froment) on hysteria in the first World War: "The hysterical symptoms observed at the present time . . . appear to develop chiefly as the result of moral and physical strain, and of commotions which demand the physical resistance of the individual and predispose him to nervous disorders of this kind, however unsusceptible he may appear . . . It is undoubtedly one of the most widespread affections and for my part I am inclined to believe that there are very few individuals who escape when placed in certain circumstances, and under the influence of more or less active occasional causes." (6)

The British psychiatrist, Dr. Frederick Mott, demonstrated the psychological character of a great majority of so-called shell shock cases and emphasized the importance of moral and hospital atmosphere in the treatment of war neuroses in general. Another war experience was the breakdown of soldiers with symptoms of dementia praecox who recovered on return to the United States.

The theoretical structure of psychoanalysis was also changed by the war. Freud no longer considered the erotic drives to be the only source of motivation but included aggressive drives as a determining factor in personality development. After the war, Freud's studies of transference and Harry Stack Sullivan's elaboration of his concept of psychiatry as the science of interpersonal relations brought psychiatry another step closer to the social sciences. Another development after the first World War was the founding of a psychoanalytic sanatarium in a suburb of Berlin, under the direction of Dr. Ernst Simmel. The problem of 24-hour care of patients was one hitherto not encountered by psychoanalysts. It became immediately apparent that the course of a patient's illness was in considerable measure dependent upon relationships with other patients, attendants, and nurses as well as on his relationship to his analyst during the interview hour. In 1937, a psychoanalytic sanatarium began operation in the United States—the Menninger Clinic in Topeka, Kansas. The experience of this clinic highlighted the need for

research to learn what sort of social environment was therapeutic. This led to an attempt to prescribe the kind of attitude
personnel should have toward each patient, known as "attitude
therapy." The concept of "milieu therapy" also appeared.

In 1938, the first papers appeared reporting social research
of interaction processes in mental hospital wards (40). Since
that time, an increasing amount of such research has been done.

Psychiatric progress from the time Meyer began his work
was largely in the form of increased knowledge of the role of
psychological factors in mental illness and in histologic studies,
showing the absence of organic brain changes in so-called functional psychoses. Research in metabolism, endocrinology, and
neurophysiology, however, was going ahead during the same
years but with results of little immediate importance to psychiatry.

The contribution of neurophysiology to psychiatry has its
origin with Hughlings Jackson's work, showing the hierarchical
organization of the central nervous system and Sherrington's
work, showing the inhibitory action of higher centers on lower.
This work was followed by John F. Fulton's research on the
frontal lobes of chimpanzees. Sections of the frontal lobes lead
to more tranquil behavior, a result which led the Portuguese
physician, Egaz Moniz, to try lobotomy on chronic psychotic
patients, a venture which had promising results. Another area
of physiological research of importance to psychiatry was that
of Walter B. Cannon, showing the relationship of the autonomic
nervous system to epinephrine, a finding which was followed
by further studies showing the disrupting effect of fear states
and of epinephrine on adaptive behavior. This latter finding
led to Manfred Sakel's theory that in schizophrenia an epineph-
rine-like substance is impairing cellular function of the cerebral
cortex, a theory which led him to give insulin (the "antagonist
of epinephrine") to schizophrenic patients. The surprisingly
good recovery rates achieved by this treatment led to its widespread adoption after the middle 1930's. Shortly thereafter,
Meduna theorized that schizophrenia and epilepsy were antagon-
istic conditions and attempted to treat schizophrenic patients
with convulsion-inducing doses of metrazol. This method also

achieved good results. Shortly thereafter, Cerletti and Bini used electric shock to induce convulsions and obtained similar results. This treatment was then tried in manic-depressive psychosis and found to be even more effective in that condition. Thus research in physiology led to many "hunches" in treatment which were effective and contributed further to psychiatric progress.

Research in psychology and psychopathology has shown that mental illness in an individual cannot be understood without taking into account his interactions with his family and with society. Research in physiology and psychosomatic medicine, on the other hand, has demonstrated the effect of emotions on body functions, while new knowledge of endocrine secretions has provided a rationale relating body chemistry to body build (Kretchmer). The picture of mental illness which is emerging from research in the now strongly related fields of psychiatry, physiology, and sociology is one in which a circular series of events occur, beginning with social factors which produce psychological changes. These psychological changes then, depending on the individual's constitutional inheritance, alter physiological function which is accompanied by further psychological changes. Change in behavior elicits further reactions from society which once again produce psychological changes in the individual and repeat the cycle.

With progress of research, it is becoming increasingly clear that the treatment of mental illness involves the development of techniques for interrupting this cycle at one or the other or all of these levels. In some forms of mental illness, judicious change in the social environment alone will arrest the disease process; in others individual psychotherapy or group psychotherapy may be needed in addition. More severe forms of illness may require electric shock, insulin coma, or even psychosurgery.

The rapidly growing knowledge of the profound effects of personalities on each other is the most challenging aspect of modern psychiatry. Hospital atmosphere, morale, *esprit de corps* and motivation of all personnel who contact patients are matters of immense importance. Of even greater importance is the need for perceptiveness and intelligent understanding of patients by all who come in contact with them. A modern mental hospital, to perform its functions, must be a perennial enterprise in social engineering and education. Consequently, administrative psychiatry assumes a new importance in the treatment of mental illness. It is a little humiliating to realize that modern psychiatry is fast approaching a point of view similar to that of moral treatment as it was practiced by the founders of the American Psychiatric Association well over one hundred years ago. Though our knowledge of mental illness today is more precise and more explicit in many areas, it is doubtful that our philosophical background or human understanding is significantly greater.

The great gains made in psychiatric knowledge in the past fifty years would be valid grounds for hope and optimism were it not for the discouraging fact that only a small minority of mentally ill patients in America benefit from the knowledge gained. Indeed, conditions in mental hospitals are so unacceptable that they were referred to, as recently as 1948, as the "Shame of the States." (11)

To understand why the majority of American mental hospitals are not providing the standard of treatment achieved by a small minority would require a large scale sociological study.

The modern concept that mental illness is a reaction to past and present relationships with other people is understandably repugnant to our society, since such a view implies that our society itself is the ultimate cause. It means that we actually do "drive" our close associates insane—something we admit only in jest. Furthermore, modern concepts of treatment which hold that mental illness is curable through relationships with other people place the responsibility to provide such relationships squarely upon our shoulders. We become even more uncomfortable when faced with the proposition that sanity and insanity are not a matter of black and white, but a relative affair depending on the adjustment of individuals to each other. Such a proposition raises the question of our own mental health. Indeed, the whole issue of mental illness becomes so unsavory at this point that we would rather put it out of mind altogether.

We have pretty much succeeded in keeping mental illness out of sight and out of mind for several generations. Medicine and law have rendered committed patients almost impotent to obtain a hearing in their own behalf. In spite of their relative helplessness they have made themselves felt, for by their very increase in numbers and failure to recover they have come to cost our society more than we like to pay for their keep. The time is at hand when we cannot afford to continue managing their lives as if they all had hopeless structural brain defects. We have long enough permitted ourselves the luxury of isolating the mentally ill to spare ourselves the shock of seeing in them our own unacceptable traits and motives. We have long enough blinded ourselves to their great sensitivity and need for companionship with the rationalization that they were "too far gone" and insensible of their surroundings to benefit from anything we could do.

Mental hospitals which have investigated the modes of dealing with patients among hospital personnel have learned that the course of mental illness is intimately related to the relative availability of means which meet the minute by minute psychological needs of individual patients. Whereas interpretation of the patient's behavior has been the emphasis of modern dynamic psychiatry, research in the social psychiatry of hospital wards is showing the importance of the patient's interpretation of the behavior of those who control him. This brings to the fore the necessity that those who attend the mentally ill understand their own behavior in order to avoid obstructing the recovery of patients. The humility required of mental hospital personnel to achieve knowledge of self is a serious demand paralleling that placed on individuals who dedicate their lives to religious or military service.

The keen perceptivity to human needs which mental hospital personnel must achieve in order to do justice to patients presents a challenge to our entire society; for it indicates how little human needs are met in other institutions, including families, schools, offices, and factories—from where patients come. Psychiatry has the responsibility of informing the public of the needs of the mentally ill. Psychiatry also has the function of training those members of society who are motivated to work toward the recovery of patients. The community has the ultimate responsibility of seeing to it that the means are provided for *applying psychia-*

*tric knowledge.* Mental illness to a greater extent than any other is, from inception to cure, *primarily* a social problem.

It is over 50 years since modern scientific psychiatry recognized the importance of total life experience in the etiology of mental illness. It is only recently that psychiatry has begun to appreciate the significance of *total life experience in the treatment of mental illness,* and to understand how impersonal custodial care en masse only prolongs, or produces another kind of, mental illness.

# IX

**The Problem of
Treatment in the
Traditional Mental Hospital**

The history of institutional care of the mentally ill may be separated into three phases: 1) the moral treatment phase, 2) the custodial non-treatment phase, and 3) the custodial re-education phase. Today we are on the threshold of a fourth phase, namely that of therapeutic research.

Modern therapeutic research in psychiatry embraces three scientific disciplines: the physiological, the psychological, and the sociological. As such it presents the first opportunity in the history of medicine for the development of an integrated approach to the scientific treatment of mental illness.

The inclusion of social science theory and methodology in psychiatric research introduces a new basis not only for evaluating the needs of patients but also for evaluating psychiatric theory and practice. It is particularly pertinent to the study of institutional psychiatry, for it provides a frame of reference for identifying habitually unrecognized and unquestioned values and attitudes, and for determining their effects on the social adjustment of patients.

Viewed from the perspectives of social science, the history of institutional psychiatry becomes intelligible in terms of the social and psychological effects of medical concepts of mental illness, regardless of their scientific validity. From this point of view the significant aspect of the earliest phase of institutional psychiatry, that of moral treatment, is that it had its origin in

ST. ELIZABETH HOSPITAL
SCHOOL OF NURSING LIBRARY
1044 BELMONT AVENUE
YOUNGSTOWN, OHIO 44505

the pre-scientific era of medicine and drew its inspiration from the same philosophy of human equality and individual rights that gave rise to our democratic political institutions. It belonged more to the humanitarian liberal movement than to medical science. As such it paid full attention to patients as persons.

The custodial non-treatment phase of institutional care was concurrent with the early phase of scientific medicine and was conditioned by the impersonal outlook of an emergent technological industrial society. The authoritative scientific verdict that mental illness was due to incurable brain disease eliminated the belief, on which moral treatment was based, that patients were capable of responding as persons to sympathetic human understanding. Since no scientific treatment for mental illness had yet been discovered, mental hospitals became mere receptacles for the incurable.

The re-educational phase of custodial care represented a more hopeful positive attitude toward patients in that they were regarded as teachable. Occupational and industrial therapies were formally recognized and introduced as treatment measures. Acceptance of the idea of re-education or training as treatment did not, however, indicate a change in the medical attitude that the lesions of mental disease were incurable. At most it amounted to a concession that patients could be taught to behave *like* rational human beings.

Adoption of the view that the goal of the mental hospital was to train patients to do useful work placed patients in a new relationship to the hospital. Since all the training they received was in those occupations necessary to the operation of the hospital, the patients found themselves to be participants in the business of keeping the hospital going. The fact that the greater proportion of the actual work done in mental hospitals came to be done by patients demonstrated the economic success of the training endeavor. The patients benefited from the measure of self-respect they gained from being contributing members to the hospital society. Regardless of how well they did their work, however, professional concepts of their mental condition prevented their being fully accepted as co-workers or as persons.

Professional belief in the permanence of the lesions of mental disease was attended by a reluctance to release patients from the hospital even though they performed the same duties as normal rational people. The resulting accumulation of patients inevitably led to a large pool of unemployed and hence unfavored patients. These patients constituted a social class which ranked at the bottom of the hospital caste system.

The concept that mentally ill patients were incurable but teachable accelerated the development of the mental hospital into an authoritarian stratified class society, governed by the principle of punishment and reward in pursuing its goal of controlling and training the lower classes. The living conditions of the lower classes were characterized by austerity, deprivation, and bleakness. Such living conditions were entirely consistent with the value judgment that patients were less worthy and less able to appreciate the better things of life than the upper classes.

This value judgment was, in fact, reflected in *all* relations between hospital personnel and patients. The sheer multitude of patients as compared with the personnel was in itself a contributing cause to remote impersonal attitudes toward patients. Belief that patients were intrinsically irrational and unpredictable completely undermined any spontaneous inclinations on the part of personnel to treat patients as persons in their own right. The attitudes of personnel, derived from such belief, indicated to the patient that he lacked some essential human quality, and that his only hope for approval lay in obeying orders and deporting himself as an impersonal, unquestioning individual.

The system of mental hospital management, in the course of its development, has adopted many of the practices of business, industry, and scientific agriculture. Today the mental hospital with its farms, truck gardens, shops, and power plants is a complete community operating at a high level of efficiency. In some respects it is typical of many large American enterprises and takes pride in its bigness. But from the standpoint of modern psychiatry and sociology it is anachronistic and unproductive, for it neither gives patients the benefit of the best treatments known to psychiatric science nor employees the benefits of modern democratic principles of industrial organization. From the perspective of modern history, furthermore, the mental hospital stands almost alone as an example of an institution which invests its energies in preserving customs and traditions rather than in making progressive innovations.

Absence of the treatment motif in mental hospitals places all professional personnel in a contradictory role, but it is the attendant who occupies the most difficult and frustrating position. He serves as guard and taskmaster whose duty it is to preserve order by restricting patients' spontaneous movements to a minimum and by closely supervising any duty he directs the patient to perform. He is the most important person in the patient's life, but his position in the hospital hierarchy is of the lowest order. He is subjected to a rigid discipline which requires him to maintain an impersonal relationship with patients and holds him responsible for any mishap which occurs. He must constantly be on the lookout lest some patient acquire a bit of glass, a length of rope, a sliver of wood, or a supply of matches; for every patient is suspect of harboring violent tendencies or desires to escape. He must even restrict conversation between patients lest altercations result. He is fulfilling his duties well if he is observed to be presiding over a scene of somber silence when the supervisor, nurse, or physician "trips" through his ward. All told, his task is a thankless one, for like the patient he remains in good standing only so long as there are no mishaps. There is no way he can progress or better himself. At best, his prospect is the monotony of uneventful life on a "well-managed" ward. His very acceptance of low pay bespeaks in his own mind and in the mind of others that his work is little respected. And in the public mind his capacity to endure close association with the fancied depravity of the mentally ill places him in a category as uniquely stigmatized as mental illness itself.

In order to preserve self-esteem the attendant explains his work in a way which implies admirable qualities of some sort in himself. He emphasizes to others the hazards of his job and pictures in detail the savage cunning or impulsive violence of his patients. He thereby attributes to himself the socially valued qualities of shrewdness and courage, and casts himself in the role of protector of society against madmen. In order to keep intact this version of his role, he must conceive his relationship to patients to be that of perpetual warfare or at best an armed truce. His chief weapons in this warfare come to be a severe countenance and a forbidding manner betokening mastery over the patients. The sounds of enraged pounding and loud cursing emanating form the seclusion rooms are convincing evidence to patients of the futility of anything more than passive resistance.

The connotation that an attendant's friendship with a patient is a reflection on his own mental health is a force which preserves the ever-present barrier between patients and attendants. Indeed, the attendant who does become friendly with patients not only runs the risk of being an outcast among his fellow attendants but also risks reprimand by the ward physician. The capacity of a patient to form friendships with hospital personnel represents a threat to the impersonal authority of the hospital. Anyone less well trained than the physician is automatically considered susceptible of being "taken in" by a patient's efforts to demonstrate his sanity and the injustice of his incarceration. On the other hand, the long-standing distrust of the attendant's character raises in the physician's mind the question of the harmful effect on the vulnerable patient of anything more than an impersonal relationship with attendants. To the extent that this bias is in any measure justifiable, it is a consequence of the hospital's own policy of selecting for attendants individuals who are forced by circumstances to work for low pay in the degrading environment of ward life.

This policy reflects the attitude that neither the mentally ill nor those who will accept work close to them are to be trusted. Indeed, the attendant charged with preventing violence is under constant suspicion of using force and violence himself. He is furthermore subjected to the control of the professional registered nurse and placed under restrictions which often vary only in degree from those inflicted on patients. In some hospitals the male attendant is not even permitted to associate with nurses or other female personnel, such as office workers who "outrank" him. His position, except in his relation to patients, is largely that of a flunky who may be summarily discharged for not "knowing his place."

The nurse in the mental hospital has, except in the infirmary, little to do with the patient as a sick person. Her chief function is that of providing more complete medical control and authoritarian discipline throughout the hospital than physicians can achieve unassisted. The physician as a healer of the mentally sick, also has nothing to do with the patient. He performs the function of guardianship over the patient's physical health and safety.

The mental hospital's relationship with its patients is entirely predicated on the thesis that the patient cannot be trusted and must therefore be kept under complete control. Indeed the very essence of the function of the mental hospital is that of controlling and protecting. The attendant controls the patients and protects them from each other. The nurse controls the attendant and protects the patient against his harshness or laxity. The physician controls the nurse and protects her against supposedly unprincipled attendants, while the superintendent controls his physicians and protects them against the critical public.

The energies of the hospital staff are expended in maintaining personnel at a high pitch of alertness to all signs of impending violence of patients. The prevailing psychological climate is one resembling military vigilance against attack. High value is placed on unquestioning obedience to authority, and traditional hospital customs and procedures are revered for their ostensibly time-proven worth in averting disaster. Proposed changes are viewed as threats to the security of all concerned. The entire hospital society has a vested interest in the status quo and looks to the superintendent as the greatest single stabilizing force assuring its preservation.

The modern psychiatrist who assumes the role of superintendent of a traditional mental hospital and makes plans for giving his patients the benefits of a full psychiatric treatment program thus finds himself confronted with the problem of how to change the structure, the function, and the attitudes and values of a deeply rooted social system. He cannot leave it unchanged and attain the quality of interpersonal relation and social atmosphere essential to psychiatric treatment.

He is faced with the immediate and vital necessity of firmly establishing, in the minds of all, his own and the hospital's

attitude of respect for patients—by raising the standard of their
living accomodations to the level which is customarily expected
by self-respecting citizens; by securing facilities for vocational
training, education, recreation, and entertainment which are on
a par with those available to the general public; by sparing
patients the indignity of indiscriminate detention behind locked
doors; by recognizing the right of patients to participate in their
own government and in the administrative affairs of the hospital.
Once these steps have been taken, the superintendent can pro-
ceed in his plans for imparting to all personnel a wholly new
philosophy of mental illness and an understanding in its treatment.

Yet even these necessary and elemental steps cannot be
taken without a large increase in the funds made available to
the hospital. At present the average public mental hospital must
hold its *weekly* operating expenses per patient to a figure less
than the *daily* operating expenses of the average general hospital.
Such a small budget forces the superintendent to improvise, and
offers little prospect of doing more than raise hopes which end
in frustration and discouragement. A possible alternative is that
of diverting funds from the care of chronic cases and applying
them to a treatment program for acute cases. This alternative
could be supported on the grounds that no program of treatment
has yet been developed for chronic cases comparable to that
known to be effective with acute cases. It has, however, the
unpalatable aspect of depriving the many for the benefit of the
few—an aspect which could be obviated by research in experimental development of life experience treatment programs for
chronic cases.

Another major obstacle to the establishment of full treatment
programs in mental hospitals is the shortage of trained professional psychiatric workers. Solution of this problem at the
level of the mental hospital calls for research in methods of
educating non-professional personnel in the psychiatric care of
patients.

Modern psychiatry, as it has been developed in the teaching
centers of the world, encompasses so many scientific disciplines
that it is beyond the capacity of any one man to master all of

it. This raises the question of whether the traditional hierarchical organization of the mental hospital does not have disadvantages which impede its growth as a scientific institution. The superintendent is legally charged with full responsibility for every patient committted to his hospital. He is not free to delegate this responsibility to his staff; he can only delegate authority to act. This state of affairs favors reliance on routine and established precedent; it prejudices against acceptance of new concepts and procedures. There is, however, as yet no basis from experience for concluding that a different form of organization would be more conducive to psychiatric advancement. The example of the general hospital suggests that greater advances are made when professionally independent physicians work together as members of autonomous and competitive medical services and are served by a superintendent whose chief role is that of providing them the means for achieving their goals.

In his over-all endeavor to bring modern treatments into the traditional mental hospital the superintendent is impeded not only by deeply rooted attitudes within the hospital but also by equally fixed attitudes in the general public. Public attitudes toward the institutionalized mentally ill lag far behind advances in psychiatric thought. They are an echo of psychiatric attitudes, current 50 years ago, when "insanity" was considered to be an untreatable disease of the brain. To the public mind, mental illness does not carry the connotation of an illness which anyone may have; it designates rather a class of human beings membership in which differentiates an individual as immutably as does race membership. The public mind also characterizes the mentally ill patient as being so completely untrustworthy, unpredictable, and dangerous and indecent that he must be kept under control at all times. These misconceptions of mental illness are serious enough because of the unjust and false stigma which they place upon a large number of our citizens; but of greater importance is that the traditional mental hospital of today operates in accordance with these same misconceptions.

The superintendent who would make modern psychiatric treatment available to his patients must recognize that the community cannot reasonably be expected to change in attitudes or alter its social or financial relations with the hospital on demand. His position is analogous to that of the modern medical emissary to a primitive land who must demonstrate to the people the advantages of modern medicine over primitive medicine before he can win their support in founding a modern medical clinic. The superintendent of the mental hospital must go a step beyond this, for his treatment of patients is not limited to technical matters which need not be understood by the community. On the contrary, he deals with problems which cannot be solved without community understanding and participation. His professional function is not limited to treatment of patients in the hospital but includes treatment of the attitudes of the larger community of which the hospital is a part. These problems of community dread of the hospital, misconceptions about its patients, and the general poverty of the hospital are also due to the pathologic conditions which require research and development of therapeutic skill.

The superintendent's success in securing treatment for his patients hangs largely on his success in establishing multiple points of close and enduring contact between the mental hospital and the community. The more intimately acquainted socially active members of the community become with patients, the more opportunity they will have to acquire an appreciation that the mentally ill are people in painfully difficult situations of a complexity that would defy anyone's capacity for explanation and impair anyone's ability to get along in a society blind to the complexities of human relations. Such appreciation can win patients the respect and consideration which are their due both as sick people and as members of our society.

Growth of understanding in the community that mental illness has to do with the frustrations, disappointments, and injured sentiments which people unwittingly inflict on each other can lead to recognition that sub-standard living conditions and imprisonment only add injury to the patient's already damaged self-esteem. From acquaintanceship with recovered patients can come a general realization in the community that mental illness is not incurable but that its cure requires far more of human thought and effort in behalf of patients than is now given.

The policy of inviting the community to participate in the daily life of the mental hospital allows the public an opportunity to discover that their "good Samaritanism" does not go unrewarded. Visitors can learn that patients in their efforts to get well have done a great deal of creative thinking about human relations and can teach others much that will help them in their own life situations. This positive aspect of the mental hospital provides a basis for its development as an educational center of great value to the community. Indeed, it is not an extravagant speculation that mental hospitals will be a nucleus of future progress in man's understanding of man, for they are natural centers for study and research in human relations.

One lesson which can be derived from the history of institutional care of the mentally ill is that human beings are molded by whatever authority they respect, and that ideas about human beings of authoritative origin eventually influence human behavior in a direction which confirms the authoritative idea.

Psychiatry as a member of the science family enjoys immense prestige as the final authority on illness of the human mind. People with sick minds, moreover, are highly sensitive to the opinions and attitudes of other people. They are profoundly affected by the fact that the law of the land has committed them to the care and custody of the mental hospital and are even more profoundly affected by the hospital's opinion of them. The history of institutional care demonstrates the different effects of optimism and pessimism. Recovery was far more frequent during the optimistic era of moral treatment than it has been since the advent of the pessimistic era of custodial care.

Modern psychiatry, founded on psychology and the social sciences as well as physiology, is alert to the role played by attitudes and interpersonal relations in determining the course of mental illness. Research studies in social therapy have led to the adoption of treatment programs which have greatly increased the frequency of recovery. At present such programs of treatment are to be found in only a few teaching hospitals. Over 99% of the mentally ill in America receive nothing more than custodial care of low standard. The real problem of mental illness today is that of motivating our society to re-instate the human rights of this great number of patients and to provide them with psychiatric treatments which have already proven their worth.

Respect for the feelings of mentally ill patients has already begun to increase scientific sensitivity to the psychic pain and emotional suffering which underlies distorted thinking and behavior. Search for chemical means for allaying such pain and suffering has established the new field of research called psychopharmacology.

The fact that this research has resulted in the discovery of drugs which have contributed greatly to the well-being of thousands of patients over the past decade is convincing evidence that serious attention to the simple human needs of the mentally ill should be a matter of great concern to everyone.

# X

## Toward a New Moral Treatment

The elapse of more than 15 years since the writing of Chapter IX, and of about 20 years since the compilation of the statistical data in Chapter III, provides a timely opportunity to give some account of the developments that have taken place during those two decades.

The events leading to what are now called the mental health services delivery system bear sufficient similarity to the early history of moral treatment to warrant referring to developments since 1960 as the New Moral Treatment Era in American psychiatry. The old moral treatment developed over a period of nearly 50 years and reached its climax around 1850. In 1855 Congress passed a large-scale mental health act (the Twelve-and-a-Half Million Acre Bill), which was vetoed by President Franklin Pierce on the grounds that there were no means (i.e., professional and trained manpower) to implement it. (That the President suffered from alcoholism, and that his wife failed to recover from an involutional psychosis, are factors that may also have influenced his veto. Perhaps, too, the gathering clouds of enmity between North and South affected his decision, since it had to do with public lands in the West as a source of revenue—lands over which the North and South were competing for control.) In the twentieth century, however, a bill for improving the care of the mentally ill did pass. The National Mental Health Act of 1946 established the National Institute of Mental Health. The act creating the Joint Commission for Mental Health and Illness was passed in 1955 and the work of the Commission resulted in passage of the National Mental Health and Retardation Act of 1963, which provided funds for community mental health centers.

The following sections of this chapter describe five present-day programs as moral treatment endeavors. *

## I. WORCESTER STATE HOSPITAL

A critical factor leading to passage of the act that funded community mental health centers was Worcester State Hospital's record, in the 1950's, demonstrating the efficacy of new approaches in reducing a hospital's census. For those with a bent toward history, it is certainly interesting that the first home of moral treatment under state auspices should also take the lead in developing the new moral treatment.

Figure 4 shows what happened at Worcester State Hospital from 1950 on. It is an extension of Figure 1 (see Chapter III). Figure 4 shows a most remarkable and dramatic change in average daily hospital population for the decade ending in 1962, and an even greater change in the eight-year period ending in 1970. As is readily seen, the average daily population for the decade ending in 1952 was 2,773. The average daily population for the eight-year period ending in 1970 was 1,155. The single year with the highest average daily population in the history of the hospital was 1950, when the figure was 2,858. As of this writing, the single year with the lowest daily population since then was 1970, when the figure was 932—one-third what it was 20 years earlier!

Admission rates also changed remarkably. The average annual admission rate for the decade ending in 1952 was 770; in the eight-year period ending in 1970, the average annual admission rate was 1,238—an increase of over 75 per cent.

The rising rates of admission to Worcester State Hospital are especially significant in view of a great growth in the numbers

---

* Readers interested in acquiring a fuller picture of the beginnings of our present day transition toward moral treatment are referred to two books which came out of Boston Psychopathic Hospital in the 1950's: *"From Custodial to Therapeutic Care,"* by Greenblatt, York, Brown, and Hyde; and *The Patient and the Mental Hospital*, edited by Greenblatt, Levinson, and Williams.

of voluntary admissions and a decline in the number of commitments. For example, commitments constituted more than 75 per cent of all admissions in 1956, but in 1970 they made up less than 10 per cent.

## INTRODUCTION OF RENEWED
## MORAL TREATMENT

The high-water mark of Worcester State Hospital's average

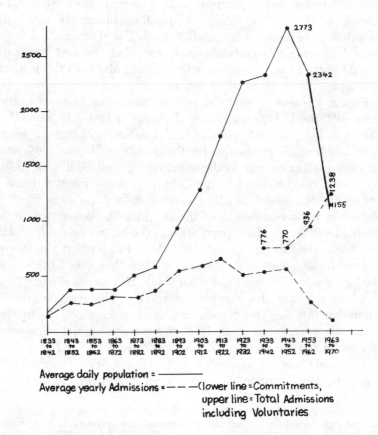

Average daily population = ————
Average yearly Admissions = — — —(lower line = Commitments, upper line = Total Admissions including Voluntaries

FIG. 4. Resident Population and Yearly Admission Rates of Worcester State Hospital 1833-1970.

daily census was 2,858 in 1950. In 1951, this figure decreased to 2,822, and then to 2,810 in 1952, only to rise in 1952 to 2,842. The year 1953, however, witnessed a trend that has not reversed itself: a decrease in the average daily census, followed each succeeding year *ever since* with a further decrease. The average daily population figure for 1953 was 2,777. As mentioned above, the figure for 1970 was 932.

During those many years, the admission rates to Worcester State Hospital increased at almost as rapid a pace as the average daily population decreased. Voluntary patients increased rapidly after 1956, while commitments decreased greatly: from 460 in 1956 to a low of 72 in 1970. (See Figure 5.)

From these data, one can readily surmise that a change in outlook and administrative practice took place at Worcester State Hospital in the early 1950's, a change that has made a considerable difference to the people living in the area served by it. In this regard, it is worth noting that the superintendent of Worcester State Hospital during this period, Dr. Bardwell Flower, was also the state's leading forensic psychiatrist. His knowledge of legal matters was invaluable in enabling him to act on his belief in patients' rights and in their capacity to respond beneficially to their release back into the community.

## THERAPEUTIC EMANCIPATION

Dr. Flower's approach to bringing relief to his patients was a straightforward attack on the overcrowded, substandard living conditions they were forced to endure. He applied a number of measures to accomplish his goal, fully utilizing opportunities as they arose. When federal funds became available for the support of elderly patients in nursing homes, he embarked on a program of placing patients over 65 in nursing homes in their own communities. As the hospital population decreased, nurses previously involved in caring for the elderly were freed for other duties. Since the hospital lacked enough social workers to carry out Dr. Flower's program of large-scale placing of patients in the community, nurses were assigned to duties usually performed by social workers. Nurses were also trained for duties usually con-

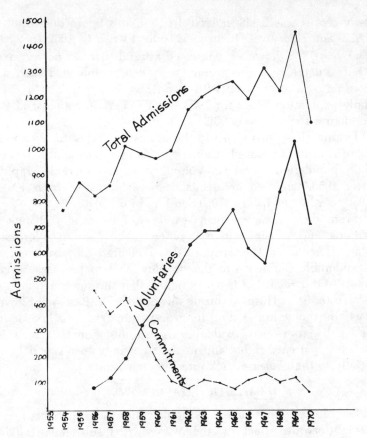

Fig. 5. Use of Voluntary Status vs Commitment 1956-1970, Worcester State Hospital.

sidered the province of psychiatrists: individual and group psychotherapy. As personnel became better acquainted with patients as individuals, it became obvious that many were ready for release from the hospital. Accordingly, medical staff and experienced nursing personnel were assigned the task of reevaluating *every* patient in the hospital. As the reevaluation progressed, it was observed that the patients in the worst mental condition were those located in the least desirable surroundings—the most remote back wards. This led to Dr. Flower's most strategic move—now referred to as the "Big Switch"—the transfer of the patients residing in the back wards to the newly built admission building. Newly admitted and convalescing patients were simultaneously moved to the back wards. At first the move evoked such protest from the new patients and their families that political pressure was brought to bear on the hospital to reverse the action. The protest died down, however, when the over-all benefit of the move became apparent. The increased attention received by the former back ward patients soon bore fruit in the form of improvement, and large numbers of long-term patients were released from the hospital each year. Some of these patients were placed in nursing homes and some in "family care." The latter is an arrangement whereby improved patients with no homes to go to are placed with families who are compensated by the hospital for the patients' keep.

Although the beginning of therapeutic emancipation was actively under way prior to the arrival of the new tranquilizer drugs in the mid-1950's, the decrease in the hospital population occurred at an accelerated pace as increasing use was made of these effective anxiety-relieving medications.

The great increases in mental hospital discharge rates beginning in the late 1940's and the early 1950's cannot justifiably be credited to any single factor. Improved environmental care and new administrative philosophies, such as moral treatment, included the use of discharge itself as a therapeutic method. The recoveries due to somatic treatments, such as electric shock, contributed to a general optimism regarding recoverability; this, in turn, increased the inclination of physicians to respond favorably to patients' requests for discharge. The arrival of tranquilizer drugs accelerated the recovery of many patients who would have recovered over a longer period of time with moral treatment alone. In addition, some patients responded to transquilizer treatment who would not have recovered without it, or who would have relapsed without it. The latter, however, often needed the rehabilitation measures of moral treatment to restore them to productive life in the community.

Worcester State Hospital's success in reducing its patient population is particularly interesting because it was the first hospital
in the country to show a downward trend in its census, and because it reduced its level well below the state and national average. The state hospital system of the Massachusetts Department
of Mental Health as a whole showed a similar decrease in census
from 1954 on, going from 24,000 patients that year to 13,000 in
1970. As of 1955, state and county mental hospitals throughout
the country showed a decrease, going from 559,000 patients that
year to 367,000 in 1970. Worcester State Hospital's decrease from
1953 to 1970, it will be remembered, was much more marked:
from 2,777 to 932.

FACTORS INFLUENCING THE
WORCESTER STORY:
GENERAL AND PARTICULAR

An adequate understanding of the Worcester story is hardly
possible without some knowledge of the larger picture of what
was happening simultaneously at the national and state levels.
It is important to begin the story with the knowledge that the
hospital's large population in 1950—the year with the highest
average daily population in its history—was the result of an
unprecedented accumulation of patients during World War II,
and was directly related to the loss of hospital personnel to the
military. At the end of the 1940's there were 300 positions
vacant, 14 of which were left open by physicians who had left on
military leave of absence and had not returned. The hospital's
problems, however, were far from solved with the ending of
the war.

Indeed, with the rapid upswing of the economy and a higher
general income, the hospital was unable to compete on the open
market for employees—especially professional people. It was not
until 1949 that state employee salaries were increased by the
legislature. With improved salaries to offer, Dr. Flower was able
to recruit a fair number of people who had been trained at Wor-

cester State Hospital. Since the hospital's long history and reputation as a training center placed it in the favored position of having many alumni, it was considerably more successful than most state hospitals in acquiring staff in the early 1950's. Of particular importance was the fact that the psychiatrists returning to the hospital from the military were a spirited, enthusiastic group, interested in getting the hospital back on its feet as a therapeutic institution. The spirit of activism was strengthened by the return of the hospital's former clinical leader, Dr. David Rothschild. The staff members began in earnest to "dig out from under"; like Dr. Flower, they were disturbed by the excess of patients and by the negative effects on them of overcrowding and substandard living conditions.

In the course of reevaluating the mental and physical condition of the patients, team members developed an intuitive ability to detect, even in a relatively brief contact, patients who were on the threshold of recovery and able to benefit by release. The immediate outcome of the reevaluation program was a reorganization of the ward services on the basis of a classification of patients in terms of their nursing care needs.

The establishment of ward services staffed to provide several categories of nursing care led to the observation that many patients were suitable for care in community facilities. As a result, cadres of nurses were formed to conduct a search for local facilities for the patients. Within a relatively short time, these nurses became expert in selecting the local facility most appropriate for each patient. On the basis of this experience, the clinical director formulated a policy under which no patient remained in the hospital if his condition was such that he could receive care in a community facility equal or superior to Worcester State Hospital. And many such facilities were found.

One lesson learned from the experience of moving large numbers of long-term patients out of the hospital was that which the clinical director termed the "cream-skimming phenomenon" of ward sociology. This refers to the fact that when the most competent ward patient is moved out to the community, his position is filled by another patient who comes up the ladder of improvement soon after he has left.

Another project that influenced program development at Worcester State Hospital was a survey undertaken by a member of the senior medical staff to ascertain the nature of admissions into the hospital. This survey concluded that the psychiatric condition of 40 per cent of admissions did not warrant their being hospitalized as inpatients. It became evident from this, and from the need of discharged patients for aftercare services, that a day hospital and an outpatient department were needed. These services were put into operation in the early 1960's.

An important factor in influencing the utilization of Worcester State Hospital was a change, in the early 1950's, in the state regulations regarding voluntary self-commitment. The requirements were liberalized so that any person, however ill, could be admitted to the hospital if he but made a written application. Prior to this liberalization, hospital superintendents were restricted in their use of voluntary status to patients with milder degrees of mental disorder. The increase of voluntary admissions after the liberalization pushed total admissions in the 1960's to nearly twice what they had been two decades before.

The experience of Worcester State Hospital has, perhaps, a rather unexpected moral: the doctors and nurses of a mental hospital found they could not do right by their patients without taking on the roles of *social planners* in the patient's behalf and finding places and activities for them in the community. This is all the more significant when we consider that for over 50 years social planning was the province of the trained social workers of the mental hospital's Social Service Department. The overwhelming magnitude of the task confronting the medical and nursing staffs at Worcester State Hospital forced them into social planning. Their success would seem to indicate the necessity for a social conscience in medicine and nursing, and a social component in their thinking about patients.

Can it be that the spread of social concern for patients from the field of social work to other health professions is the process underlying the emergence of the new moral treatment?

## II.  BOSTON PSYCHOPATHIC HOSPITAL

In 1943, when Dr. Harry C. Solomon assumed directorship of Boston Psychopathic Hospital, American psychiatry had taught for nearly half a century that mental illnesses were disorders of the total personality that could be understood in terms of the patient's life history and treated by such psychological means as psychotherapy, occupational therapy, and habit training. Indeed, the most pernicious of mental diseases, dementia praecox, had long been considered by some authorities to be a habit disorder. More recently, many had considered it to be a product of unfavorable interpersonal relations. American leadership in the field of mental health rested largely on its development of dynamic psychiatry, that is, psychologically oriented psychiatry based on Meyerian psychobiology and Freudian psychoanalysis. The strength of dynamic psychiatry rested on its value not only as a theoretical framework formulating a plausible human etiology of mental diseases, but also as a method for discovering their treatment. The general principles of treatment had, in fact, been known for several decades and had been applied by many psychiatrists in a variety of mental disorders. One group of mental disorders, however, had largely gone untreated because of the shortage of psychiatrists—namely, the major psychoses.

In 1943, Boston Psychopathic Hospital undertook to apply, as fully as possible, the principles of dynamic psychiatry in the treatment of severely psychotic patients. The chief obstacle to this venture was the absence of a physical and social setting consistent with an attitude of respect for patients demanded by dynamic psychiatry. The hospital wards were relatively barren and lacked sufficient means for breaking the monotony of doing nothing. Patients had a choice of either sitting on hard, heavy benches or pacing the floor. Their days were characterized by deadening monotony, punctuated by the regimented activities of rising in the morning, going to meals, and returning to bed early in the evening. Patients were dealt with on an entirely impersonal basis: nurses and attendants rarely spoke to them other than to make specific requests connected with hospital routines. On the acute services, patients were allowed no private possessions, not even their own clothing; and the clothing provided for them was ill-fitting and unsightly. Nor were they allowed a moment's privacy or escape from the watchful eyes of attendants. The governing principle of patient care was, in short, the purely negative one of preventing the patient from doing anything that could possibly lead to his getting out of control or harming himself. The patient as a "total personality" was completely neglected except for, at most, a few hours a week of psychotherapy with his ward physician. And whatever benefits the patient gained from psychotherapy were nullified by the demoralizing effect of the hospital environment on his self-esteem.

The steps made toward achieving an environment consistent with psychotherapeutic principles were based on the common-sense idea that hospitalized patients have at least as great a need for an opportunity to form their own interests and relationships as do healthy individuals. The first action taken toward altering the environment in the wards was to supply a few playing cards to the patients. This small attempt to enrich ward life immediately brought to the fore the complexity of the problem to be faced when established institutional habit patterns are altered. Ward attendants, nurses, and physicians resisted the innovation on various grounds: the floor would become littered with playing cards and look unsightly; cards would be lost and new decks would have to be bought; competitiveness and disagreement would arise among the players; patients might get out of control, for they would no longer be in their places on the long benches against the walls; small tables used for card playing were light enough to be lifted and used as weapons, etc.

When the next step was taken—the introduction of checker games—there were more objections: patients might swallow the checkers or throw them at each other. It was evident that hospital personnel feared any departure from established routine. It was also apparent that nurses and attendants had been denied the opportunity to gain an up-to-date understanding of mental illness and the needs of patients. Traditional mental hospital practice had relegated the role of attendants and nurses to that of limiting the patients' freedom of movement and guarding against every possible mishap. Hence, anything approximating normal social life for patients could not be achieved without including attendants and nurses as professional partners who had positive roles to play in the care of patients. Indeed, they had been so thoroughly indoctrinated with the necessity of keeping the patients immobilized, and so completely trained to do nothing with patients in the absence of express orders by the physician, that no change could be made without discussing its rationale with them. It became clear that normal social life could not be provided as long as ward personnel were limited to obeying orders, were not allowed to act on their own initiative, and were prevented from contributing ideas and asking questions.

Once the personnel became used to cards and checkers and participated in these games with the patients, these activities were accepted as a matter of course. Resistance again cropped up, when Horse Race and similar table games were introduced. Again, the basis for resistance was concern about the danger and nuisance that new paraphernalia might bring. When pictures were hung on the walls, it was said that patients would break the glass and use it to cut themselves or each other. When window drapes were introduced, there was concern that patients would use them to hang themselves.

The very difficulties that arose in attempting to create a normal social life for patients revealed how little the hospital personnel, including the psychiatrists, respected the capacity of patients to appreciate living conditions considered essential by other people. In principle, such lack of respect for the feelings of the mentally ill was not far removed from the ancient superstition that lunatics are insensible to cold. Bit by bit, however, the entire staff began to share the improved morale of the patients. As the realization grew that life in a mental hospital need not be somber and barren, it became increasingly possible to allow the patients greater mobility and more opportunity for socialization. The Occupational Therapy Department, which had previously been open only to well-behaved patients with mild disorders, was officially made available to all patients. When the chief occupational therapist insisted that each patient who came must have a specific

prescription from the ward physician, this presented no great
obstacle: physicians merely changed their habit of writing practically no occupational therapy prescriptions to one of writing
blanket prescriptions for every patient. They recognized that
there were no genuine criteria for writing occupational therapy
prescriptions in the first place, and that there were no reasons
for withholding its possible benefits from patients. The long-
established custom of sending female patients to occupational
therapy in the morning and male patients in the afternoon
was more difficult to overcome. Both the supervisor of nurses
and the chief occupational therapist objected to allowing
both male and female patients in the occupational therapy
department at the same time. They were not, however, adamant
in their stand; first one and then the other would vacillate and
admit the unnaturalness of having only one sex in the department
at a time. When the move was finally made, the resistance of the
nursing service was such that patients least capable of self-care
were picked to be present on the first day of coeducational
occupational therapy. The almost complete absence of decorum
that ensued was deemed to be a sufficient demonstration that such
activities were not possible in a mental hospital. Certainly, it was
a clear example of the ability of personnel to undermine and make
difficult any departure from established custom. It was a short-
term defection, however. Today, none of the personnel could
conceive of the Occupational Therapy Department being other
than coeducational.

The strong tendency on the part of personnel to adhere to
established custom was more the result of long indoctrination
than a matter of personal preference. Indeed, not a few of the
attendants had long harbored the private opinion that patients
were unnecessarily deprived of the most ordinary satisfactions,
and some had even bought newspapers and magazines for them
with their own money.

Yet it was not until personnel of all ranks felt genuinely free to
express themselves that the hospital's administrative officers became fully aware of the extent to which the natural sympathy of
personnel for patients had been discouraged by prohibitive rules

and regulations. When personnel were taught that their relationships with patients were an important part of treatment, an interest in dynamic psychiatry was aroused that could not be satisfied by a few didactic lectures. It was soon recognized that there was a need for regular staff conferences of attendants, student nurses, head nurses, and social workers, where the interpersonal relation of patients and personnel could be thoroughly discussed. As the principles of dynamic psychiatry permeated the hospital, the needs of individuals in both groups were more readily recognized and acted upon.

By focusing attention on the emotional needs of individuals and by carefully appraising different points of view in open discussion, it was realized that patients face problems that differ only in magnitude from those faced by personnel and other nonpatients. The open-forum character of these staff meetings, furthermore, gave everyone a voice in policy-making.

One of the benefits of providing a basis for mutual respect among attendants, nurses, social workers, and physicians was that it led quite naturally to encouraging patients to form a self-administered organization of their own; this became known as "patient government." This body governed its meetings according to parliamentary procedures, passed resolutions concerning its own affairs, and made recommendations to the administrative officers of the hospital. The recommendations were given full attention and, if feasible, were acted upon; if not, a full explanation was given to the officers of patient government. This democratic privilege restored to the patients some of the self-esteem they had lost in the process of being admitted to the hospital. The very provision of a means whereby all ranks of personnel and patients could make recommendations that would be seriously considered by the administrative psychiatrists was a powerful stimulus for patients and personnel to assume responsibility. A heightened self-esteem and an increased willingness to take responsibility served as valuable preparation for dealing with individuals from the community—volunteer workers and students of medicine, psychology, sociology, and theology—who were invited to take part in the life of the hospital.

The extremely positive and optimistic attitudes toward mental illnesses that were engendered by the concept of their being, to an important degree, due to the patient's personal problems were greatly strengthened by the introduction of a more extensive use of somatic treatments and by the experience of seeing remarkable improvement in those suffering from the most severe psychoses, i.e., general paresis, psychotic depressions, mania, and schizophrenia, then being treated with fever-penicillin therapy, electric shock, and insulin coma. The effectiveness of somatic treatments in making patients more communicative not only aroused optimism but also acted as a challenge to stimulate personnel to apply their personal skills to help patients regain their capacities to relate successfully to others.

The growth of motivation in personnel to deal with patients on an individual basis contributed to the final elimination of every measure of restraint. The use of continuous tubs and wet-sheet packs passed completely out of use. Indeed, even the use of sedative drugs was abandoned, although not without considerable resistance on the part of nurses and house physicians. Within a year the number of hours that patients were locked in seclusion rooms (bare rooms that contained only a mattress) per month dropped to one-quarter of the former level. In every respect, the skill and tact of hospital personnel proved to be far superior as a method of meeting the needs of acutely disturbed patients than all the traditional measures hitherto used to quiet them.

Within two to three years, the patterns of human relationships in the hospital changed completely. Research began to include investigations into the group dynamics and social structure of the hospital. New treatment methods such as group therapy, socio-drama, and psychodrama were adopted. There was, moreover, no decrease in background activities as these more specific therapeutic methods were developed. On the contrary, recreational activities steadily increased in number and variety, and continuous improvement was made in the comforts, conveniences, and esthetic appearance of the wards.

Special attention was also given to the individual needs of patients with respect to the outside community. A full-time social worker was employed to function as an intermediary between each patient and his family and employer. She introduced the patient and his family to the hospital and began, on the very day of admission, to make the preparations necessary to ensure the patient's readjustment at the time of his discharge.

The great improvement in the behavior and morale of patients that accompained these changes was conclusive evidence of the effect of environment on mental illness. While such environmental processes are not always sufficient therapy for recovery, they play a large part in producing a setting in which spontaneous recoveries can occur and in which specific therapies can be fully effective. Of even greater importance, however, was the knowledge, derived from experience, that the hospital "'environment'" would easily slip back into a stereotyped routine and again fail to adapt to the needs of individuals if vigilant and thoughtful attention to the details of hospital life failed to be given by its leaders. The whole emotional impact of the hospital on patients was found to depend largely on whether each detail in the hospital-patient relationship signified an attitude of respect for the patient or whether it betrayed an attitude of disregard for individual sensibilities in favor of technical considerations. This hospital's experience clearly shows the role played by administrative psychiatry in patient therapy and indicates the importance of further research in the social psychiatry of mental hospitals.

The wholesale shift in the functioning of Boston Psychopathic Hospital to a large-scale intensive treatment program during the 1943-1950 period represented a departure from its original purposes. When it was founded as a "psychopathic" hospital some 30 years before, its function was to serve as a diagnostic clearinghouse and as a center for teaching and research. At that time, relatively few patients remained at the hospital under regular commitment. From 1912-1942, the yearly admission rate was 2,000 or more, of which only 150 or less remained under commitment—about 7 per cent. By 1950, there were about 1,000 admissions a year, of which about 300, or 30 per cent, remained for treatment under commitment.

The results of the total treatment program that the hospital undertook are probably most objectively indicated by the changes in the discharge rates of regularly committed patients. In the years 1925-1944, these discharge rates were between 33 and 37 per cent. During the five-year period, 1945-1949, in which the total treatment program was first put into effect, the discharge rate was 62 per cent. These rates refer to the proportion of patients admitted who were discharged from the hospital's books after a trial visit in the community of one year's duration. By 1948-49, this figure had risen to 70 per cent. Twenty years previously (i.e., 1928-29), the comparable figure was 31 per cent. During the 1950's and 1960's, discharge rates continued to rise to a point where, in the year of this writing (1971), over 90 per cent are expected to be discharged back into the community. Indeed, the proportion of patients needing continuous hospitalization for an indefinite period after their admission is now less than 5 per cent.

From the vantage point of 1971, it seems obvious that the changes instituted in the 1940's by Boston Psychopathic Hospital in its approaches to patients was an important early experiment in social psychiatry, with radical implications. In effect, it was also an experiment in therapeutic emancipation which was accompanied by microsociological studies, on the one hand, and followup studies on the other. This experiment showed conclusively that mentally ill patients respond positively to a policy that affords them maximum freedom and opportunity to develop their abilities. They do *not* misuse the trust placed in them by the hospital; but they *do* seek help for their emotional problems, they *do* take initiative in helping themselves, and they *do* demonstrate organizational ability and administrative capacity. This experimental program was, therefore, successful in motivating mentally ill patients to make an effort to reestablish effective relationships with others.

The total treatment program developed at Boston Psychopathic Hospital during the 1940's has many points in common with the moral treatment hospital of the early 1800's. The success of the underlying principles of both programs, so widely separated in time, indicates that there has always been hope for the mentally ill, a hope that does not depend upon the discovery of new drugs, such as the tranquilizers that appeared in the scene in the mid-1950's.

Indeed, the great comfort that the phenothiazines brought to patients and their families and hospital personnel has had rather mixed consequences—some positive, some negative. While it has, on the one hand, encouraged the development of interpersonal relations and social participation, it has, on the other, tended to impress upon the patient and his associates an attitude that detracts from the importance of his development as a person in relation to others. The latter is exemplified by the priority given to getting the patient to take his medicine over respecting the validity of his feelings. More often than not, for example, an expression of strong feelings on the part of the patient leads those who feel responsible for him to request his physician to increase his medication.

As at Worcester State Hospital, the application of Boston Psychopathic Hospital's version of the new moral treatment was characterized by the superintendent stimulating the social conscience of the medical staff. The small size of Boston Psychopathic—120 beds—and its large staff of 175 plus social science students from many Boston campuses, made for a vastly different situation than that at Worcester. Indeed, where Worcester applied what might be called a macrosociologic approach to upgrading treatment efforts, Boston Psychopathic's approach was microsociologic. The major interest of the staff professionals and the students was focused on the intrapsychic dynamics and interpersonal relations of patients—to the degree that they could be learned in interviews with each patient. Patients' families were similarly interviewed, thus providing detailed knowledge of each patient's life. Perhaps the most significant feature of the developing program was the emphasis it placed on the treatment of patients with major psychoses, especially those schizophrenic disorders traditionally considered essentially untreatable. In the view of the superintendent and clinical director, such pessimism was unwarranted, since the failure of these patients to recover could be ascribed to therapeutic neglect. Schizophrenic patients were recognized as persons with unique life problems, but with a considerable capacity for recovery in a social milieu directed to problem-solving. The total treatment approach was a thorough-going moral treatment program enriched by twentieth-century psychoanalysis and social science concepts of human behavior. (At Worcester State Hospital the staff also applied the total treatment approach whenever it was possible to do so, but, faced with thousands of patients to treat, they mobilized their major resource, namely, nursing personnel, to do the job.)

The division of treatment programs at Boston Psychopathic will be of interest to planners of mental health centers. It was essentially a tripartite division, each under physician leadership. The milieu therapy program was largely the responsibility of the assistant superintendent, who worked closely with the nursing and occupational therapy departments. The individual psycho-therapy program was organized and supervised by the clinical director, who worked mainly with psychiatrists and social workers. The somatic treatment program was under the supervision of a senior neuropsychiatrist, who worked with senior residents especially interested in physiological research.

In retrospect, it would appear that the common denominator in the Boston Psychopathic and Worcester programs was the presence of people in key positions who had an enduring empathic curiosity about their patients and in whose minds psychological and social serendipity could merge and be quickly translated into action in a manner reminiscent of the early days of moral treatment.

## III.  BUTLER HEALTH CENTER

In 1957, Dr. Robert W. Hyde left his position as assistant superintendent of Boston Psychopathic Hospital to become the new superintendent of Butler Health Center in Providence, Rhode Island. The American Psychiatric Association had recommended that psychiatric services be developed in the buildings of historic Butler Hospital to meet the needs of the surrounding

Rhode Island communities, and because of Dr. Hyde's unique experience and qualifications, he was named to head the program.

From the outset, prior to the admission of patients to any of its clinical services, a general understanding was shared by the administrative staff and heads of clinical departments that the philosophy of total treatment would guide the development of the new mental health center in its handling of internal affairs and in its community relations.

Since Dr. Hyde and his staff were well acquainted with the history of moral treatment, its name was often used in referring to the center's policy of making therapeutic use of every person in contact with patients, but the term "social psychiatry" was more often used as a modern synonym. Social psychiatry then acquired a local definition: it was the name given to the art and science of recruiting individuals to play psychotherapeutic roles in dealing with patients.

Social psychiatry at Butler became more broadly defined as the art and science of producing a social climate in which mental illness is divested of its traditional capacity to keep other people at a distance. Mental illness was reduced to its component parts, which were familiar to everyone as the troubles endured in everyday life. The patient was recognized as being overburdened with troubles, and treatment was recognized as being a thoughtful giving of effective help in personal matters. These definitions were based on the wholesale assumption and unspoken premise that everyone possesses some degree of motivation to give psychological aid to others, and that everyone has a combination of personality make-up, mode of thinking, fund of knowledge, and backlog of experience that can have a psychotherapeutic value for appropriately selected emotionally disabled persons. The superintendent and clinical director thus regarded their tasks as twofold: the first was to acquire a staff with a variety of personalities to work with patients; the second was to learn which personnel were of psychotherapeutic value to particular patients.

The small size of the professional staff at Butler Health Center and the circumstance of starting a completely new organization favored the growth of thoroughgoing communication and discussion of ideas among its members. As a result, ideas about patients' needs rather than precedent or habit tended to predominate in determining the course of everyday action. In this context, the idea of making therapeutic use of all individuals, regardless of educational background, was at first accepted in theory, and later in practice, by newcomers who joined the professional staff.

With an increase in the size of the clinical staff and in the number of patients served, a discernible pattern began to take shape along more or less functional lines, and areas of need in the community were designated which the Butler staff found itself attempting to meet.

## SECTORS OF SOCIAL PSYCHIATRY

Social psychiatry is divided into three parts: preventive psychiatry, milieu therapy, and rehabilitation. Each of these divisions requires the collaborative endeavors of many people.

### Preventive Psychiatry

The first major service opened to the community was the outpatient department. The staff soon found itself dealing with requests for advice and help that were later formulated as belonging in the area of *preventive psychiatry* as a sector of social psychiatry. Inquiries were made by telephone and in person by individuals who sought advice for themselves or for a relative or friend. These inquiries pointed up the importance of easy accessibility to psychiatric service so that cases of incipient emotional impairment could be readily spotted. They also brought to the fore the multiplicity of ways in which certain words and actions of individuals are misunderstood in situations that are relatively stressful to the individual but that go unrecognized as such by their associates. In some respects, seemingly minor and brief discussions with people who make informal inquiries to psychiatric workers provide the clearest examples of social psychiatry in everyday practice. The response of the psychiatric worker is automatically aimed at turning an individual's relationships to a therapeutic purpose.

By and large, the outpatient department did most of the preventive work. To increase its effectivenesss, it adopted two important policies: 1) immediately providing at least psychological first aid and evaluation, and 2) establishing a helping relationship of some kind even when a full program of treatment could not be provided.

## Milieu Therapy

The second major service opened to the community was the day program. In the early months of this program, prior to the opening of the inservice unit, the staff became involved in intensive relationships with both patients and their relatives. During this period, a pattern of patient care and treatment emerged that carried over to the inservice unit and was maintained in both services thereafter. As has been noted, the staff held to the premise that every individual, irrespective of training, was endowed with therapeutic potential. With the opening of the day program, this premise was applied to the fullest, not solely as a matter of principle but also as a matter of necessity. Occupational therapist and social worker, psychologist and sociologist, nurse and psychiatrist all found themselves working together as an intimate group, continually discussing ways and means to use their personal resources in allaying the severely disturbed behavior of a relatively small number of psychiatric patients. The experience gained in this effort clearly demonstrated to the staff's satisfaction that patients could be successfully treated without the help of locked doors or the use of physical force. It also demonstrated the role played by each staff member's personality in the treatment and recovery process of every patient. Getting "through" to a patient and winning his trust was clearly a matter of personality and personal motivation rather than a matter of formal psychiatric training.

With the opening of the center's 40-bed inpatient service, licensed practical nurses and attendants who had had no previous psychiatric experience were added to the staff. Here again the positive psychotherapeutic value of psychiatrically untrained people was repeatedly demonstrated. Thanks to this firsthand experience, neither the trained nor the untrained personnel saw any mystery or anything abstract about the idea of milieu therapy. It came to be a rather frequently used term for thoughtful attention to all concrete events occurring in minute-by-minute dealings with patients. (For more details, see Chapter XIII.)

Several times a day, the superintendent of Butler's Health Center, its clinical director, and its staff psychiatrists all took part in informal discussions with ward personnel about the behavior of problem patients. Scheduled formal staff meetings were later adopted to assure contact among all personnel dealing with patients. The majority of these meetings discussed the roles played by personnel in the treatment of particular patients. Relatively little time was spent on the classical presentation of cases. The diagnoses were the results of the experience of the staff, *as a group*, with each individual patient. Treatment planning became a matter of determining, through discussion, the roles to be played by individual staff members and by the group as a whole in their relationships with each patient. The manageability of such detailed planning was possible because of the small size of the inpatient service—40 beds.

## Rehabilitation

Rehabilitation had an early beginning at Butler Health Center due to joint planning with the Rhode Island Division of Vocational Rehabilitation before the clinical services were started. This close liaison with a rehabilitation agency resulted in the admission of patients to the day program with a variety of problems not ordinarily dealt with in a purely psychiatric service. Since these patients were unable to hold jobs, the presence of a vocational counselor on the permanent staff provided an opportunity to work out methods for correcting motivational disorders concurrently with the treatment of mental illnesses. Rehabilitation clients were placed in activity areas of the health center along with psychiatric day patients and inpatients. Many of these clients had personality make-ups and reactions that fit more or less satisfactorily into a wide range of diagnostic classifications; some had character disorders, some had physical handicaps, and others had chronic psychoses or had had relapses of psychosis since their discharge from public mental hospitals. Some had motivational problems difficult to match with any of the formal psychiatric diagnoses.

The presence of a varied group of rehabilitation clients along with regular psychiatric patients accelerated the adoption of goals and the development of ways of dealing with patients that were recognizably different from those associated with treatment. As staff members became aware that the purpose of their relationships with these patients was rehabilitative rather than therapeutic, some of the distinctions between therapy and rehabilitation became apparent. Relationships of therapeutic value came to be thought of as those that aimed at giving relief from psychic pain and eliminating psychopathology. Relationships of rehabilitative value, on the other hand, came to be thought of as those that aimed at strengthening the patient's ability to cope with the world at large by providing direct aids, by coaching him, and by giving him practice in fending for himself by serving as his sparring partner. In actual practice, treatment and rehabilitation were carried out by patient-centered teams that developed in the course of staff discussions. Some of the members played therapeutic roles, while others played rehabilitative roles. In most cases, treatment and rehabilitation proceeded concurrently. In some cases, there was a phase during which all staff members felt called upon to play a therapeutic role until such time as they felt the patient was able to benefit from rehabilitative relationships. In other cases, the most effective procedure was for a certain staff member to alternate in playing both roles.

Frequently, the distinction between milieu therapy and milieu rehabilitation was not immediately apparent in the management of specific patients. The rule-of-thumb criterion that therapy should relieve pain and rehabilitation should elicit motivation often led to philosophic dilemmas—staff members sometimes had opposing views as to how sick a patient was or how much hidden pain he suffered. A series of staff group discussions on a single patient were often necessary before workers dealing with the patient could arrive at an emotional orientation toward him that was reasonably free of ambivalence. Such discussions were essential for integrating the efforts of rehabilitation-minded personnel with those of their therapy-minded colleagues.

## METHODOLOGY IN THE PRACTICE
## OF SOCIAL PSYCHIATRY

As stated previously, social psychiatry may be defined as the art of producing a social climate that divests mental illness of its capacity to keep other people at a distance. The methods used to elicit such a climate have been briefly mentioned in this chapter. The keystone of methodology, as it took shape in Butler Health Center's experiment in social psychiatry, was active involvement in the total treatment program by the superintendent, who was also the psychiatrist-in-chief. He made himself continuously accessible to personnel for free discussion of problems concerning the care of patients, a policy that led to the emergence of group discussion as a means of supervising the psychotherapeutic relationships of all personnel with patients and of decision-making on administrative matters. The informality of the meetings, the general freedom of individuals to attend or not to attend, or to have private discussions with the psychiatrist-in-chief—all contributed to the development of spontaneous involvement of the majority of personnel in helping patients with their troubles.

The precedent of accessibility for discussion set by the psychiatrist-in-chief had the effect of stimulating similar accessibility on the part of the clinical director, the staff psychiatrists, and the heads of service departments. This compounding of spontaneous patient-centered discussions served to reinforce the motivation of all personnel to relate with patients and to maintain a high level of interest in them. The accessibility to personnel of a number of senior staff members provided a much-needed freedom for personnel to select the person with whom they could most easily discuss personal matters.

## Development of Personnel

The use of informal free discussion as the basis for guiding the affairs of the clinical services resulted in a rich flow of information about the patients and in the acquisition of a more complete picture of their daily lives. It also facilitated recognition of specific social influences that had a bearing on the behavior of patients, key influences that would not ordinarily have come to light. The importance of the personality make-up of personnel for the patients' recovery process was repeatedly demonstrated. Recognition of this was the first step in identifying the factor of greatest importance to the success of social psychiatry—the manifestation, by those in authority, of genuine respect for human individuality. Such respect was demonstrated by enlisting the individual worker as a consultant in any planning that would benefit from his experience. It was shown most explicitly by the energy invested by those in authority in learning the assets of each worker and in seeking means for his maximum development.

In open group discussions, the investment of energy in developing the assets of personnel tends to motivate staff members with different professional backgrounds to exchange knowledge and techniques, and to pass them on to those colleagues who lack formal psychiatric or psychological training. The absence of an opportunity for such a learning experience, on the other hand, fosters a tendency for the staff to stress a narrow, status-invested interpretation of their respective professional and nonprofessional roles. If this tendency is unchecked, barriers to communication arise and often lead to conflict between different professional groups.

The experience of Butler Health Center indicates that the success of social psychiatry depends to a great extent on a desire by those with the most training to teach and a desire by those with less training to learn. If the desire of the personnel to help patients is not equaled by a desire to learn from each other, their value to patients is considerably reduced. The most fundamental and most important rule derived from the Butler experience is that respect for the patients' individuality and personality assets is not forthcoming unless personnel experience the same respect from senior staff members. The use of personality matching based on such respect is discussed in Chapter XIII, which deals with milieu rehabilitation.

### THE PROBLEM OF RESISTANCE IN
### THERAPY AND REHABILITATION

The failures of mental health workers to provide firsthand service to patients are very rarely due only to an insufficiency of skills, knowledge or techniques. Failures are much more frequently traceable to strong sentiments, harbored by all of us, *against* giving service. This asserts itself forcibly in a variety of circumstances and in a variety of forms. As staff members, we are not all motivated purely by the joy of giving service. Many of us are noticeably aggressive and do not, frankly, at all times *enjoy* giving service. We should not be blind to the human propensity to occasionally enjoy dominating those in need of service. Although mental health workers soon become experienced in coaching other people in the art of handling themselves more effectively as persons, they are, at the same time, reluctant to strengthen the other fellow's hand to the point of his getting the upper hand. In our dealings with each other and with those in closely related professions, we tend to hold back our trade secrets—not because we fear their use will not be properly understood, but because we feel they will be far too well understood! We are all in the business of maximizing human creativity, but we delude ourselves if we forget that our other reason for getting into it was to acquire the know-how to excel over others. We cannot help guarding ourselves against being intimate and becoming too well acquainted with other people. We cannot afford to risk other people knowing our vulnerabilities.

Competitiveness is by no means the only source of resistance to giving service. Even stronger resistance arises from a variety of fears—fears, for example, that a patient will be overly dependent and make excessive demands, or that a relationship will lead to embarrassment. If the patient has an appealing, heartwarming personality, we may keep our distance from him to avoid unfavorable comments by our co-workers and superiors. If the patient has a contentious personality, we keep our distance to avoid altercations that might bring on criticism by others. Our general tendency to play it safe by keeping our distance is in itself a resistance to doing the work with patients that needs to be done. Resistance in the form of fears and antipathies not only prevents our getting well enough acquainted with our patients to discover their hidden assets, it even blinds us to their obvious assets.

The Butler experience clearly demonstrated that there is no substitute for getting well acquainted with patients if we are to serve them well. Like the rest of us, they are in the dark in a number of ways: they are uncertain about how much they know, they have no clear picture of their own personality make-up, and very little idea of how people estimate their personality. We have an advantage over patients in that we have more ready access to sources of enlightment from each other. In turn, we are the patient's source of new perspectives about himself. It is our job to know patients well enough and to see to it that they know us well enough for them to take us seriously and allow us to discover assets they have not discovered in themselves.

The need to know our patients well in order to serve them well, and the presence of resistance against knowing them well, is the crux of the problem we all face in our daily work. To solve this problem, the policy adopted by Butler Health Center was for top staff to provide those who gave direct service to patients the same respect that the workers were expected to provide patients. In brief, the resistance of the individual worker to giving service to patients is expected to be a direct consequence of the resistance of his superiors to giving service to him. Explicit communication of this expectation by those in charge of a service group makes the topic of resistance a matter that can be openly discussed. In turn, this enables the group to identify various types of resistance and to endeavor to reduce them to a minimum in caring for each patient.

*SOCIAL PSYCHIATRY: FURTHER*
*CONSIDERATIONS*

For those who shared in the Butler experience, it became increasingly evident that social psychiatry was a matter of working with patients in a thoroughgoing and socially relevant manner. The basic emphasis of this kind of psychiatry is on comprehensiveness, that is, on total treatment of the total personality. It does not confine itself to the relief of symptoms or even to the cure of the patient's illness, both of which are regarded as the province of psychiatrists specializing in particular methods of treatment. The social psychiatrist sets himself the task of going beyond the patient's illness to study and explore the two areas of major importance to the patient: 1) his make-up as an individual, and, 2) his particular personal environment.

Exploration and study of the patient's make-up place relatively little emphasis on his illness; instead, they concentrate on his personal likes and dislikes, on his assets and liabilities, and on his aspirations and the obstacles that prevent him from attaining them. His successes and failures and his sources of enjoyment and disappointment are looked into with particular care.

Exploration and study of the patient's environment focus on the patient's place in the home and community and seek to discover those elements that improve his morale. Among the questions needing answers are: Does the community facilitate or impede the patient's utilization of his assets? Does it demand performance in areas in which he has no aptitude? Does the patient occupy a position of usefulness to others to any important extent, or does he occupy a position that requires him to be relatively helpless and play a role that provides others with the satisfaction of being useful? These questions offer a glimpse of the challenge involved in sizing up a person and his life situation.

As has been previously mentioned, social psychiatry could just as well have been called moral treatment or comprehensive psychiatry. The latter term implies that to be effective it requires the participation of many people, not only in giving particular services to patients but also in assisting in the development of an intelligible philosophy of social psychiatry by taking an active part in the ever-progressing research process that is both the foundation of, and the justification for, the continued existence of social psychiatry.

The value of social psychiatry and, for that matter, that of the whole of psychiatry itself derives ultimately from the willingness of relatively untroubled people to use their life experience and their capacity to think in behalf of people who are more troubled. All people have done more thinking on some topics than on others, and have arranged their lives in a way that favors having certain kinds of experience rather than others. Mental health workers are people who have selected experiences and topics for thought that they believe have increased their capacity to help emotionally troubled people. Whether their selections actually do provide the best basis for being helpers or not is an open question—and a subject for research in its own right. Of even greater importance to the general welfare, in terms of mental health, is the consideration that many people who have not deliberately or consciously sought to be mental health workers may have had the experiences and possess the personality and the habits of thinking that will allow them to become very effective helpers of people incapacitated by emotional disorders.

## TREATMENT RESULTS

Treatment results at Butler Health Center were almost identical to those at Boston Psychopathic Hospital—over 90 per cent of inpatient admissions were discharged to their homes. The average length of hospitalization of inpatients was considerably shorter, however—about 35 days compared with 90 days currently at Boston Psychopathic. It would appear that the much smaller size of Butler—40 beds compared to 120—was strongly conducive to a shorter length of stay.

The matter of optimum size of mental centers and hospitals is one of central importance. It was a topic of considerable discussion in the early days of moral treatment, especially when political pressures were brought to bear to increase the bed capacity of hospitals. It is probably not possible to name a fixed figure for optimum bed capacity, since treatment programs depend so much on the quality of leadership, on the personality make-up of hospital staff, and on esprit de corps. It is also not possible to make fair comparisons between facilities short of comprehensive research endeavors, which control for such factors as illness categories and socioeconomic conditions of patient populations. Generally speaking, the larger the bed capacity of the hospital, the lower the staff-to-patient ratio. And the larger the hospital, the lower the discharge rates also tend to be and the longer the average length of stay.

Modern era "moral treatment," with its attention to higher standards of environmental care, has been under development all over America since the mid-1950's. By and large, greatly increased discharge rates and shortened lengths of stay are now the rule practically everywhere. Marked reduction in hospital census has resulted in improved staff-to-patient ratios, with consequent gain in capacity to provide better treatment.

### PROMINENT FEATURES OF THE
### BUTLER PROGRAM

The uniqueness of Butler as a mental health center derived from a number of factors: the application of approaches learned at Boston Psychopathic Hospital, the small size of the center, the shared interest in social psychiatry—milieu therapy as a latter-day version of moral treatment—and the circumstance that the staff lived on the grounds of the center, within short walking distance of one another. All these factors strongly influenced the development of the most important attribute of the Butler clinical and administrative staff, namely, the high degree of acquaintanceship of staff with patients and the enormously greater amount of time devoted to staff communication about patients and to joint thinking about their problems and about ways to solve them.

Butler's uniqueness was also due to the superintendent's project-and-research approach to the center's operation. Every aspect of the program was part of one of the three demonstration projects funded by the National Institute of Mental Health and the Office of Vocational Rehabilitation. The operation of the center's various services, on the basis of goal-directed project designs with ongoing documentation of several kinds of activity, resulted in sustained staff interest and morale of an exceptionally high level. It took no great strength of the imagination to feel a kinship with the original era of moral treatment, for Butler Hospital was one of the original moral treatment hospitals. Its library—the Isaac Ray Library—is    a treasure house of psychiatric literature dating from the beginnings of moral treatment. Indeed, the sense of continuity was quite marked, as can be seen in the following quotation from the opening paragraphs of Dr. Hyde's *Annual Report* for 1958:

"One hundred years ago Isaac Ray reported for the year of 1858 that on the 31st of December, 1857, there were in the house 140 patients. During the year ending on the 31st of December, 1858, there were admitted 47, making the whole number under care, 187. There had been discharged 52. Of those discharged, 22 had recovered, 7 were improved, 14 unimproved, and 12 died.

"One hundred years later I wish to report that on December 31, 1957, there were in the house 26 patients. During the year ending on the 31st of December, 1958, there were admitted 188 patients, making the whole number under care 214. Of these 188 patients, 160 came directly from the community while the remaining 28 came from outpatient or day services. There have been discharged 180. Of those discharged, 6 had been in the hospital for observation only, 8 went to other hospitals, 5 of which were state mental hospitals, 4 died, 50 were recovered, 103 were improved, and 9 were unimproved.

"This service to residential patients represents but a part of the service of the center in 1958, for in addition to this, 287 other patients came first to the outpatient department and 64 came first to the day program. This makes a total of 511 different persons who were admitted to Butler Health Center in 1958. As 100 patients were already in active treatment from the previous year, a total of 611 different patients received psychiatric service at Butler during 1958.

"As many of these patients were transferred for further treatment to a service other than the one to which they were first admitted, the total service rendered was far greater than that represented by these figures; or 390 admissions to outpatient, 116 to day service, 228 to residential service, or a total of 734 admissions to these different services of the center.

"In 1958 this service was rendered in the same building, on the same grounds, and by the same organization of trustees and corporation. What then has changed to account for the greater number of persons served by Butler?

"We have learned that the patient's recovery involves more than simply the doctor and the patient; it involves the entire community, both the hospital community and the outside community. Any degree of consideration and understanding from friends and relatives frees the patient of the isolation of being different and segregated. Acceptance on the street and in the neighborhood reduces feelings of strangeness and difference.

"The broad clinical goal of the hospital is to consider the total man and his environment, man as a physical, psychological and social being; as part of a family and community.

"When we compare the extent of our work at Butler in 1958 with those in 1858, we are not measuring simply the growth of our psychiatric skill, we are measuring the growth of enlightenment, understanding and consideration of the people of Providence and Rhode Island (2)."

The system of management put into effect by Dr. Hyde in reopening Butler Hospital and Butler Health Center has proved to be of considerable durability. The basic program is still in operation even though a decade has lapsed since Dr. Hyde and his original team left to establish programs elsewhere.

## IV.  CUSHING HOSPITAL

Moral treatment, it will be recalled, ceased to be a success when it encountered "foreign insane pauperism" (a term once frequently used in state hospital annual reports) and when the organic brain disease theory of mental illness became widely accepted by physicians. It is also noteworthy that moral treatment, in the earlier and most successful decades of its practice, had practically no contact with geriatric patients. This was partly because there were fewer old people in the general population then, and partly because the practitioners of moral treatment believed, with Hippocrates, that the mental ills of the elderly stemmed mainly from bodily deterioration. Furthermore, it was customary for enfeebled, senile persons to be cared for in the homes of their adult children or other relatives, and to be treated by the family physician. In short, the socially displaced, homeless old person was a rarity.

It was not until the twentieth century, with its rapidly growing proportion of elderly people and its increasingly mobile population, that many people reached an advanced age without a family circle to which they could belong. The practice of mandatory retirement at 65 further aggravated the situation. Thus large numbers of elderly persons now endure idleness and loneliness as well as the hazards and drawbacks of advancing age. A social remedy for this unsatisfactory state of affairs remains to be developed. In its absence the one avenue left to many of the elderly, even when their major life problems are not of a medical nature, is to use the only living accommodations available in today's industrial community: medical care facilities, i.e., hospitals and nursing homes. Having a diagnosable medical ailment at least has the merit of allowing a person to gain entry to a setting that provides human contact and care.

In the decades following World War II, it became apparent that there was more incentive for the elderly to emphasize and nurture their illnesses than to exercise their strengths. By the mid-1950's, the Massachusetts Department of Mental Health found itself contending with a rapid increase of elderly patients in its state hospitals. In these circumstances, the problem confronting state mental hospitals when they admitted elderly patients was that *success in treatment* by whatever means did not solve the elderly patient's life-problems, for it did not change the social reality that these patients had no place in the community. Indeed, it often developed that they found themselves having more of a life in a state hospital ward than they had had anywhere else in years!

Thus did it happen that hospital personnel saw success in treatment becoming a painful mockery. Inescapably, participation in such a mockery is accompanied by feelings of shame and guilt. The prospect of admitting an elderly patient brings immediate feelings of dread and frustration when one knows in advance that one will be unable to change his social reality no matter how successful treatment may be. It is, moreover, almost always the nurse or the social worker who must tell the hospitalized older person, "There just isn't any place for you to go on the outside." Faced with this situation, it is not surprising that nurses tend to do what they can to make elderly patients feel as much at home as possible.

The change in the extent, and hence in the nature, of this problem is reflected by a consideration of the number of persons involved. In 1937, for example, there were 1,176 admissions to Massachusetts state hospitals of patients over 65. In 1945 this figure was 1,721, and in 1955 it had increased to 2,007. The number of admissions under 65, on the other hand, showed an increase from 5,142 in 1937 to 5,867 in 1955, an increase of about 14 per cent. The increase from 1937 to 1955 for those over 65 years of age was 70 per cent, or five times as great as for the younger ages.

The circumstances described above were clear indications to the Department of Mental Health that the time had arrived to make special provisions tailored to the needs of the elderly. This obligation required, furthermore, that recognition be given to the fact that a previously most rare category of geriatrc patient was making an appearance in numbers warranting special consideration. These were the patients in their 80's and 90's. In 1947, for example, only 91 patients over 85 years of age were admitted to all Massachusetts state hospitals combined. In 1960 there' were 269 such admissions, a threefold increase. In 1937 the total number of patients cared for who were over 80 years of age was 838; in 1955 this figure had increased to 2,962—three and one-half times as many as in 1937.

One of the early measures taken by the Massachusetts Department of Mental Health to meet the needs of elderly patients was the creation of geriatric units in state hospitals and the construction of completely new medical-surgical units. While this ameliorated the condition of elderly patients in state hospitals, it was not appropriate to the needs of those who did not require commitment to mental hospitals but were extremely vulnerable to mental and emotional breakdown, partly due to advancing age and partly to physical disease processes that reduced their capacity to withstand the stresses of the unsatisfactory physical and social environment of their daily lives. This group of the elderly required a service that could provide care appropriate to their physical condition and simultaneously attend to their psychosocial needs.

The realization that mental impairment in the elderly is caused not only by physical disease and aging processes in the central nervous system and other organs, but also by increased vulnerability to environmental stresses and hazards due to social isolation, led to the suggestion that facilities for their care be developed in a new and special institution devoted entirely to the elderly. Such an institution could give undivided attention to developing methods for coordinating mental health care with medical and surgical services that had not yet been developed in general hospitals, chronic disease hospitals, or traditional mental hospitals.

In 1955, the Department of Mental Health acquired Cushing Hospital from the Veterans Administration. The hospital was completely remodeled and renovated, with facilities especially designed to meet the particular needs of patients suffering from physical handicaps, physical diseases, and susceptibility to confusion and other mental impairment. The clinical staffing of the hospital was planned with the consideration in mind that proper care of physically fragile, brain-damaged, and emotionally disturbed patients requires special personnel trained both to protect the physical health and safety of such patients and to deal therapeutically with unpredictable behavior resulting from such states of mind as confusion, excitement, despondency, or ill temper.

The personnel quotas allotted to Cushing Hospital to achieve these goals therefore included not only personnel for a medical department and a nursing service, but also a psychiatrically trained director of nurses, an occupational therapy department, a psychiatric social service department, and a psychology department. When the hospital opened its door to patients in 1957, these services were organized under the direction of its psychiatrist-superintendent and surgeon-clinical director. Experience gained since that time has demonstrated the great importance of paying continuous attention to the physical and social milieu of hospital life on the one hand and to physical disease processes among patients on the other. This experience suggests that future developments in the geriatric programs of the Department of Mental Health will be in the direction of greater integration of medical and surgical practice with psychosocial approaches to patient care.

The vulnerability of the elderly to mental ills, the frequency with which they suffer physical ills, and their rapidly growing numbers were a combination of factors that placed a major burden of responsibility on the Department of Mental Health to provide long-term geriatric care to the elderly of Massachusetts. In 1970, about 6,000 geriatric patients over 65 years of age were cared for in the Department's 12 state hospitals. Cushing Hospital, with about 650 patients, was the first hospital of the Department designed to integrate the medical, surgical, and psychiatric care necessary for the proper management of elderly patients suffering from both physical and mental impairment.

## CONSIDERATIONS UNDERLYING PLANS FOR THE FUTURE

Nineteen sixty-three was the year in which, for the first time, a patient at Cushing Hospital reached the age of one hundred years. Her birthday party was sponsored by volunteers and attended by hospital staff and patients as well as by her own family of four generations of descendants, including a son 75 years of age. This patient's hundredth birthday helped to publicize the fact that Cushing Hospital was then the residence of more than 40 men and women between the ages of 90 and 100. The presence of so many people so far advanced in years emphasized the obligation of the hospital to deal with human problems that had not been adequately solved anywhere; the staff had a fore-taste, on a relatively small scale, of coping with what will surely be a very major and widespread social problem of the future.

Clearly, the loneliness, reduced vigor, and limited mobility of infirm elderly citizens cannot reasonably be regarded by anyone as *solely* a medical or psychiatric concern even where diagnosable physical or mental afflictions are also present. Nevertheless, social pressures are such that Cushing Hospital, in common with all other geriatric facilities, is required in most cases to take full responsibility for *all* aspects of the geriatric patient's life *for the rest of his life*. What does this mean in practical, functional terms? One finds the answer when one realizes that hospital staffing patterns are still based almost entirely on the inescapable necessity of providing around-the-clock physical care of patients, the burden of which falls squarely on nursing personnel. The demands of physical care are of such major proportions in themselves that they tend to overshadow the personal and social needs of patients. Indeed, the patients' distressingly complex private affairs and deep personal needs may remain completely hidden from view in the absence of *active* intervention by others. The magnitude of these nonmedical needs is as yet but partially known. The bearing that such unmet needs have on patients' physical and mental health is, however, certainly considerable.

The basic deficiency of facilities such as Cushing Hospital is a shortage of personnel in the fields of social work, psychology, and occupational therapy, and in the volunteer services. The corps of workers in these fields is small, too small in fact even to ascertain the full extent of patient needs in these areas. The vitally important contribution made by this small corps points up the necessity to acquire the means to enlarge its numbers with both trained personnel and volunteer apprentices.

So little is known, academically or otherwise, about a society in which a large proportion of members reach an advanced age, or about the sociology of the oldest segment of that population. Certainly the problems faced by families of four or five coexistent generations are but little appreciated. This is more fully realized when it is discovered that the children of geriatric patients are themselves becoming patients in geriatric hospitals.

The personnel of a geriatric hospital are continually confronted with events that leave little doubt that they are seriously involved in the personal lives of patients with respect to matters other than those that are purely medical and technological in nature. Some of the most inescapable and distressingly painful moral and legal problems arise in the context of unspoken assumptions, misunderstandings, and fundamental disagreements on the subject of prolonging life versus withholding treatment and permitting its end. There is a set of parallel problems that also demand full consideration; some families oppose treatment, rehabilitation, or remotivation programs for patients whose deaths are *not* likely to occur in the foreseeable future. Contained within all of these problems are questions of psychiatric diagnosis and psychopathogenesis in relation to functional mental depressions, psychosomatic disorders—and the fundamental matter of the patients' will to live.

Elderly patients with a tendency to memory loss, who have been hospitalized for a number of years, almost inevitably lose contact with society at large, including their own community. They also cease to exercise their rights of citizenship and lose status as communicants of their church. In a very real sense, elderly patients with memory loss tend to become children of the hospital by being entirely habituated to the methodical hospital routine as passive recipients. It is evident that their memories of community life need to be refreshed, that dormant interests need reviving, that long-procrastinated decisions and solutions regarding personal problems need to be worked on and settled. In short, the tedium of hospital life fosters apathy and atrophy of all the faculties of which the adult personality is composed. It is equally obvious that our corps of workers in the fields of social work, psychology and occupational therapy could never be large enough to counteract the forces of apathy and atrophy on a direct, individual basis. This corps must, however, be increased to a size sufficiently large to recruit and guide the human resources of the community on a scale required to maintain the roles of patients as persons and social personalities. That some patients seek out personal relations with the staff of a hospital's business office, dietary service, or maintenance department, and that these personnel make a valuable contribution in return, is convincing evidence of the great distance we have yet to go in meeting the social needs of patients.

Thus, Cushing Hospital has two major roles: 1) that which hospitals of the medieval period had when the entire task of the hospital was full care of the patient rather than of his disease, and 2) that of the modern scientific hospital, the entire function of which, in its own estimation, is ordinarily the cure of particular diseases only. This dual role of Cushing Hospital has the paradoxical outcome that the hospital still has the responsibility of full care of the patient—even after it has cured his disease—simply because there is no appropriate place where he can be accepted as a functioning member of society outside the hospital!

The fact that Cushing Hospital exists at all as a high-standard, full-fledged hospital facility reserved solely for the aged is a reflection of a major contemporary trend toward a reawakening of respect for the elderly, respect for our historical roots as a state and nation, respect for the inner feelings and mental health of the individual, and respect for religious and spiritual values. Such factors as the knowledge explosion, the population explosion, the scientific revolution, the destructiveness of nuclear war, the amorality of totalitarian political systems, the rapidity of upward social mobility, the generation gap, the achievement of affluence, and a continuing pervasive decrease in our sense of security and peace of mind have all contributed to a greater readiness to search elsewhere for values that today's society fails to provide.

Looking back on Cushing Hospital's brief history and the much longer history of its parent body, the Department of Mental Health, one becomes acutely aware of how damaging are the social, psychological, and spiritual effects when communities choose the course of total institutional segregation and custody as a method of dealing with their problem people. It seems fully apparent that high standards of patient care cannot be met by

medical and surgical means alone. Experience teaches that
standards of care will deteriorate to the lowest, most degraded
level unless a continuous effort is made to attain the highest level.
There is an obligation to seek genuine moral solutions to situations
that deny patients their full rights with places of their own in
this world, not just beds in a hospital. The moral problems of
patient management will remain hidden from view unless, as a
beginning, recognition of the psychological and emotional needs
of patients is shown by greater participation of all hospital personnel. Spiritual advisors should also be active partners in the
care of individual patients, in the development of hospital policy,
and in the establishment of community relations.

PRIMACY OF MORAL CONSIDERATIONS
AS BASES FOR GERIATRIC CARE

As an agency charged with the total care of large numbers
of elderly individuals for the remainder of their lives, Cushing
Hospital has responsibilities beyond the cure of diseases. It has
the obligation to protect its charges against deprivation of their
human rights, an obligation that includes moral and spiritual as
well as civil and legal rights. There is no longer a place for that
habit of mind, of modern origin, that regards the hospital as a
specialized service organized to provide only the material and
technological services rendered by scientific medicine and surgery
and their subspecialties. Furthermore, it is important to recognize that hospital professionals in the various patient-care disciplines cannot have full responsibility for, or assume themselves
to have the competence to deal with, many of the vitally important moral issues and problems that continually arise in a
geriatric hospital. For example, there are problems that emerge
with the imminence of a patient's death or with the mistaken
assumption on the part of a patient's relatives of the imminence
of his death.

PSYCHOSOCIAL NEEDS

The establishment of services that give individual attention to
the aged person's morale was accomplished at Cushing Hospital

by adopting measures that diverge somewhat from standard practice in mental, chronic disease, or general hospitals. These measures fall into four categories:

1. Orienting the Social Service Department in the direction of community organization and social group work by placing this department under the direction of a head social worker experienced in the field of community organization.

2. Orienting the Psychology Department in the direction of social psychology and research in developmental psychology as a means of identifying the needs of the individual as a group member.

3. Orienting the Nursing and Occupational Therapy Departments toward consideration of psychiatric aspects of patient care by making psychiatrists and psychologists available to these departments as consultants for specific problems and as instructors in clinical psychiatry and group dynamics.

4. Fostering attention to the motivational as well as technical aspects of physical rehabilitation by making the services of a board-certified physiatrist available to nursing, occupational therapy, and physical therapy personnel of the Special Rehabilitation Ward.

As in the case of physical-medical needs, the meeting of the psychosocial needs of long-term patients is largely approached by directing the continuous and pervasive influence of nursing personnel on the lives of patients. A fundamental factor in directing this influence is the highly important matter of responsiveness on the part of hospital administration to spontaneous proposals made by nursing personnel for improving the psychosocial climate of life on each of their wards. An example of this is the support given to the nursing personnel when they wished to redecorate their respective wards after they were painted. Color schemes for new overdrapes, spreads, and bedside curtains created considerable interest. One ward acquired an aquarium, which stimulated patients to read a great deal about tropical fish. Another ward acquired a new resident—a parakeet whom the patients named Sam Junior, in honor of a much-loved physician. In other wards, hanging baskets of plants appeared; in still others, pictures appeared on the walls.

Perhaps the most striking example of unusual inventiveness in improving the morale of patients was when the nurses on Ward 305 prevailed on the ward physician to write prescriptions for adequate "doses" of good-quality beer for the patients. In the words of the nurse in charge, "The idea of introducing beer to the patients was to create an atmosphere for them other than that of a hospital. If the patients could not get a change of environment, then we would help them recapture the good times they had in the past and probably would still enjoy." Interestingly, it was found that nurses of shifts other than the shift that served beer reported that the patients were less agitated, that medications for restlessness were reduced, that the patients slept better at night, and that there was even less incontinence.

### SPIRITUAL NEEDS

The spiritual and religious needs of a geriatric hospital require far more than routine consideration. The large proportion of deaths (one-quarter of the patient population each year) and the large number of patients enduring preterminal illness require the full-time attention of clergymen who are especially suited to minister to the elderly and their families. Patients undergoing rehabilitation also need help in maintaining or reestablishing bonds with their home community churches. There are many problems of a moral nature that cannot be properly handled without the presence and assistance of the clergy. Cushing Hospital has adopted a policy of encouraging the active participation of chaplains in the care of individual patients, and in bringing the chaplains into professional contact with nurses, social workers, psychologists, and psychiatrists. There is a need for a full-time chaplain in most geriatric hospitals. Experience thus far gained suggests that there should be a closer working relationship between clergymen and clinical and administrative staff than is the rule in either general or mental hospitals.

## SUMMARY OF THE GOALS OF ORGANIZATION
## AND OPERATION PLANNING

During the first seven years of its existence, Cushing Hospital identified and clarified its goal. In the beginning, the hospital had the obvious duty of providing care and treatment, in the usual sense of those words, to persons compromised by the illnesses of advanced age. For the first few years the traditional medical habit of mind prevailed; the physician came to the patient's side when he was called by the nurse. He provided treatment and follow-up until he was no longer needed for the complaint in question, and then he dropped out of the picture.

This noninvolvement of the physician continued for some time without being identified as a policy not consonant with the best interests of chronically ill patients. Once it became so identified, however, the goal to be sought became clear, namely, to effect a transition from a passive mode of operation by all clinical disciplines to an activist mode. In practice, pursuit of the goal meant that physicians assumed leadership roles in planning and implementing activities in the insititutional life of the hospital and in the personal lives of individual patients. Planned activity, then, became conceptualized partially as a nonspecific, and at times even as a specific, means to improve states of mental and physical health. The psychological climate of activism, so to speak, was accompanied by an active search for pathological conditions that could be repaired surgically or by other medical means.

As might be expected, this activist method of improving the condition of patients was considerably advanced by encouraging each of the clinical disciplines to vie with one another in searching out and meeting the needs of patients.

The degree of success achieved in making a transition to the activist mode was also reflected in an increased flexibility and versatility in adapting to the changing demands placed on the hospital by other public and private agencies.

The most significant aspect of Cushing Hospital's activist development is that it occurred within the context of federal and state legislation providing new support for active assistance to the aged. Much of our progress in the care of the aged in Massachusetts can be traced to the wisdom of the General Court in enacting legislation in November, 1960, to implement the federal Kerr-Mills Act, which provides medical assistance to the medically indigent aged.

## MORAL TREATMENT AND THE COMMUNITY

In his effort to apply a program of moral treatment as a solution to the mental ills of elderly persons, the superintendent of Cushing Hospital found that the best that could be accomplished was a discharge rate back to their homes of only ten per cent of each year's admissions. The daily reminder of the psycho-physiological fragility of large numbers of the patients, the high proportion of patients with underlying depression who sought to conceal it so as not to be a burden on others (but whose emotional needs could only be met by the initiative of specific people outside the hospital), the somewhat substantial proportion who were fortunate enough to enjoy reasonably good morale because personnel had become their family, and the ever-growing demand of general hospitals and nursing homes to send terminal cases to Cushing for deathbed nursing—all this converted what was intended to be a program of moral treatment into a program of dealing with moral-ethical dilemmas. Solutions at best were a matter of learning what lesser evils to choose from among the many that constantly beset the patient's life. There was no escaping the conclusion that moral treatment could only succeed if it could include the patient's family and neighborhood. The socioeconomic realities of modern life are such that no hospital staff, however expert and large, could ever find or create a social situation appropriate to each patient's needs. The elements that can dissipate the demoralization of the elderly are missing in hospital life. Some of these needs are obvious; many are yet to be identified. Most of the infirm elderly are treated in ways that diminish their self-esteem and their sense of having dignity in the eyes of others. Can it be that this problem will diminish with the passage of time? Are the elderly of today a unique, one-time-in-history, dispossessed generation, a product of the drastic social rearrangements that have occurred since the World War II period? Can it be that future generations will not suffer such a degree of displacement and dispossession in their old age? If so, the present generation of elderly are paying the scientific and social costs that will benefit future generations; costs that no generation may have to pay again, at least until another exceptional period of drastic change occurs.

Obviously, many events have combined to cause the isolation and neglect now suffered by our eldest generation—a neglect that has led to guilt-ridden restitution that, rather than dealing with the needs of individual personalities, takes the form of spending money on mass measures to "correct a social condition."

The experience of an unsuccessful attempt to bring moral treatment to bear on the mental ills of the elderly teaches a lesson that has a wide application in the mental health endeavor in general. First of all, it teaches the tragic, damaging fallacy of offering the citizenry a program that represents itself as having the know-how to meet a specific need or solve a specific problem when the name or label of that need or problem is in fact a misnomer, for it does not actually stand for *a* need or *a* problem but, rather, for innumerable complex needs, problems, and relationships. The truth of the matter is that nowhere in the modern world does a program exist capable of meeting such needs or solving such problems. This is true because no society has given any program the sanction, the resources, or the powers to alter the very composition of that society itself. Furthermore, if such sanction, resources, and powers were to be assigned to a program, the program leader would not know what to do, beyond a few palliative measures, measures with unforeseeable complications that would possibly only make matters worse.

The tragic and damaging fallacy involved here is that people have been led to believe that the needs and problems they have in mind, in relation to a service program, are ones that can be handled by others endowed with special know-how. The individuals who make up the population thus quite reasonably believe

it appropriate to refer these needs and problems to the announced
authorities. As a result, the one thing that might improve a situation is left undone, namely, the application of individuals' own
resourcefulness toward solving the problem. Thus, it can be
envisioned how, despite their good faith, individual service-givers
and service-receivers may end up wholly disillusioned, angered,
frustrated, and demoralized, or resigned to hopelessness.

As indicated above, the goal of applying enlightened programs
of a new moral treatment buttressed by modern concepts of social
psychiatry can only be successful for certain kinds of mental ills
and life situations. These successes are, furthermore, usually
partial in that the original manifest disturbance is dissipated
without fundamental changes being made in the underlying conditions that engendered the disturbance in the first place.

Americans used to think of themselves as exceptionally re-
sourceful, independent, and self-reliant individuals. It was not
until the Great Depression and the scientific advances associated
with World War II and the space program that they began to
take, in great numbers, their life problem to professionals for
solution. It has not yet come fully into awareness that professionals and their institutions have little more than partial and
temporary contributions to offer.

The question we now face is: What could a new moral treatment endeavor be if vast numbers of people put all their life
problems in the laps of professional service facilities? The answer
that forcibly suggests itself is that new moral treatment endeavors
would not be successful if left to professionals and specialized
institutions. But a new moral treatment that *could* be successful
would be a moral treatment perspective applied as a matter of
public policy throughout every sector of community life.


## V.  SOLOMON MENTAL HEALTH CENTER

In 1958, when Dr. Harry C. Solomon retired from the chairman-
ship of the Department of Psychiatry at Harvard Medical School,
he immediately assumed the duties of Commissioner of Mental

Health of Massachusetts, the oldest department of mental health in the nation. That year he was also president of the American Psychiatric Association and, in his presidential address at its annual meeting, he presented a recommendation that had an electrifying effect on his audience.

"The large mental hospital is antiquated, outmoded, and rapidly becoming obsolete. We can still build them but we cannot staff them; and therefore we cannot make true hospitals of them. In this year of 1958, after 114 years of effort, rarely has a state hospital an adequate staff as measured against the minimum standards set by our Association, and these standards represent a compromise between what was thought to be adequate and what it was thought had some possibility of being realized. Only 15 states have more than 50% of the total number of physicians needed to staff the public mental hospitals according to these standards. On the national average, the supply of registered nurses is calculated to be only 19.4% adequate; that of social workers, 36.4%; and of psychologists, 65%. Even the supply of the least highly trained, the attendants, is only 80% adequate. I do not see how any reasonably objective view of our mental hospitals today can fail to conclude that they are bankrupt beyond remedy. I believe therefore that our large mental hospitals should be liquidated as rapidly as can be done in an orderly and progressive fashion.

"In our present system it seems unlikely that there can be much improvement in the staffing of our conventional institutions. Our young physicians specializing in psychiatry are not heading toward our large hospitals, nor are the other categories of personnel. In many of our hospitals about the best that can be done is to give a physical examination and make a note of the mental condition of each patient once a year, and often there is not even enough staff to do this much.

"The first signs of self-liquidation are already evident. For example, in Massachusetts, until half a dozen years ago, there was a steady increase in the number of patients in the hospitals each year. Then a period of stabilization followed. In the last several years there has been a reduction at the end of each year, as compared with the beginning, in the number of patients in hospitals. Moreover, this has occurred with an increasing number of admissions and a decreasing death rate, indicating a higher discharge rate. This suggests that if the trend continues, less bed space will be required. This process of liquidation could undoubtedly go faster were staff and personnel more numerous, but, as I indicated before, this does not seem probable in our present large hospital system.

"We are now in a period of hopeful change, however, in treatment facilities for the mentally ill. Psychiatric wards are being opened in the general hospitals; outpatient clinics are increasing in numbers; day hospital and night hospital facilities are being provided; halfway houses are being experimented with; the place of an extension service whereby the hospital provides service to patients living at home is being studied on models provided by our English colleagues. Psychiatrists in private practice are equipped for and interested in treating patients in their homes. Liberalization of insurance plans to provide care for mentally ill individuals makes possible greater utilization of wards in general hospitals and private mental institutions. Small intensive treatment units are being provided either as independent hospitals, or as a portion of the large hospital providing a more rapid turnover of patients. Rehabilitation services and aftercare clinics help to support patients in the community who previously would linger in the hospital. An atmosphere of greater optimism about the outcome of psychoses leads to an attitude of greater liberalization in the discharge of patients and a willingness of hospital authorities to take certain calculated risks. Several states are experimenting with new types of facilities for those among our aged people who show some signs of mental deterioration but who are not disturbed enough to find the wards of our mental hospitals a suitable haven. All of these factors have favorable potential for reducing the number of chronic patients and to lessen the need for beds. These are the hopeful aspects of the current movement in our field.

"As the new facilities increase in number, it may be presumed that, more and more, acutely ill persons will seek their help. The readily recoverable will be treated in them and returned to home and community.

"What of the less readily recoverable, however? Their prospect remains grim unless new ways are found to meet their needs. They will be sent to the large mental hospitals, where they will accumulate in an atmosphere of gloom, despair, and deterioration. We cannot allow this to happen.

"If my description is correct and my projections reasonably accurate, a new attack on the 'care and custody' of the long-term ill must be attempted. Unpalatable as it may appear, one must face the fact that we are doing little by way of definite treatment of a large part of our chronic hospital population. It is not even the case that we are providing them with first-class environmental care, much less loving and tender care. Therefore, I suggest we take a new look at the problem.

"I tentatively suggest that facilities be established devoted to care and custody of a group of chronically ill individuals for whom, at the present time, we have no clear-cut definitive medical or psychiatric treatment. I suggest that such facilities be planned as a colony or home rather than as a hospital. I suggest that a new discipline be developed for the proper management of these individuals. I am not ready to define the details of this discipline nor from whence they should be recruited; but I think of the possibilities of drawing on the knowledge of city planners, group social workers, educators, public health personnel, sociologists, specially trained administrators, and so on. I conceive of such facilities being of moderate size. In each such community there will be a hospital section staffed by visiting surgeons, internists, psychiatrists, and other specialists. To the hospital section with its outpatient clinic would be referred those individuals for whom some specific medical treatment was indicated. Rehabilitation activities would be in the center of the scheme, both vocational and social rehabilitation. I would offer a working definition of rehabilitation in this setting as the best utilization of the capacity of a disabled individual.

"Thus, within this framework of the community-oriented intensive treatment facilities on the one hand, and a new type of facility for the long-term ill on the other, we would differentiate between psychiatric treatment and 'care and custody.' This mechanism would allow for the most effective utilization of the skills and training of highly trained physicians, nurses, social workers, and others in the treatment of the readily recoverable; it would create a new specialized group of workers for the rehabilitation and development of the maximum potential of individuals whom we are not yet capable of leading to full recovery."

Dr. Solomon's recommendation that the large mental hospitals be liquidated as rapidly as could be done in an orderly and progressive fashion had a considerable impact on members of the Association. Some expressed enthusiastic agreement and support, while others were entirely opposed.

## A RETURN TO SMALL FACILITIES

One of the first actions Dr. Solomon took as Massachusetts Commissioner of Mental Health was to conduct a survey of the urban communities of the Commonwealth to ascertain those with the greatest need for mental health services. His purpose was to lay the groundwork for establishing community mental health centers, to be patterned after the Massachusetts Mental Health Center (the new name, adopted in 1957, of Boston Psychopathic Hospital). As a result of the survey, Lowell and Fall River were designated as the cities with the greatest over-all need. Lowell was chosen as the site of the first mental health center largely because it had the distinction of being most neglected by the state mental health system due to its being furthest from the state hospital (Worcester State Hospital, about 50 miles away) serving its population.

In October, 1965, the Commissioner requested the writer, then Superintendent of Cushing Hospital, to begin making plans to assume responsibility for putting the mental health center program into operation when its building became available for occupancy in 1966. In January, 1966, the writer was transferred to the central office of the Department of Mental Health to make preparations for opening the center.

## PRELUDE TO SERVICE

At the central office, January to September, 1966 was a period of particular importance in two respects: 1) close working relationships were developed with the business division of the Department of Mental Health, with the state administrative departments of the executive branch, and with members of the legislature; and 2) in frequent conferences, perspectives on the needs of Lowell area residents were acquired. It was the aim of Dr. Solomon, assisted by Dr. Robert W. Hyde (formerly of Butler Center in Providence), to effect a transition from custodial to therapeutic care (25) in the department's mental hospitals and schools for the retarded. Conferences revolved around the fundamental question of how to bring moral treatment into the life of an industrial community beset with serious social problems, including a disproportionately large number of mentally ill persons in the state hospital and in the community.

## A BRIEF SOCIAL HISTORY OF LOWELL

In 1817, Francis Cabot Lowell studied the characteristics of the Pawtucket Falls on the Merrimack River. The area immediately surrounding the Falls was then inhabited by about 250 farming people. Lowell found the Falls and the series of falls downstream from it to be well-suited to power a number of mill operations. He then proceeded to draw up plans for a complete industrial community, making provisions for meeting all the necessities of the community's future inhabitants, including education, recreation, and the chaperonage of the young women who would operate the looms of the new cotton mills (10). The plans were put into action in 1821, after Lowell's death, and within a few years the population grew to 2,500. The community, which was named Lowell, was in effect a total institution, with the entire population wholly dependent on the Merrimack Valley Corporation. A few years later, in 1839, it included health care provided by the Lowell Corporation Hospital.*

It would appear that Lowell was a successful example of early American industrial social idealism, an idealism that very likely had its origins in the moral philosophy that also gave rise to moral treatment hospitals, first in Massachusetts and then elsewhere in New England.

Industrial idealism seems to have suffered its breakdown from some of the same influences that underlay the breakdown of moral treatment: ethnic and religious bias and Social Darwinism. In any event, the harmonious life of the Lowell industrial community appears to have been more difficult to maintain after the arrival of immigrants following the Irish potato famine of the 1840's. Further difficulty and hardship entered the picture with the unemployment caused by the cessation of Southern cotton shipments to Lowell during the years American society was torn asunder by the Civil War. The last three decades of the nineteenth century, while characterized largely by industrial recovery, were marked by growing labor strife. The arrival of French Canadians in the mill towns of New England was opposed by mill workers who feared their damaging effect on wages. The established population of Lowell, along with those of other New England mill towns, came in conflict with several such immigrant groups whose cultural backgrounds were so different from their own.

In developing broad social programs today, it is important to review the sequence of events that occurred in Lowell. An effort should be made to understand why paternalistic industrial idealism did not work out as Lowell had planned. Perhaps comprehensive studies would show it unlikely that any other approach to industrialization would have had more foresight in contending with unpredictable demographic and social movements associated with technological development.

* The significance of this particular instance of comprehensive industrial organization in the earliest years of America's industrial revolution is reflected in the title of a book published years later: *Lowell—An Industrial Dream Come True,* by H. C. Meserve. Boston: National Association of Cotton Manufacturers, 1923.

### LEGACY OF THE BREAKDOWN OF
### INDUSTRIAL IDEALISM

Of greatest concern to us was the magnitude of the human problems to which the Greater Lowell community is heir. The level of endemic poverty has been high in Lowell due to recurrent periods of large-scale unemployment. Alcoholism has been a serious problem there for over a century. Incurable mental illness was reported to have been on the increase for many years by Dr. Nathan Allen, a Lowell physician, in his paper published in 1876, "The Treatment of the Insane" (1). It would appear, on the basis of observations made in relation to patients from Lowell in the post-World War I period, that organic brain disease due to syphilis may well have been on the increase since the Civil War. The medical personnel of Worcester State Hospital have long commented on the high prevalence of general paresis among patients from the Lowell area as compared with other population centers. Another problem that has seriously disrupted life in Lowell for many decades is desertion of families by fathers; this was often associated with unemployment and alcoholism.

Thus, Lowell's population has long been discouraged and demoralized by problems, beyond those borne by other communities, stemming from mental illness. Two factors have contributed to its disadvantage in this regard: 1) as has already been noted, Lowell's greater distance from its state hospital than other population centers in the Commonwealth; and 2) the establishment, in a bordering town, of the Tewksbury Asylum for the Chronic Insane in 1866, an institution whose reputation influenced adversely the morale of Lowell people regarding insanity. Tewksbury Asylum was described by Dr. Nathan Allen in his 1876 paper as follows:

"It is connected with the state almshouse as a department, though in a separate building, but is a part of the same institution, under the same management and officers. It provides for about 300 insane persons, all paupers" (1).

There can be little doubt that an institution where insanity became associated with the obloquy of pauperism had an adverse effect on the minds of Lowell citizens. The change that had occurred in the mode of treatment for the insane from the era of moral treatment can be sensed in the following quotation from Dr. Allen's paper:

"On no one point are we so sensitive as on that of *personal liberty*. The idea of having our liberty—our freedom—forcibly taken away, of being confined by bolts and bars, shocks our sensibilities. This is perfectly natural; it accords with our best instincts of self-respect and self-government. In cases of the insane surrendering up their personal rights—their liberties—may not the change in many instances aggravate or increase their derangement, and serve as a powerful hindrance to the restoration of health and sanity? . . . All moral, civil and social provisions and agencies must have a powerful influence to improve both physically and mentally the chronic insane. And just as long as they are treated as criminals, as prisoners, as dangerous persons who must be confined, placed under guardianship and constantly watched, just so long will their physical energies suffer and be cramped, and their spirits languish and be depressed.

". . . there are large numbers among the chronic insane; if they could have the same kind treatment, and useful employment, the same confidence and freedom as are accorded to sane people, what a surprising change it would soon make in their conduct and character. It would not only improve their health and spirits, making them more contented and happy, but would doubtless restore some of them to sanity, usefulness and self-support. Such a boon, we believe, will yet come to many of the chronic insane. . . . Wherever the rights and liberties and the interests of any class of persons are invaded or are suffering, whether inside or outside of an institution, such a state of things cannot always continue. Reform sometime must and will come."

Dr. Allen's prediction that *"reform sometime must and will come"* has indeed come true—albeit nearly a century later! It may prove helpful to our perspective to quote further from him:

"On account of the great aggregation of numbers in lunatic hospitals, and the multiplied duties and responsibilities of the superintendents, would not the individual treatment of a case be well-nigh impossible? Would not more cures be effected, and greater success follow treatment, if the best medical skill and attendance could be brought to bear more directly and personally upon every patient? It is not easy to divide such labors or delegate to others such experience and skill. The truth of this position is manifest if we apply it to the treatment of other diseases, or to medical practice generally, or to the various departments of business, whose special knowledge and personal attention are found requisite for successful results. Besides, is it not a fact that the *smaller* hospitals have generally reported a larger per cent of cures? Also the report of the larger institutions do not show so great a per cent of recoveries, as they did twenty or thirty years ago, even of patients admitted from year to year, and under treatment.

"Since the hospital is generally regarded as the only proper place to cure insane patients, it should be so managed as to do this very work in the best possible manner . . . the objection to a large number of patients does not apply wholly to the duties of the superintending physician, but it has another side, in its effect upon the sick insane, causing an impression, if not frequently a conviction, in their minds, that but little (comparatively) is done for them, and that their individual case is of small or no consequence . . . *that treatment* which inspires the most personal interest, confidence and hope . . . is, of all others, the most successful, and should be employed to the greatest extent. On this account, small hospitals have altogether the advantage. In fact, if these institutions are to be regarded as hospitals expressly for the cure and treatment of the insane, they should be small. This was once the prevailing sentiment, and is still the opinion of some of the best judges, but, for various reasons, the general custom of late years has been to build large hospitals and, frequently, to make the small ones still larger."

The discontinuities of social endeavor in America over the past hundred years are indeed thought-provoking. Dr. Allen's observation on the need for small mental hospitals was not an isolated instance; it was in fact an example of what was felt by many Massachusetts physicians and welfare workers of his day. It is interesting to digress for a moment and contemplate the

irony of the way in which Massachusetts finally, in 1912, acquired
the first small mental hospital since the early moral treatment era—
Boston Psychopathic Hospital. One might with good reason
assume that this new mental hospital of 120 beds was modeled
after Massachusetts' first experience with mental hospitals, the
Worcester State Hospital, which also began as a 120-bed facility.
The fact of the matter is, however, that the model after which
Boston Psychopathic Hospital was patterned came out of Germany—Emil Kraepelin's clinic in Munich. Thus it would appear
that it was not possible to put humanitarian considerations into
operation until resistance could be overcome by invoking science-
based considerations. The worldwide reputation enjoyed by
German science at that time was apparently such that it provided the leverage needed to win support for a German-type
psychiatric facility in Massachusetts. Also, the original pre-World
War I plan in Massachusetts was to establish municipal psychiatric facilities in every large urban center of the Commonwealth.
Since Boston Psychiatric Hospital turned out to be the first *and*
*the last* of such facilities to be built, one could surmise that the
occurrence of World War I and the development of negative
feelings toward things German contributed toward abandoning
the original plan. In any event, it was not until 1966 that the
Commonwealth established its second small-size, state-operated
municipal mental hospital—the Dr. Harry C. Solomon Mental
Health Center in Lowell.

### SOLOMON CENTER IN OPERATION

During the early phases (January-September, 1966) of preparing to begin operations, a crucial decision was made, namely, to
give priority to Lowell area patients in residence at Worcester
State Hospital. Consequent to this decision was the assignment
of the center's personnel, mostly nurses, to duty on the wards at
Worcester State Hospital, where they could become acquainted
with Lowell area patients.

When Solomon Center's outpatient department began offering
services in September, 1966, arrangements had been worked out

whereby Lowell area patients at Worcester were discharged to Solomon Center for aftercare on an outpatient basis. Services were also offered simultaneously, through the hospitals and social agencies in Lowell, to citizens of the city and of the eight surrounding towns designated by the Department of Mental Health as belonging to the Lowell Mental Health Area.

All problems brought to the center were handled on an outpatient basis until March, 1967, when a small day program began operation. The staff soon learned to improvise in caring for applicants with all varieties of problems and severities of emotional disturbance and mental illness. The outpatient clinic functioned on the premise that anyone who called the center or came as a "walk-in" was contending with a crisis of some kind. A policy was immediately adopted of promptly responding to bids for help and of placing no one on a waiting list. A division of responsibilities soon took shape spontaneously: social workers responded to every request from the community, while nurses responded to aftercare requests by patients discharged from Worcester State Hospital. Ex-patients of Worcester who called from the community were referred to the nurses by the social workers. Psychiatrists functioned as consultants whenever their colleagues in the other disciplines encountered problems that appeared to be of a medical nature, or to involve a risk requiring a psychiatrist's attention. Thus they provided back-up services to both social workers and nurses—but mostly to nurses, since they were dealing almost entirely with patients under treatment for psychoses. Psychologists also provided back-up service—but mostly to social workers who referred patients with psychoneuroses.

After five months of operation, new patients were being admitted from the community at the rate of 35 per month and ex-patients of Worcester State Hospital were being admitted to the aftercare clinic at the rate of 33 per month. Based on a study of these five months of outpatient clinic service, it was possible for the head social worker to report as follows:

"The presence of a local psychiatric resource that includes emergency care would itself appear to have a deterrent effect on hasty hospitalization. Some figures obtainable eight months after

services were offered at the center showed there was a definite
dropping off of patients admitted to and applying for admission
to Worcester State Hospital. There was also a discernible lessening of panic-button reactions on the part of relatives and by social
and law enforcement agencies, and less reluctance by families to
receive patients back into the home after short-term treatment at
the State Hospital."

By the end of the fiscal year, there had been 857 admissions to
the center during ten months of operation. Admissions to the
outpatient department totaled 758; to the day program, 22; and
to the inpatient department, which had been opened in April, 77.

In the center's *Annual Report* for fiscal 1967, the following
commentary was made in regard to the mode of introduction and
orientation of personnel to exploratory approaches in meeting the
needs of applicants for mental health services:

"It is important that the attitudes of the personnel of a mental
health center be regarded as the leading subject of concern in the
minds of those bearing final responsibility for operation of the
center. Good fortune in recruiting key personnel with down-to-
earth, practical, and accepting attitudes toward patients and
acknowledgment of the almost entirely exploratory state of mental
science has more to do with future development of the center than
any other single factor. The acquisition of a director of psychiatry, director of nurses, and a head psychiatric social worker, who,
on the basis of experience, firmly believed that personality make-
up was a factor at least as important in helping patients as the
factor of specialized education, made unusual flexibility possible.
This flexibility and readiness to attempt to meet the needs of
troubled people provided a capacity to respond to all applicants
for service whether such applicants actually had a specific need
for psychiatric services or should be referred elsewhere. As the
social service and nursing service departments grew in size, they
were encouraged to function in a spontaneous manner and to
offer immediate appointments to all applicants who called in on
the telephone, and to further offer to come to the applicant's own
home, if this appeared to be indicated. This spontaneous mode of
operation led, in effect, to establishment of a social service department, which functioned initially as a family service agency,
and to a nursing service which functioned initially as a nurse

clinic and a visiting nurse service.

"Our experience thus far suggests that this center may operate most effectively as a federation of disciplines in which each discipline is fully responsible for maintaining constructive relationships with, and to make appropriate use of, other disciplines in the care of patients. It is expected that acquisition of further experience in operating as a federation will enhance the development of collaboration with health and social agencies in the community by each of the professional disciplines of the center."

Another commentary from the 1967 *Annual Report* discusses the effectiveness of the program as reflected by statistical follow-up of inpatients:

"The manner in which the inpatient service of a mental health center is utilized is of crucial significance in determining the over-all benefit provided the community by the center. However, there is some basis for questioning whether an inpatient service is *absolutely* indispensable for a mental health center to accomplish its mission. There have, at any rate, been a number of demonstrations that it is not impossible for skilled, highly dedicated mental health personnel to handle severe emotional crises without admitting the person afflicted to any hospital facility at all. In actuality, the inpatient service is less a means of definitive treatment than for reducing the stress of a patient's emotional crisis to a level that spares both the patient and those directly involved with him from undue fatigue and exhaustion. In other words, inpatient units will be needed only as long as there are insufficient numbers of people endowed with the skill and endurance to last out severe emotional crises in the community outside such units. The occurrence of a number of successes in the handling of such crises by the personnel of the mental health center during the seven-month period preceding acquisition of inpatient service facilities suggests that the presence of skilled personnel in the community may obviate the need for inpatient units in the future. At present, however, the inpatient service is responsible for the care and treatment of two broad categories of people residing in the Lowell Mental Health Area; namely, those suffering severe new attacks of mental illness and those who have had incapacitating mental illnesses for many years. Some of the patients handicapped for a long time are in residence at Worcester

State Hospital, while others reside in local communities. Many of
the latter are socially and occupationally incapacitated people,
who in the past suffered severe exacerbations of their illnesses
due, in part, to the unfeasibility of providing them with adequate
aftercare at such a great distance from Worcester State Hospital.

"As described above, 65 patients were admitted to the inpatient
service. Data presented in Table 6 provide comparison of the
average number of days that patients in the several categories
spent in residence on the wards of the inpatient service of the
mental health center. The number of days in residence tallied
for each patient included *not only* the number of days in
residence for his *initial* admission to the center, but also the
number of days he was in residence in each subsequent readmission (if any) during the six to eight-and-one-half month follow-up
period.

"The most striking data in Table 6 are the great span between
the average number of days spent in residence by first admission

TABLE 6.—INPATIENT DAYS AT 6–8½ MONTHS FOLLOW-UP
(BY SEX AND ADMISSION CATEGORIES)

| | Number of Individuals | Still at LMHC 12-31-67 | Trans. to WSH* | Average Number of Inpatient Days at LMHC |
|---|---|---|---|---|
| First admission—males | 9 | 1 | 0 | 29 |
| First admission—females | 17 | 0 | 0 | 41 |
| Subtotal | 26 | 1 | 0 | 37 days |
| Readmission—males | 9 | 1 | 0 | 66 |
| Readmission—females | 10 | 0 | 1 | 51 |
| Subtotal | 19 | 1 | 1 | 58 days |
| Transferred**—males | 5 | 2 | 0 | 121 |
| Transferred—females | 15 | 2 | 1 | 113 |
| Subtotal | 20 | 4 | 1 | 115 days |
| TOTAL | 65 | 6 | 2 | 67 days |

* This column indicates the number of patients in each category who were
transferred *to* Worcester State Hospital for longer periods of treatment.
** The term "transferred" indicates patients admitted directly from
Worcester State Hospital.

males as compared with transferred males (i.e., admitted directly from Worcester State Hospital)—29 days compared with 121 days! In the case of females, the span is between 41 and 113 days. Readmissions for both males and females ranged between these figures; 66 days for the former and 51 for the latter. Perhaps the most significant difference, from a practical and statistical point of view, is that which obtains between patients with no previous admissions (totaling 26 patients) and those who had had previous hospitalization in mental hospitals (totaling 39 patients). The average days in residence for the former was 37 days; for the latter, 83 days. These figures might be interpreted to suggest that the proximity of the mental health center to the population it serves may favor admission earlier in the course of illness and, with it, earlier recovery. The figures show that only six of the 65 individuals still required hospitalization at the end of the follow-up period of six to eighth and one-half months.

"These data (especially the over-all average length of stay of 6 days) suggest that the mental health center's program is somewhat effective in reducing the time that patients must occupy hospital beds. Of much greater significance, however, is the fact that transferred patients and readmission patients occupied hospital beds much longer than did first admissions. The "transfers" and "readmissions" were people who had been away from home at the State Hospital for rather long periods of time and had established reputations as being mentally ill. Their comparatively long stays in the inpatient service of the center were only in part due to the tenacity of their illnesses. The more important factor was the great difficulty encountered by the center in its attempt to place patients back in their own homes or elsewhere in the community when their improvement had reached a point no longer requiring hospitalization. As might be expected, hospitalization beyond this point became, in itself, a new impediment to full actualization of the patient's recovery potential."

The great difficulty the center had in placing its recovered inpatients back in their own homes or anywhere else in the community was paralleled by the experience of the Social Service Department; this was reported by the head social worker in her special study of applicants to the outpatient clinic during the first five months:

"In the initial phase described, it was obvious we were functioning simultaneously as a combined family agency, evaluation, information and referral agency, and outpatient psychiatric clinic. An overview of the types of problems brought to the center at its inception and early days points up various areas of greatest vulnerability among the residents of the community and also spotlights the lacunae in the spectrum of social and other caretaking services. The only clear-cut and incontrovertible conclusion that can be drawn from the study is the *absence* or *inaccessibility* of alternative services to meet the wide range of distressing conditions and states of mind among people "afloat on a sea of troubles" and who, in the resulting stresses, saw fit to turn to a new resource designated as a mental health center."

## *Diagnostic Categories: Inpatients*

Classification of patients by diagnostic categories, admission status, and sex are presented in Table 7. Although the small number of patients involved tends to decrease their significance, they do provide some basis for predicting future trends. It should also be noted that these figures do not represent a random sampling of the population of the Lowell Mental Health Area. For example, the entry containing the largest number (9), representing schizophrenic reaction among transferred female patients, is an artifact produced by an administrative decision to transfer female patients with major mental illnesses from Worcester State Hospital to the mental health center as its first complement of patients. This decision was made because it was thought to be somewhat less difficult to work with female patients, and because our nursing service had no male personnel at the time of the opening of the inservice department.

Forty-five of the 65 patients were afflicted with major mental disorders (schizophrenic reaction, 25; affective reaction, 14; chronic brain syndrome, 6). Perhaps of some significance is the

TABLE 7.—Diagnostic Classification by Sex and Admission Status (Inpatients)

| Diagnostic Category | 1st Adm. (Males) | 1st Adm. (Females) | Readm. (Males) | Readm. (Females) | Trans. (Males) | Trans. (Females) | Total |
|---|---|---|---|---|---|---|---|
| Schizophrenic reactions | 1 | 4 | 3 | 5 | 3 | 9 | 25 |
| Affective reaction | 2 | 2 | 2 | 4 | 0 | 4 | 14 |
| Chronic brain syndrome | 3 | 3 | 0 | 0 | 0 | 0 | 6 |
| Emotionally unstable | 1 | 3 | 0 | 0 | 0 | 2 | 6 |
| Psychoneurosis | 0 | 2 | 1 | 1 | 1 | 0 | 5 |
| Adult situational reaction | 1 | 3 | 0 | 0 | 0 | 0 | 4 |
| Schizoid personality | 0 | 0 | 2 | 0 | 0 | 0 | 2 |
| Passive aggressive | 0 | 0 | 0 | 0 | 1 | 0 | 1 |
| Inadequate personality | 0 | 0 | 1 | 0 | 0 | 0 | 1 |
| Personality pattern disturbance | 1 | 0 | 0 | 0 | 0 | 0 | 1 |
| TOTAL | 9 | 17 | 9 | 10 | 5 | 15 | 65 |

Males—23
Females—42

fact that first admission females greatly outnumbered first admission males—17 versus 9—and that half the females had disorders in the categories of: emotional instability (3), adult situational reaction (3), and psychoneurosis (2). There seemed to be a strong tendency for females to outnumber males among patients admitted directly from the community: of 45 such patients, 27, or 60 per cent, were females. Two-thirds of the patients admitted directly from the community (29 of the 45) were afflicted with major mental disorders. This suggests that a community-based mental health center's inpatient service should not expect to deal primarily with incipient or lesser mental disorders.

*CLINICAL STAFF*

The average number of clinical staff in service during the ten months the center was open in fiscal 1967 was 36, distributed as follows among the disciplines: medical, 3; psychology, 3; occupational therapy and rehabilitation, 2; social service, 5; and nursing,

23. Those trained in the behavioral sciences and experienced in serving the mentally ill (in addition to the psychiatrists and psychologists) included 1 occupational therapist, 2 social workers, and 4 nurses. In other words, the ratio of those with experience in the mental health field to those without experience was 13 to 23. During April, May, and June, when the inpatient service was in operation, the average total of clinical staff was 52, with 16 experienced and 36 inexperienced personnel.

A review of the center's first ten months by the heads of the professional disciplines brought a number of considerations to light. Social workers were particularly cognizant of the insufficiency of human services in Lowell and of the consequent utilization of the center to meet needs that could be met by nonpsychiatric social agencies. They were especially concerned with the frequency with which they discovered inpatients to have no home to which they could return on discharge; finding a residential placement for such patients constituted a major difficulty. This was seen as related to the community's long-standing habit of sending patients to Worcester as a permanent dwelling place. Nurses, on the other hand, were primarily concerned with the overtaxing of ward personnel who were trying to carry out the open-door policy and contending with aggressive "acting-out" behavior among patients. This concern led to a demand that more experienced psychiatric nurses be hired who could conduct much needed inservice training of ward personnel. That the community also needed these nurses was evident from the reports of nurses who were already providing evaluation and consultation services to nursing homes, the local Visiting Nurses' Association, and the nursing services of the general hospitals. Psychologists were sensitive to still other issues, especially the need for more community programs and for continuity of patient care. In regard to the latter, they felt that the compartmentalization of services by the established three-part division of the center's services into outpatient, day program, and inpatient service was a definite drawback. They recommended that more attention be given to the psychologist's role in research and in interdisciplinary educational programs.

The three psychiatrists were mainly concerned with the fewness of their numbers and with the heavy burden of interviewing patients at the center as well as consulting with physicians on their patients in general hospitals. They particularly regretted the absence of time to develop educational and research activity. Rich opportunities for research in social psychiatry had to be passed by.

The Catholic and Protestant chaplains had been serving the center only a few months by the end of the fiscal year (both had attended clinical pastoral training courses at Massachusetts Mental Health Center). Their particular areas of contribution had, however, already begun to emerge: pastoral counseling of inpatients and liaison with the clergymen of Greater Lowell. Their liaison role also represented an important beginning in the development of community mental health.

The importance of rehabilitation services was recognized from the very beginning of the center's activity. The Massachusetts Rehabilitation Commission assigned the District Supervisor of Mental Disabilities of the Lowell District to the center on a part-time basis until a rehabilitation counselor was added to the center's staff. In less than three months he interviewed 33 patients, 12 of whom were accepted for Massachusetts Rehabilitation Commission services; 6 of these were Lowell area patients at Worcester State Hospital. By the end of the fiscal year (June 30, 1967), the new rehabilitation counselor, who had arrived in January, had counseled 97 patients; of these, 40 were referred to the Massachusetts Rehabilitation Commission, which accepted 30 for services. Of the 74 patients referred for employment, 32 were accepted. Of the 97 patients counseled, 58 had records of hospitalization at mental hospitals prior to their admission to the center.

Based on their experience during the first year of operation, the clinical staff could say, regarding the needs of Lowell area citizens, that they were beginning to see the below-water part of the iceberg. Two major needs that could be met outside the center were marriage counseling, on the one hand, and vocational and employment counseling on the other. Within the center, the outstanding need was for more people experienced in relating to acutely ill patients to support those ward personnel who had no prior experience.

Community programs had their spontaneous beginnings with the activities of clinical staff members who now resided and had lived in Lowell for years prior to the opening of the center. This was true of the nurses and chaplains and, to a lesser extent, of the social workers. It was usually not true in the case of psychiatrists and psychologists. From this emerged what would perhaps be recognized as facts of life about mental health endeavors: 1) there is no real substitute for years of living in a community as a neighbor or work-associate of persons who come to have a need for mental health services; and 2) the mental health professional's knowledge of the behavioral sciences is limited in application unless he has a close ongoing collaboration with co-workers who have lived for a long time in the community to be served.

## WORK PROGRAM

A general awareness, among personnel and patients alike, that indolence and loneliness were not conducive to good morale resulted in repeated efforts to engage patients in useful work activities. These efforts were successful for only short periods of time and among only a few patients. The need for a larger effort to coordinate the work activities of the center with other treatment programs led to the formation of a work program committee composed of the rehabilitation counselor, the head occupational therapist, the recreational therapist, a psychologist, and a social worker. The social worker served as chairman of the committee's weekly meetings and as group leader of weekly meetings with maintenance and housekeeping personnel. In between meetings, she also functioned as work activities and patient-personnel coordinator. As a result of these efforts, a stable work program emerged in which the daily attendance was equal to three-fourths of the inpatient census.

## SHELTERED WORKSHOP

The need for light industrial work for which patients could be paid was long recognized by the center's personnel. A beginning toward meeting this need was made when the Rehabilitation Committee of the Mental Health Association of Greater Lowell, Inc., became interested and offered to sponsor a sheltered workshop.

### COMMUNITY PROJECTS

The groundwork for participation in community-based projects was prepared by the center's head psychiatric social worker. Arrangements were made to set up a social service information and advice station.

### MOST OUTSTANDING ACCOMPLISHMENT OF THE YEAR: ITS SIGNIFICANCE

The most outstanding accomplishment of the first year's work was the relatively large number of individuals served and the small number transferred to Worcester State Hospital. Of 1,430 admissions (involving 1,200 individual patients), only 10 were transferred. The latter made up less than 1% of the total number of individuals served and only 2.5% of admissions to the center's inpatient service.

The extent of this accomplishment is revealed by the results of a special study* showing the over-all effect of the center's operation on the number of patient days that Lowell area residents are hospitalized at Worcester State Hospital. A comparison of the number of admissions and the number of patient days of hospitalization of Lowell area patients is as follows:

|                          | Worcester State Hospital Admissions | Worcester State Hospital Patient Days |
|--------------------------|:-----------------------------------:|:-------------------------------------:|
| July 1965-December 1965  | 111                                 | 19,200                                |
| July 1967-December 1967  | 53                                  | 3,670                                 |

During the period July-December, 1967, the center's inpatient service admitted 158 patients, who were hospitalized a total of 6,410 patient days.

---

* This study was performed by a consultant sociologist to evaluate the social contribution of the center.

These data show that the center has contributed to reducing the number of admissions to Worcester State Hospital and to shortening the average length of hospitalization of Lowell area residents there from 180 to 70 days. This reduction may be attributed to the availability of aftercare services at the center.

From the above, it would appear that the center provided services of tangible worth in reducing the amount of time that Lowell area residents were denied family and community life by prolonged hospitalization.

It is especially significant to consider these results as related not only to staff effectiveness, but also to the fact that the personnel who performed the bulk of the work—and hence made highly effective contributions—were those who had little or no experience, training, or education in the care of the mentally ill or in study of the mental sciences prior to their employment at the center. This suggests that the department heads of the clinical services were singularly successful as on-the-job trainers and motivators of their personnel. It also indicates that we have much to gain from trying to learn the varieties of leadership by which citizens of local communities could develop their own helping approaches to mental illness.

One factor that may foster development of a helping approach is awareness of the natural tendency of the most acute and severe mental illnesses to be self-limiting in a relatively short period of time *if the patient is not rendered helpless by physical incarceration or by psychological indignities.* Such knowledge is born of efforts to maintain an open-door policy and to make the surrounding community accessible to the patient. The desirable effect of these efforts appears to result from their tendency to reduce whatever fear there may be regarding mental illness among patients, personnel, volunteers, and visitors.

Also of help, perhaps, is an outlook based on the fact that recovery from psychosis often occurs independently of scientific intervention. Indeed, the fact that recovery from psychosis has occurred in every culture and society in history indicates that we might well benefit from studying the responses to mental symptoms of the various cultural groups of our own local communities. Certainly, we could benefit from making more of an effort to share common ground and common language with the people we serve, especially those most isolated from the mainstream of productive community activity.

## QUALITY OF SERVICE: A DEBATABLE ISSUE

The quality of service rendered citizens of the Lowell Mental Health area by Solomon Center is not simple to ascertain. The psychodynamic purist would withhold judgment until each patient had been thoroughly studied by a fully trained psychotherapist. The physician who tends to credit recoveries to the healing powers of nature, even when specific remedies are applied, would be less apt to demand that one be able to explain recoveries in order to accept them as an accomplished fact. For such a physician, quality of service to the mentally ill can be measured by the extent to which a patient is free to get over his ailment on his own and is protected against insults to his sensibilities.

The experience of Solomon Center suggests that situational conditions may contribute more to a patient's capacity to recover than the advanced academic training his care-givers may have undergone. Certainly, the relatively small amount of psychotropic medication used and the very small number of patients treated with electroshock suggest that factors other than these must be operative with considerable effectiveness.

It has been argued that reduction of patient days in the state hospital is meaningless and that both patients and society would be better off if the former remained in state hospitals for much longer periods of time. This argument cannot be refuted without knowing the facts of each patient's situation for months, and even years, after discharge from the center. The determination of such facts requires that a systematic and long-term follow-up review be undertaken by teams of personnel who are placed on special assignment to perform such studies.

Follow-up studies may show that significantly large numbers of patients are substantially free of mental illness for many years after their discharge from the center. The implication of such an outcome would be of considerable importance in view of the fact that these results are produced by personnel, most of whom have not had prior advanced academic training.

## ADMINISTRATIVE COMMENT

The administrators of the center believe that no one organizational format is known to serve the interests of patients better than another. They also tend to the view that administration serves best when it administers the least. In line with this view, all development of direct services to patients has been accomplished by department heads in the process of responding to patient demand. Very few specific requests have been directed to them by administrative authority. In turn, they make few specific requests of the personnel responsible to them. Practically every demand made on personnel is made by the patients, by their families, pastors, and physicians, and by community agencies.

The existence of the above-described sentiment suggests that exercise of authority is rarely needed. In practice, it has happened that events have required no more than a veto—mostly to proposals that would seem, in practice, to decrease the speed or amount of direct services to be provided to patients. By the end of the first *full* fiscal year of operation (fiscal 1968), it appeared to be more in the interest of all concerned to continue investing center staff time in meeting the needs of patients coming for help rather than in prevention programs.

As has been stated, practically all of the demands made on personnel are those made by patients. There has been, however, some pressure exerted on the staff by the administration to maintain adequate clinical records and to undertake research. The subjects of record keeping and research are serious problems awaiting solution. The top priority assigned to meeting patients' demands has resulted in an extremely active patient turnover. On the average, there are about 1,200 interviews or sessions each month (distributed among almost 400 individual patients). At present, only three clerical personnel are available for record keeping or research functions. In addition, a considerable amount of their time is, of necessity, required for preparing reports for the Department of Mental Health. There exists, therefore, a pressing need for clerical personnel trained in medical stenography and medical record keeping. There is further need for a statistical clerk and a statistical analyst if we are to acquire anything more than superficial knowledge of our own clinical operation.

### THE GROWTH OF GROUP APPROACHES: A MAJOR TREND

The emergence of group work is perhaps the most significant development in the life of the center. Group work—or, more accurately, working groups of clinical personnel—has become a method of functioning throughout almost the entire spectrum of the center's activities. Clinical management of inpatients takes place almost entirely in group meetings of personnel with patients. Reduction in the size of the groups was accomplished by dividing the personnel into four groups, each of which meets with one of four groups of patients. Each patient-personnel group has a membership of 10 to 16: 6 to 10 patients meet in the morning and afternoon with 4 to 6 personnel five days a week. Morning sessions are given over largely to management problems arising out of everyday difficulties encountered by patients in adjusting to one another and to the center routine and activity programs. Afternoon sessions are devoted to patients' personnal problems.

The work program is planned and administered by a group—designated as the "work committee"—which is headed by a social worker and includes the rehabilitation counselor, the head occupational therapist, the recreational therapist and a clinical psychologist. Another group of personnel meets with the rehabilitation committee of the Mental Association of Greater Lowell to develop a sheltered workshop. Personnel representing every clinical discipline conduct group therapy sessions—always with no less than two personnel present, who function as "co-leaders." Indeed, group therapy has become a recognizable competitor with individual therapy. For example, in the last six months of the year, figures indicate that, on the average patients served by the center attend one group session each month as compared with 2.3 personal interviews. Group supervision of individual therapy has also come into the picture.

Another area characterized by group activity is a monthly meeting with personnel of other agencies. A group of center personnel confer with their community counterparts to discuss mutual concerns in meeting the needs of citizens.

The chaplains have also contributed to group endeavors by serving as co-leaders at seminars for clergymen of the area. They formed a committee in the Greater Lowell area to bring patients to their own churches. These efforts were supplemental to their liaison activity in arranging for consultations with the clergy at the center, and to their pastoral counseling services to patients.

These group endeavors raise the question of why groups were selected as the preferred method of approach in discharging the duties of clinical administration as well as in providing treatment to patients. An answer that suggests itself is that heightened concern regarding patient care began to appear as the center accumulated experiences with treatment failures, experiences which are less frequent during the early days of a center's existence. The acquisition of greater numbers of clinical personnel (the average number in service increased to 65 from 38 the preceding year) with less experience with mentally ill patients, and the even greater increase in admissions (from an average of 86 per month to 120), combined to put greater stress on personnel. Since "misery likes company," it is not surprising that clinical personnel found themselves forming groups to pool their thinking and to share responsibility.

### TREATMENT VERSUS PREVENTION

The problems of treatment presented by the appearance of more intractable mental ills and by greater firsthand contact with a greater variety of human life and misery tend to forestall an investment of effort in applying the generally prescribed prevention approaches. There is, however, an associated lack of clarity as to what treatment is and what preventive measures are. In some respects a focus of attention on the treatment of a wide variety of emotional strain by collaboration with personnel of other agencies, clergymen, and volunteers also contributes to prevention. In the second year of the center's existence, 1969, the community became more aware of its services and made a greater demand on them. The clinical staff, now faced with greater work loads and beginning to feel the effects of being taxed beyond capacity, began to question the division of labor among professional disciplines and services as well as the sense of various treatment approaches. The occurrence of open expressions of disagreement and altercation among factions of the staff served, however, to point up their main characteristics as a functioning body: their resilience and stability. It would appear that these desirable staff qualities could be credited to their having adopted a multiplicity of group settings to deal with management and therapy problems during the preceding year; these forms had also become well established as informal mechanisms of self-government, self-determination, and decision-making with respect to policy development.

## DIFFERENTIATION AND DIVERSIFICATION

Disagreement among clinical personnel was but one aspect of center development during the year. Differentiation of effort manifested itself in the adoption of such new programs as the alcohol clinic; in liaison with the district court and the Lowell police department; in collaboration with Lowell high school guidance counselors; in collaboration with the clergy in forming volunteer organizations; and in support to the establishment and maintenance of a pastoral counseling center in Lowell. A program of case-finding was also instituted in conjunction with Lowell General Hospital, Lowell Visiting Nurses Association, and Community Teamwork, Inc., Lowell's anti-poverty agency which jointly sponsored Well Baby and Cancer Detection Clinics. Another program of collaboration with Community Teamwork involved the training of ten New Careerists at the center for the purpose of manning self-help centers in the community. Also undertaken during the year was a graduate social work student training program. Altogether, about 40 different groups were established.

### CITIZEN NEED FOR COMMUNITY CONCERN VERSUS GROWING COMMERCIALIZATION OF HUMAN RELATIONS

Like the morale of clinical personnel in a mental health program, social morale cannot be expected to be on the plus side when citizens are confronted year after year with more stresses and higher tax levels— and without any indication that there will be fewer needs in the foreseeable future. The seeming inevitability of rising costs, even in the face of high-speed, automated mass production, may suggest that we are unwittingly—perhaps even unwillingly—slipping into a new mode of living in which aspects of human interchange become increasingly commercialized and service industries swell to the size of large manufacturing enterprises. Tasks that once were accomplished by way of neighborly sociable helpfulness cannot now be done without purchase of services.

Our present commitment to a humanistic-humanitarian concern for the individual requires that we be sensitive to the inescapable fact that the morale of a society varies in direct proportion to the kindness and dignity of the arrangements it makes to assure that the idiosyncratic needs of its more helpless members are perceived and met.

In this connection, it might be expected that there are components of our society—especially of our health, education, and welfare systems—that clash with each other in a way that is demoralizing to our social life. In addition, it may be that our most important task is to prepare ourselves to endure certain facts of life, namely, that some social enigmas are insoluble. Just as we admit political democracy to be less than perfect but prefer it to alternative forms of government, so it may be that we must revise our expectations and admit that our public mental health establishment has inherent limitations. An attitude of respect for human individuality, and for social efforts to preserve it, seems to be the indispensable ingredient for continued social progress.

## INHERENT CONFLICT OF INTEREST: THE PERMANENT DILEMMA

The commercialization of human interchange referred to previously may be partly attributed to the rapid growth of professional technical specialization in more and more areas of human relations. Trained specialists must, of necessity, be remunerated for their services. The higher their training, the fewer their numbers and the greater the cost to those who obtain their services. It follows inescapably that only a few of those in need of a special service can be fortunate enough to have access to it. Thus, it would appear that recent advances made in various areas of human relations give rise to *new* inequalities that *add* to the disruption of social life. In other words, advances in knowledge in the area of human relations, rather than being helpful, may actually turn out to be damaging to the human relations of the populace as a whole. Could it be that, when it comes to benefiting the average citizen, progress in the behavioral and social sciences is a wholly different matter from progress in the physical sciences? This question brings up the matter of *who is to decide* how scientific knowledge of any kind is to be applied. Apparently, recent advances in nuclear physics, tissue transplants, and genetics are leading physical scientists to suggest that the areas of *future scientific research effort* should be selected by the people as a whole through the exercise of democratic political processes. Similarly, it is suggested that the assignment of priorities in the *application of already existing scientific knowledge* and *in the selection of those to benefit from such application* should be made via the political process. Hence, these are signs of a growing recognition among experts in the physical sciences that they may not be as well equipped with decision-making apparatus as the citizenry as a whole is when matters affecting the public interest are involved—even when these matters are of a highly scientific-technical nature.

There are signs of a tendency in the *opposite direction,* however, among experts in the *human relations sciences.* Since the latter are relative newcomers in terms of occupying positions of public importance, they would tend to be correspondingly less mature, less secure and, consequently, more aggressive. In any event, even with the security of full maturity, there would probably always be a strong tendency among human relations experts to resist the idea that the people are better equipped than they are to make decisions in the realm of human affairs. This is certainly not at all surprising, for quite reasonably the human relations expert could, at least from an abstract theoretical point of view, contend that since the political behavior of the people is one of his objects of study, it is he who has the more comprehensive basis for judgment and that it would accordingly be his role to tell the people what to do rather than the reverse. Thus, we are faced with the irony that the human rights of citizens and the vested interest of human relations scientists threaten each other. The very existence of such an essential conflict of interest in itself suggests, perhaps, that much of *human relations research should be performed under the control of elected representatives of the people* as a preventive measure; this is preferable to the emergence of behavior control technologies in the hands of those strategically situated and motivated to put doctrinaire or theoretical systems into effect at the cost of eliminating the democratic process.

### REBIRTH OF SOCIAL CONSCIENCE
### IN THE BAY STATE

The above deliberations may, perhaps, be brought into useful perspective by returning to psychological, social, and historical considerations, some of which are mutually supportive while others are mutually contradictory. It is well to be reminded first that, for the past three centuries, the care of nervous and mental disorders was removed from the folk culture of European peoples by governments and by the clerical, legal, and medical professions. This was sometimes done to correct abuse of the afflicted by an ignorant populace. Many of the earliest removals, however, appear to have been effected by an oppressive church and state in search of heretics and practitioners of witchcraft.

It is well known that in the early history of rural Europe, the family and the clan managed the problems of nervous and mental disorders. It was an intrafamilial matter first and foremost, and only rarely did it go so far as to become a village or neighborhood concern. The early history of Massachusetts is also characterized by home care of the mentally ill by the family, the minister, and the family physician. The community-sense of village life was particularly strong at that time, for villages were groupings of people who had chosen to come together for religious reasons. The religious community and the political socioeconomic community were one. Indeed, there is good reason to ponder the fact that Massachusetts grew and prospered for 200 years without a mental hospital of any kind!

It is important to our thinking today to consider that community-sense and concern for the individuals of Massachusetts villages lost strength when new religious groups came into their midst and villages increased in size to the maximum point where villagers could not know one another personally. Apparently, these two factors were instrumental in interfering with the capacity of families to care for their own members during mental illnesses.

Community-sense, solidarity, and neighborliness are of critical importance to us today, when citizens are beginning to seek each other out to form new community organizations to correct old evils. This tendency is being encouraged by the ecumenical spirit of the churches and spurred to action by the discovery of longstanding social neglect of people who are far more disadvantaged than those more fortunate have been prone to believe. Our political bodies can ill afford to allow these beginnings to go unnoticed. Timely support might well lead to the unprecedented mobilization of community concern for families and individuals who have become social casualties.

## THE NEW SHAPE OF COMMUNITY ACTION

There is a growing indication that today's newly forming groups are organizing around a shared respect for the needs and problems of individuals, and that such groups are aware of the necessity to steadfastly and slowly work out the development of means to meet needs and solve problems. Most important, however, is the fact that they seem fully aware that the acquisition of funds is not the be-all and end-all of their efforts. They do not automatically assume, as was the case even in the recent past, that the answer lies solely in acquiring salaries for specialists to provide essential services. Quite to the contrary, there seems to be a growing sentiment that volunteerism is a value of specific effectiveness in its own right. Like group psychotherapy, volunteerism is on the threshold of being fully recognized on the basis of its definitive effectiveness rather than as a substitute brought into the picture because of insufficient funds with which to pay professionals.

It may be visionary to see this revolution-filled period of world history as the beginning of a cultural metamorphosis in American life. The citizen as a unit of political power is no longer content to be the passive object of social planners located in governmental bureaus. He is, perhaps, intensely aware that the checks and balances which hold traditional political manipulation within safe limits may not yet have been invented to hold computer-armed social scientists within correspondingly safe limits. He shows signs of feeling himself fully involved and desirous of more active participation in the political process at all levels, *including* his local community. As he becomes more active in politics on a local level, he also becomes more aware of the problems and needs of other citizens and of the absence or inadequacy of community programs to assist an increasing number of such fellow citizens. This new awareness leads the citizens into joining or organizing volunteer groups that provide direct personal assistance by the volunteers themselves.

One may speculate that this trend to offer voluntary service to problem-ridden fellow citizens may grow to a point where the voter is so often a volunteer provider of direct services that

political and social service realms will blend and lead to the
emergence of a new self-concept of citizenship as defined by the
citizen himself and to a new brand of politics more intimately
concerned with the varied status of individuals in relation to
the ever-accelerating pace of social change.

Thus it may be the better part of wisdom for our present
mental health program leaders to consider the probability that
the development of community concern for the individual citizen
may be more to the point than the development of mental health
service as such. The art of mental health leadership may well be
the art of sensing when timely withdrawal from the social scene is
indicated.

## THE PERMANENTLY IMPAIRED
## CITIZEN'S SPECIAL NEED FOR
## COMMUNITY CONCERN

Solomon Center is impelled by humanistic-moral considerations to give priority to those citizens in the Lowell Mental
Health and Retardation Area who are most handicapped by
irreversible impairment of the nervous system. Such handicaps
are suffered at all stages of life, but it is at the extremities of the
human life span that the greatest need for care exists. Accordingly, young children and the very elderly, who cannot speak for
themselves, have the greatest need for thoughtful provisions by
others to bring them comfort in dignity. Perhaps the greatest
need of all, however, is to bring our social leadership to admit
that, as a rule, a state of physical and moral neglect obtains
among these two groups, the most severely handicapped of
humankind. Not until this admission is made—and it is not
made without considerable inner resistance derived from knowledge of the truly great quantity of tax dollars already being
spent for the handicapped—is it possible to begin to grasp
the magnitude of the problems presented by the varieties and
degrees of nervous-system and psychological impairments suffered
by fellow citizens. Such a beginning is assisted, perhaps, by
attempting to identify as many as possible of the various sub-
categories which comprise all the nervous and psychological

ailments generally known to exist, and by dealing with them as various combinations of four broad categories:

| | |
|---|---|
| General behavior disability | Specific partial behavior disabilities |
| General learning disability | Specific partial learning disabilities |

It is probably fair to say that our present mental health programs include the responsibility of attempting to improve society's bungling efforts to compensate for the cruelties of biological mishap, on the one hand, and the aging process on the other, to the degree that they affect the human nervous system. Nature does not permit even the most socially and economically favored of us to escape both.

Community mental health, in itself indefinable, might profitably be equated with life betterment for everyone. If that is the case, one cannot afford to overlook the fact that psychological and social forces are so interrelated that neglect in any one area may vitiate even the most generous provisions for another area of human need. The presence of inequities and unfairness is always demoralizing, yet shame and guilt almost always inhibit corrective action. Witness the searing welter of feelings suffered by parents who visit children—or by children who visit parents— committed to institutional confinement. It is not difficult to perceive such an experience as adequate to precipitate anyone into a life of benumbed or desperate nihilism. It would, accordingly, not seem reasonable to expect that the morale of a whole society— and especially that of a democratic one—could be much higher than that of its most neglected part, i.e., those of its citizens whose very incapacity prevents them from improving their own condition. Such incapacity, whether from developmental defect, brain damage, or psychological trauma or deprivation, warrants both social and scientific attention. The policies of the past, which tended toward wholesale concealment of demoralizing conditions among those incapacitated by psychological or central nervous system damage, has been repudiated in recent decades by citizen action. Yet great neglect and partial concealment are still very much in the picture.

## IMPLICATIONS FOR PROGRAM PLANNING

The dominant tendency, in recent decades, toward the professionalization of every helping role in American life has been accompanied by a corresponding tendency toward the commercialization of human relations wherever the label of *help* or *service* may be applied. The foregoing presentation suggests that these tendencies may be self-defeating from the point of view of both the individual citizen and the community.

The writer's experience during the growth and development of Solomon Mental Health Center has led him to the conviction that state leadership and funds are as much needed to stimulate and support local initiative in organizing community concern for the individual citizen, and for his development as a full participant in community affairs as for his care during periods of incapacity. There is much to suggest that success in this area would greatly reduce the need for mental health services per se, and that, in order to be effective, the moral treatment perspective cannot be confined within the limits of mental health facilities but belongs in the realms of public policy, public administration, and institutional administration as well.

# XI

## The American Political Heritage
## and the Training of Psychiatrists

*THE SCIENTIFIC SOCIETY:*
*A SOCIAL PSYCHOSIS?*

American medicine has been deeply affected by its membership in two cultures: the scientific culture and the American political culture. Science and scientific methods as we know them today may be said to have incubated in the universities of medieval Europe and to have grown out of prescientific intellectual activity in theology, philosophy, and mathematics. These disciplines resulted, after but a few centuries, in a rather widespread capacity for highly developed abstract thinking, a capacity first recognized and applied in interpreting religious beliefs in relation to social change. Applications soon followed in the fields of law and jurisprudence, and then in the financial and commerical activities of the Renaissance. Within a century or two, after overcoming the initial opposition of established authority, abstract thinking demonstrated its value by penetrating the secrets of nature and obtaining mastery over her. Abstract thought and esoteric concepts finally led to those problems of the modern world that result from placing a higher value on great ideas than on persons. The adoption of such a value-system was a crucial and perhaps fateful step in the history of the West.

I am taking the liberty, or perhaps the poetic licence, of diagnosing the results of this mental stance as psychotic in character. Among the self-defeating enterprises stemming from this psychotic

196

manner of thinking, I cite the developments in scientific technology that have brought about great increases in the population of the Western world; we now exist in numbers that cannot survive without total dependence on this technology. The individuals who make up the contemporary Western world have almost completely and irretrievably lost the essential freedom to derive a livelihood directly from nature. They now face the critical necessity of developing new concepts of checks and balances and a division of powers that will prevent the abstract impersonal values of the scientific society from exercising their power to inflict a new and dehumanized tyranny over the individual.

The other aspect of this cultural context, which I believe belongs in the picture, has already been touched on. I refer to the good fortune Americans have enjoyed by having, for nearly 200 years, a government whose objectives have been preventing tyranny and guaranteeing every citizen his rights to life, liberty, and the pursuit of happiness. The principle of separation of the powers of government, the principle of separation of church and state, and the careful introduction of checks and balances (wherever their need could be foreseen) have by and large served better and longer to protect our liberties than any other system of government could have done.

The broadening bands of intersection of these two cultures, the scientific and the political, as they affect medicine, have taken form as the health services and the departments of education of the state and federal governments. Government entry into the administration of research in the medical sciences and the provision of medical services constitutes a development that has long engendered strong disagreement. The pros and cons of this issue are not our subject of discussion. Its existence is noted to point up the fact that government-operated medical facilities are growing and that even though organized medicine is becoming more active, it remains, in its attempts to influence the legislative process, relatively ineffective.

The position occupied by medicine in relation to individual and public fear of disease and disfigurement, and of pain and death, is one of great sensitivity and key importance in modern life. Indeed, it may be well worth considering whether medicine, in its capacity to influence human motivation, psychologically occupies a position in modern life analogous to that occupied by religion in our earlier history. If this is so, the question should be raised as to whether the preservation of individual liberty requires the separation of medicine and state, just as our early history necessitated the separation of church and state. Can it be said that insight into our current social psychosis would lead us to this conclusion? This brings us to a concern for the state of the mentally ill.

## THE AMERICAN POLITICAL HERITAGE
## IN RELATION TO MENTAL HEALTH

The mental health establishment of the United States has undergone truly enormous growth since the turn of the twentieth century, with the greatest growth occurring during the past two decades. This growth is largely a result, and in part a source, of the ever-accelerating pace of social change that has characterized this period, and it has been greatly aided by the passage of recent federal and health legislation which gave it the funds to carry out its programs.

In the years of its deprivation, the mental health movement had its share of serious problems and failures. It has every right to be apprehensive rather than jubilant at being provided with enough funds to do its job, for it is now contending with far more difficult problems than it knew in its days of poverty.

The amount of literature on mental health matters is vast, too vast to be absorbed even by those in the field who must do its daily work. The training of mental health workers requires many expensive years of arduous effort. Yet even in the presence of this great learning and scientific productivity, the question must be put: Does anyone know how to define the functions of a mental health establishment or to designate the limits of a mental health program? That we do not is not in the least surprising, for mental health workers are the first to admit their inability to give a definition of mental health or illness that has sufficient validity to be used as a test or proof of anyone's sanity.

Our inability to define mental health and illness may lead to the conclusion that perhaps such a definition lies outside the domain and special interest of the mental health discipline. Dealing as it does with the relation of an individual to his society and of a citizen to his sovereign state, the authority and responsibility for making a definition of illness may well be recognized to lie within society itself in each instance of questionable behavior. This brings us to the vitally important matter of dealing with the psychosocial significances of the American system to the individual American. We cannot afford to overlook the historical fact that America's Founding Fathers invested their whole beings, hearts, minds, and souls in the task of building a political system on the foundation of unqualified, unconditional, full respect for the individual citizen and his rights, irrespective of his position in the social and economic system. Here was a political system based on loyalty to a principle rather than to a ruler, a family, or a cultural tradition.

The relationship of the individual citizen to the political system of his state and nation is an emotional bond greater than mere patriotism, for it is based on a deep sense of participation, however vicarious it may actually be. Indeed, there is the ever-present heartening fact that the political system itself is a portal of opportunity open to many to whom doors are elsewhere closed.

One may readily express misgivings as to whether the American system accomplishes its aims. A keystone, however, to understanding this system is the common experience that, whenever it fails to act in the best interest of the individual, it is usually immediately apparent that it is off course and headed in the direction of evil. The significance of this can be more fully appreciated when comparisons are made with political systems of other times and places that have won loud applause for their virtue on the relatively rare occasions when they *do* act in the best interest of the individual. In other words, while the American system is considered a miserable sinner if it fails at any point to benefit the individual, other systems announce themselves as saints when they, on occasion, succeed in benefiting their citizens.

How did our Founding Fathers manage to build so well? The answer lies in their attitude toward human individuality, on the one hand, and human nature on the other. This attitude asserted the indispensability of unconditional respect for the potential of the individual for growth, development, and the attainment of near-perfection. It also asserted the indispensability of maintaining full awareness of the perfidy of human nature when exposed to the temptations of unhampered political power. This attitude underlay the long labor and careful thought that were put into eliminating the temptations of arbitrary power from the machinery of government. The American political system was a carefully designed political invention for the express purpose of preventing tyranny; in no sense was it fashioned as the instrument of a preconceived national destiny. The right of the individual to work out his own personal destiny in freedom could not otherwise be safeguarded.

The fact that the American republic is still a going concern after nearly 200 years not only bears witness to the wisdom of its founders, but also demands our consideration of these founders as prototypes of those American politicians who have perpetuated the growth of our political system and its capacity to safeguard individual freedom. The Founding Fathers were men whose interests were both broad and deep. They were all versed in the science, moral philosophy, psychology, and medicine of their day. Some, like Benjamin Franklin, Thomas Jefferson, and Benjamin Rush, all signers of the Declaration of Independence, were acknowledged leaders in science and medicine. But first and foremost they were exceptionally wise humanitarians and social reformers.

This brings us to a fact that is insufficiently recognized among mental health workers and political leaders: that of the common heritage of the American mental health establishment and of American political democracy. Each has its origin in the meditations and assertions of the moral philosophers of the Age of Reason who provided the moral and rational basis for the American Revolution. They, in turn, traced their values back to the judicial thinking that evolved in the course of centuries of application of English common law and to the great influence of English, French, and Italian Renaissance literature, which reviewed the political, medical, and psychiatric thought of classical Greece.

The exceptional congruence of human values in two areas of American life that superficially appear to be entirely unrelated is worthy of much consideration. The more thoroughly one scrutinizes the principles on which the American political system and American psychiatry are built, the more they reveal themselves as the same principles.

Viewed from another perspective, it is evident that a major part of the mental health establishment is an arm of the humanitarian American state. After all, the term "state hospital" has been a synonym for "mental health" for more than a century and a half. The first hospital unit to care for the mentally ill was established at the Pennsylvania Hospital largely through the efforts of Benjamin Franklin two decades before the Revolutionary War. The first state mental hospital was established by Governor Fauquier of Virginia at about the same time. Franklin was respected as being so well versed on matters psychological that he was appointed to a board of scientists by the king of France to investigate the phenomenon of mesmerism. Franklin's reason for supporting the establishment of a psychiatric unit at the Pennsylvania Hospital was to care for, treat, and restore reason to the disordered mind of the lunatic, not to seclude him from society.

The first health services provided by the states were hospitals for the moral treatment of insanity. Indeed, within a generation after the death of George Washington, every state of the union had established a mental hospital.

These facts bring to the fore the vital consideration touched on earlier, namely, that the condition designated as "mental illness" is not primarily so much a medical concern or responsibility as it is a vital concern of the sovereign state to provide sanctuary and relief and comfort to those of its citizens who find themselves alienated from family, neighborhood, and community.

The years since the Revolution have witnessed the cultivation of more and more contacts between the state and the citizen. The state is becoming increasingly humanized and more and more a tangible and comprehensible entity to the private citizen, due partly to an increase in the services of the state to the citizen and partly to rapid advances in communications.

During this same period, when the state and the private citizen have been gaining in their sense of familiarity with one another, the stream has been running in the opposite direction with respect to the relation of the individual to the health professions.

In the early history of America, the family doctor was a personal friend of the household, fully devoted to its members in times of illness. In recent years, however, his image has become that of a remote and neutral, if not cold and impersonal, figure— the specialist who deletes the human factor from his technical and financial relations with his patients. Of even greater significance, however, is the public image of the psychiatrist as a figure even more remote and bloodless than the doctor—and yet the psychiatrist's self-avowed special skill is in the area of personal relationships! This state of affairs is largely the result of the paradoxical, self-contradictory role psychiatry adopted for itself when it began to count itself among the highly specialized sciences and sought to justify its existence as a science rather than as a humanitarian endeavor. It regards science as its wellspring, and scientizes its methods and rationale as a matter of discipline. And the more it scientizes its procedures, the more it dehumanizes them and places them in the category of impersonal technicalities. The more psychiatry pursues this course, however, the more it compounds the complexity of the misunderstandings which have confused and troubled the relationship between the physician and the lay public in modern times. These misunderstandings originate partly from the proclivity of the lay public to attribute magical powers to the medical man, and partly from the physician's tendency to foster such beliefs as a support to his role as faith-healer.

Society's exploitation of the idea of the magical powers of the physician resulted in transferring the responsibility for alienated citizens from the community to custodial institutions under medical management. This transfer created a situation in which the community could, in good conscience, wash its hands of alienated citizens on the grounds that hospital physicians had special curative powers.

In retrospect, we can see how the well-nigh irreversible process of accumulating inmates in state institutions was started. This accumulation, which continued decade after decade, inevitably led to degrading what were once hospitals into crowded slum colonies jammed with human derelicts. Such a reprehensible turn of events was able to take place under the very eyes of a thoroughly humanitarian political leadership because of a barrier that arose between the physician, on the one hand, and patients and political leaders on the other, when the physician exchanged his role of family doctor for that of medical science specialist. This barrier also intruded itself on the relation between political leaders and science in general during the latter part of the nineteenth century. In the earlier history of the country, the man of science and the political leader were not infrequently one and the same person. Later, the rapid advance of science and the specialization that accompanied it were together responsible for the near-complete break in communications between the political and scientific leadership, on the one hand, and the everyday workers in the two fields on the other. Because of this break in communications, a trend developed whereby politicians tended to overrate scientists and scientists tended to underrate politicians. For the most part, public opinion has tended to agree with both politicians and scientists in their respective views of each other. As long as this situation prevails, humanitarian considerations not only lose their priority in American life but come dangerously close to having few, if any, respected proponents due to the enormous success of science—with its avowed materialism, objective neutrality, and ideological disregard for humanitarian considerations. The public has allowed itself to become resigned to a policy of management by experts in some areas of public activity. Severely damaging misunderstandings have been, and continue to be, incorporated in the complex of attitudes that make up public opinion. Perhaps the most sensitive aspect of public misunderstanding is the mental health field and its relation to science. This misunderstanding had its origin in wholly innocent oversights not unlike those that lead to highway fatalities—not too dramatic an analogy when one considers that these oversights present the risk of destruction of our national purpose.

The issue at stake is that mental health is being represented by its experts and received by the public as a matter that lies in the domain of science, and hence is a matter to be dealt with by providing funds to the appropriate scientific specialists. We must be fully aware that this is simply not the case. The message that needs to be heard by the American public and their political leaders is a very simple one, yet it is particularly vulnerable to distortion in both the sending and the receiving. This vulnerability derives in part from the reluctance of the mental health specialist to acknowledge that mental health is in any sense a simple matter, one that is understandable to the public, and in part from the reluctance of the "public"—the constituents of each community—to acknowledge this truth, namely, that the solution of a problem does not entail special knowledge but, rather, special effort by the community.

The message is simply this: Mental health can be almost completely equated with citizen morale, and mental illness with individuals who are demoralized by alienation from family and community. Obviously, such vital and delicate matters as morale and demoralization, which lie at the very focal point of human life and motivation, are much too important to be placed in the hands of science, medicine, or psychiatry. Since they are humanitarian concerns, touching everyone's relations with everyone else, they must be primarily the concern of the sovereign state, of its political leadership, and of its local community leadership.

Where, then, do the professional specialists of the mental health sciences fit in? In an advisory capacity to community leadership. Our advice must include accurate reporting of the limits of our effective technical instruments and skills, but our greatest responsibility lies in exercising vigilance that the demoralized citizen does not wander into a no-man's land and drop into oblivion because of lack of communication between mental health institutions and the community.

Our discussion may profit by turning to the topic of mental health programming in relation to the political system. The first point we must emphasize is that a mental health service—translated as citizen morale service—is not a commodity or a performance that can be purchased from a vendor. On the contrary, it is almost entirely a matter that requires both financial support and personal participation in a manner somewhat similar to what we do when we join a fraternal organization or a church. To be specific, a community that would acquire and maintain a mental health service must contribute its leadership and enough of its membership to perform many of the tasks involved in restoring alienated, demoralized persons to their rightful places in the hearts of their families, friends, and neighbors.

The quest for more certain knowledge and for scientific status has again and again, over the centuries, led physicians and others concerned with their alienated fellowmen to delve into the mysteries of the mind by way of introspection, meditation, and speculation. This propensity is at the same time both the greatest strength and the greatest occupational hazard of mental health professionals. In the past few decades the introspective, meditative, speculative approach has again come into its own after having been discarded for about a century. Now again, as in the past, it is accompanied by an upsurge in the standards of humanitarian care demanded in behalf of the demoralized, alienated citizen. Its adoption of the introspective, meditative, speculative approach in the training centers that teach the arts of mental healing has brought with it a very great prolongation in the time required to produce qualified workers in the mental health field. In some settings, the position has been reached at which training is acknowledged to be interminable. To the uninitiated onlooker, the trainee appears to be trapped in a squirrel cage of collective introspection and to be seeking buffers to insights that strain his sensibilities.

The point that needs to be dealt with in this connection is that community leadership has a right to be confused by the contradictory messages it receives from various sectors of the present-day American mental health establishment. The political and community leader learns from one sector that mental health problems can be substantially relieved by applying reasonably comprehensible humanitarian measures. From another sector he is given to understand that successful treatment of mental ills rests entirely with those who have acquired a special knowledge that is as obstruse and difficult to attain as knowledge of nuclear physics and relativity. Such a state of affairs and the confusion it creates in the public would appear to be ample evidence that doctors of the mental sciences are not equipped, unaided and by themselves, to safeguard the commonwealth in the critical matter of citizen morale. How, then is citizen morale and mental health to be safeguarded? One answer that suggests itself is for a serious effort to be made for collaboration at several levels between political and social leadership, on the one hand, and the professionals in the mental health disciplines on the other. To be more specific, the solution may lie in the formation, at state and community levels, of permanent joint commissions of leaders and workers in politics, community life, and mental health.

It is not in the least fanciful to harbor the expectation that such commissions would derive some strength from the heritage of respect for human individuality, a heritage which the mental health professions and the American political system cherish in common as having priority above all other considerations.

## THE TRAINING OF PSYCHIATRISTS AND NEGLECT OF THE MENTALLY ILL

### The Primacy of the State Hospital's Political-Social Role

The state hospitals play vitally significant roles in the social and medical history of the United States. From their beginnings, state hospitals have, in principle, been sanctuaries for those of its citizens who became alienated from family, friends, neighbors, and community. Over the past century and a half, thousands of American citizens have retreated from personally demoralizing and humiliating situations to the state hospitals, which, at their worst, still often were havens where wounded self-esteem could heal, exhausted energies could be restored, and general health could be looked to.

From the points of view of the public interest and the civil rights of the individual, the state hospital is not adequately accounted for in terms that are applicable to other types of hospitals, which can be accurately described as workshops for physicians, existing for the convenience and increased efficiency of physicians as well as for reasons of economy. The state hospital cannot, however, be described as a workshop for psychiatrists, one that happens to be paid for out of state tax money. It is much more than that. It can be more aptly understood as a primarily political social institution with a political-humanitarian function that is part and parcel of the American political system and its longstanding traditional efforts to devise effective ways of preventing infringement of the liberties of citizens. Only secondarily is it a medical institution.

State hospitals bear the name of hospital and are, furthermore, under medical supervision and direction because physicians, as classic Hippocratic humanitarians, were regarded as capable of providing the most effective stewardship available to serve the best interests of the individual. This was, in any event, the judgment of American political leadership in the early nineteenth century, when our state hospital system was first established. One might hazard the guess that if a time ever should arrive when physicians are regarded as no longer occupying the forefront of humanitarian leadership, that may well be a time when hospitals will once more become true asylums, and members of disciplines regarded to be of a more humanitarian bent will be called on to direct them.

### Some Aspects of the Historical
### Matrix in which Psychiatric
### Education Emerged

The displeasing suggestion that there could ever be a time when psychiatrists might not be regarded as suited to direct institutions of humanitarian purpose is offered to evoke some useful background thoughts for a discussion of psychiatric training in state hospitals. This subject requires consideration of what we now regard as our models for psychiatric residency training—the psychiatric residency programs of the university teaching hospitals of our great universities. These programs are obviously of critical importance to the future of psychiatry. The problems of grasping the essence of these programs, and of explaining why they are the way they are, may in some measure be made more intelligible by first taking a look at the history of medical education in the United States in relation to the rest of the Western world. Most relevant to our purpose is the situation in higher education and in the advancement of science at the turn of the century when the acknowledged paragon of excellence was the university system of Germany and its specialized graduate schools. Among the most admired of these were the schools of medicine. At that time, most American medical schools had either no connection with universities or loose affiliations, sometimes in name only.

The preeminence of German universities and the receptivity of American university scholars to the contributions of German social scientists had a particular bearing on the social outlook of our educational leadership. This outlook was later given the name of Social Darwinism. Some of the clearest expressions of American versions of Social Darwinism are to be found in the writings of William Graham Summer, who was Professor of Sociology and Political Science at Yale University from 1872 to 1909. (See page 85.)

In the field of medicine, views were expressed in support of sterilizing the unfit as an eugenic measure. At that time our state hospitals and schools for the retarded were looked upon not only as repositories for detention of the unfit, but also as instruments for preventing their procreation—in other words, eugenics by sexual isolation. It was during those years that American intellectuals, following the lead of the universities, harbored the lowest opinion they have ever had of the people's capacity to govern themselves, and voiced the least faith they have ever had in democracy.

This climate of thought is cogent to our discussion because it has a bearing on the most important events that took place in the history of American medical education, namely, the complete elimination of half of America's medical schools and the coercion of the remaining half to revamp their mode of operation in imitation of the science-based university medical schools of Germany. The fact that a change of such magnitude could be brought about essentially by one man, Abraham Flexner, backed by funds from two of America's greatest philanthropies—first that of Carnegie and then that of Rockefeller—is most remarkable and deserves serious study in its own right.

It is important to consider this matter from the point of view of identifying certain attitudes toward human values that may have been carried over and unwittingly included in our attitudes, and also because it influenced the priorities that have emerged in psychiatric training programs in recent years.

The first point warranting discussion is the high priority given to science for its own sake by German universities in the latter part of the nineteenth century and the lower priority given to the lives of individuals as ends in themselves in their own right. The second point is that American universities tended to follow the German lead even though this led in a direction antithetical to the main current of the American cultural and political heritage. The third point is that these intellectual forces led to a disregard of the very important social fact that, in the course of the nineteenth century, the people of America and their physicians had, in over 150 localities, spontaneously developed methods to train those who felt called to the healing art, usually without the benefit of federal, state, or other large-scale direction or support. In other words, medical education had emerged within the endemic folkways of the American people in a manner that called on the physician to keep good his Hippocratic promise to teach the arts of medicine to others. In many instances, this combined the advantages of apprenticeship with those of the classroom and the demonstration laboratory. It was a method of training that was close to people, and that treated the apprentice as a person, who in turn treated his patients as persons.

The shortcomings of these 150-odd ventures in medical education is not the issue. Rather, the issue is that medical education was redefined as a matter that belonged wholly in the hands of higher authority, and as such was completely removed from the hands of people and separated from their folk culture.

The closing of the medical schools from 1900 to 1930 was perhaps a crucial step toward the consolidation of an American educational establishment that may still be on its way to becoming a monolithic hierarchic system of interlocking control centers. We may have emerging before us another example of the irony so frequently observed in the history of man's efforts to better the lot of his less fortunate fellows. I refer, of course, to the belief that education, as it was conceived by Horace Mann, would be the instrument of liberation of the individual and I contrast this hope with the evolution of education along the pathway of increasing powers, e.g., setting standards and standardizing, including and excluding—in short, the pathway of those who would erect a new hierarchy of authority.

The great questions of today may well be: "What are the checks and balances that could prevent a newly forming mammoth establishment from bringing about a new hegemony of the few over the many? Where the few ascend above the many, and where their science-based authority is remote from the people, is it possible for the few to respect the interests of the people as much as they respect knowledge and science?"

## HAS MODERN PSYCHIATRY EDUCATED ITSELF BEYOND USEFULNESS TO THE STATE HOSPITAL?

As we said earlier, there is a high degree of cogency in regarding our state hospitals as citizen sanctuaries for those alienated from their immediate family and social circle. These hospitals admit great numbers of people who are severely compromised in several dimensions of human functioning. The patients present innumerable patterns of deprivation and stress, blocked aspirations, and indignities suffered. The one thing people who find themselves in these institutions have in common is that they are social rejects. The basis for their being rejected, furthermore, is behavior that ranges from the simply tiresome to the burdensome to the terrifying. They can be equally well described as people who have reached a phase in their lives when they are singularly unattractive, unappealing, and difficult to deal with on a person-to-person basis.

My purpose in describing the patients in state hospitals in such terms is not to emphasize the lowly status they occupy in their own eyes and in the eyes of their social group, but to highlight the fact that these patients apparently occupy an equally lowly status in the eyes of a majority of our most highly educated modern American psychiatrists. It would seem reasonable to relate this state of affairs to the fact that psychiatry has in the past two decades or so won acceptance as a branch of higher learning at the upper levels of our universities. It is also note-worthy that psychiatry did not win great numbers to its ranks until it reached a high level of academic, and hence social, acceptability. Could it be that the university, the seat of intellectualism, has succeeded in intellectualizing the depth psychologies on which modern dynamic psychiatry is based? Could it happen that a depth psychology can itself be intellectualized when it is the very source of the insight that intellectualization is a defense against learning unpleasant truths?

Insofar as psychiatrists are looked to for guidance in matters of mental health and illness, do we not occupy a position of leadership that obligates us to know not only what our own underlying motives may be but what the underlying motives may be of the educational culture of which we are a part? Do we impart the spirit of this type of inquiry to the resident? Can we claim that we have studied our own educational history sufficiently to be assured that what Germans did to Europeans and what Americans did to the Japanese in the 1940's under the heading of total war were not events that can be traced to a common origin in the form of an antihumanitarian outlook among the intellectual leaders of the two countries at the turn of this century?

I trust that it is evident that I am haunted by misgivings as to why American psychiatry should fail the state hospitals at a time when it has been more successful than at any other time in its history in recruiting able people to its ranks. Hopefully, consideration of this train of thought will yield a psychological climate useful as a backdrop in discussing the subject of residency training itself.

RESIDENCY TRAINING IN STATE HOSPITALS
VIEWED FROM THE COMBINED
PERSPECTIVES OF NINETEENTH-CENTURY MORAL
TREATMENT AND TWENTIETH-CENTURY
SOCIAL PSYCHIATRY

The state mental hospitals of America offer the richest and most meaningful educational experience that can be acquired in any one type of institutional setting today. They provide a rare opportunity to learn, on the basis of direct, firsthand personal contact and observation, practically every aspect of man's condition as it is affected by the complex influences of modern life. Within the walls of these hospitals there are almost limitless varieties of unmet human needs that can provide opportunities for the creative imagination which the classrooms and laboratories of our highly structured educational systems cannot begin to match. Indeed, in many respects, these opportunities are often greatest in those state hospitals where the impoverishment is most pronounced. (The latter may be particularly well suited to the more aggressive, independent, and imaginative residents.) Yet we are all aware that this true wealth of challenging learning experiences available in our state hospitals is almost universally overlooked and disregarded.

This state of affairs can be explained, in part at least, as due to the educational policies which organized psychiatry has adopted in its efforts to acquire for itself a high-level position in the academic and medical world. The self-defeating patterns of these efforts are perhaps related to the great emphasis placed on standard-setting and standardization, on the formal accreditation of institutions as teaching centers, and on the certification of psychiatrists as teachers. Obviously, as in any situation in which many feel the call and few are chosen, the status of unacceptability is the lot of the majority. When applied to state hospitals, such a situation is especially damaging, for they have long felt the stigma associated with insanity and now feel the stinging insult of unacceptability added not by unenlightened strangers but by their own fraternity.

There is a weird feature to the story of psychiatric training in American state hospitals as it has taken shape in recent years. This weirdness derives from its perplexing schizoid dissociation from hospital psychiatry itself, which, indeed, sometimes has no relationship to the hospital's problems whatsoever except as some maverick resident seeks to forge such a relationship.

I believe that this weirdness has its origin in the inferiority feelings that have haunted American psychiatry since the breakdown of moral treatment. American psychiatry also has feelings of inferiority on two other scores—in relation to the rest of American medicine and in relation to European, especially German, psychiatry. American mental hospitals gave wholesale acceptance to Kraeplinian psychiatry without a protest; a little later, after a period of some resistance, they gave enthusiastic acceptance to Freudian dynamic psychology. That neither of these schools of thought was made an integral part of hospital practice in patient care can perhaps be partially explained by the observation that both may have been imported more to allay feelings of inferiority and to win acceptability than out of recognition of their value as instruments of better care for patients.

Perhaps less discernible to many modern psychiatrists is the fact that moral treatment did not come to a complete halt in our mental hospitals simply because it was dropped by their medical staffs. Many aspects of moral treatment have been perpetuated to this very day in our nursing services by attendant personnel whose practices were acquired by informal pathways from their antecedents. Even our worst state hospitals, during their worst years, have always succeeded in achieving improvement warranting discharge in about 50 per cent of their annual admissions.

It is at least consoling to believe that there are therapeutic forces at work in our state hospitals even when there are no staff psychiatrists or when they are playing hookey in town, busying themselves with other matters.

As a final point, let us note that our state hospitals are only now entering the early phases of acquiring the first true hospital psychiatry since the breakdown of moral treatment. This is taking place under the leadership of the new discipline of social psychiatry, to which we owe the concepts and practices of milieu therapy and the therapeutic community.

The main problem faced by the state hospital today in training psychiatric residents would appear to be in promulgating plans for training in social psychiatry. These should include training in depth psychology as the most effective means we know for sensitizing the physician to the inner experiences of human individuality.

I suggest that an immediate aim of training in social psychiatry should be to explore the means for reducing the intellectual and social distance between the residents and the personnel of hospital service departments. The elimination of communication barriers is of crucial importance, first, so that the resident can learn psychiatric lore that is otherwise almost unattainable and, second, so that he can be equipped to discharge his future responsibilities as a leader and counselor of these same personnel. It is noteworthy that the military has long recognized that the commissioned officer learns more about the craft of officership from his enlisted men than he can learn at his academy. From this one might infer that the American medical school imparts less humility than does the American military academy.

It seems apparent that a major task of social psychiatric training is to equip the psychiatrist with the mobility and versatility necessary for him to travel effectively in every human setting produced by history. We have not only a starting point, but also a staying place for our endeavors, in the persons of a half million or so patients and personnel who occupy the state hospitals of America.

*THE ESSENTIAL SKILLS OF THE SOCIAL
PSYCHIATRIST AS RELATED TO THE
TRAINING OF PSYCHIATRIC RESIDENTS*

There is as yet no wholly satisfactory definition of social psychiatry which clearly separates it from other endeavors. I would like to suggest, however, that the basic skill which needs developing in psychiatric residents lies in the area of social organization with goals that are unique to the needs of the mentally ill. Experience indicates that the essential goal is to discover those arrangements of people that, in relation to one another, produce psychological climates which are most effective in evoking the spontaneity of the individuals involved. This skill could also be described as the art of developing open societies among the mentally ill and providing them with challenges and resources that will give them the opportunity to restore their self-respect and their usefulness to themselves and others.

The state hospital is the setting in which these skills are most needed and in which they can be most effectively taught and developed. Dynamic psychiatry, on the other hand, has a strong moral obligation to contribute its share in the development of these skills, for it is perhaps the only effective means available for sensitizing and enriching the psychiatric resident's respect for human individuality.

## SUMMARY AND CONCLUSIONS

Psychiatry and, with it, psychiatric education has digressed from its fundamental task of caring for those most seriously damaged by mental illness. This digression has occurred in company with the success enjoyed by psychiatry in winning acceptance, in higher academic and medical circles. The advancement of social psychiatry and the training of psychiatric residents in social psychiatry are, hopefully, steps in the direction of a return to the fundamental task of caring for patients in state hospitals—barring a similar digression into the community, to the exclusion of the state hospital.

Today, our society is in a transitional period and is undergoing rapid changes. The rising admission rates to state hospitals, the primarily political-social nature of state hospitals, and the growing public attention to them strongly suggest that urgent action is required to establish residency training programs that are tailored to meet their needs.

# XII

## Occupational Therapy: A Neglected Source of Community Rehumanization

*THE CHALLENGES CONFRONTING*
*OCCUPATIONAL THERAPY*

In considering how to meet the new challenges confronting occupational therapy today, I would suggest that we redefine the problem as fundamentally moral rather than as professional, technical, or scientific. As I see it, this involves the moral obligation and responsibility that we, as agents of society, have to any individual whose future as a member of that society is in serious jeopardy. Occupation is central to man's social institutions—indeed, to his very existence. We must recognize that when we speak of either the will to work or the will to live, we are speaking of the same human striving.

Acknowledgment of the critical moral importance of occupation in human life demands an in-depth review by the health professions of their own value judgments and practices with respect to identifying which are the means and which are the ends of our endeavors. There remains no doubt of the capacity of science and medicine to effect repeated revolutions in our mode of human existence. Nevertheless, we adhere to the moral position that knowledge and health are not ends but, rather, means to a better life. These considerations bring us to the recog-

217

nition that occupation is an indispensable moral condition of human individuality. It is, furthermore, a condition of relationship that has no existence in itself but exists entirely through actions performed by the individual in reciprocal relations with others; hence, it is a strong determinant of his sense of personal identity.

From the foregoing it would appear inescapable that our concern with occupation carries with it a moral mandate to respect occupation as a component of individuality and, as such, as an end to which all our other measures are means. This leads us to the possibly unexpected state of affairs of having to recognize that medical endeavors must necessarily be applied in the interests of both the individual *and* his occupation. Conversely, neither the individual nor his occupation can be subverted to health or treatment ends without violating the integrity of the individual and his occupation. Pursuit of the moral position of the individual's occupation along this course brings us quickly to the view that the term "occupational therapy" is either a misnomer or a contradiction of the profession's own moral position.

As seen from this angle, the dilemma of occupational therapy becomes somewhat more visible and perhaps more definable. Occupational therapy suffers from a limitation imposed upon it by its origin in the setting of medical care, and as an outgrowth of mental hospital nursing practices. As such, it has regarded itself as part of a larger endeavor masterminded by the medical discipline. In this context, it has operated as a moral force in the interests of individuality by providing the mental hospital patient with the opportunity for occupation.

To depict occupational therapy as a moral force may or may not be agreeable to the professional occupational therapist. It does, however, help one to see how occupational therapy acquired a name that is a misnomer for its field of endeavor, and also how it was blocked from perceiving either the depth or the breadth of its role as a moral and scientific force. This role has even more central importance to future human development than could possibly be claimed by any existing scientific specialty which neither has nor claims a moral basis.

## OCCUPATIONAL SERVICE WORKER

To carry this line of reasoning along a more fruitful course, it would be helpful to recognize the modern occupational therapist as evolving a new discipline of occupational development that he will apply as an occupational service worker. In this capacity he will develop means for analyzing both the manifest and latent perceptual-motor skills of the individual as they relate to his personality and motivational make-up. He will also develop ways of analyzing the components of the occupations of the community in which he serves, and he will make it his business to know the emotional and motivational values they have in that particular community.

In this connection, we see the occupational service worker as divorced from medicine and as having his base of growth and development outside the hospital. He will belong to the educational and economic life of the community, to which he will contribute a much-needed kind of knowledge, and in which he will be a force in fostering respect for occupations.

Psychiatrists and occupational therapists may find it difficult to seriously entertain the proposal that occupational therapy should have major social responsibility outside the framework and confines of medical services. I contend, nevertheless, that occupational therapy has acquired a body of moral perspectives and occupational lore of unique value to society, and that it can be an enormous aid in facilitating the development of human individuality. It has a message that can be more effectively utilized if it is not limited to being a service solely for sick people. I contend, furthermore, that the graduation of occupational therapy to the position of an autonomous professional community service would in no way lessen its contribution to patient care in medical facilities. On the contrary, this development would in the long run greatly augment the capacity of the occupational specialist to contribute to the patient's functional and social restoration to community life.

The rationale for expecting a unique, critically vital contribution to community and national life from occupational therapy derives from the fact that occupational therapists are driven by a moral concern for the individual and for what he is doing in the here and now. This is in marked contrast to some other modern disciplines and sciences, which often give the highest priority to ideas, ideologies, theories, and personal success. Another asset that is almost peculiar to occupational therapists is their high tolerance for puzzlement, confusion, and frustration.

It is important, I believe, to remember that occupational therapy acquired its unique and valuable assets through many decades of adversity. Its origin and development in the state hospitals gave it a firsthand acquaintance with every conceivable kind of deprivation endured by imprisoned, insecure people. It was always a matter of having only a tiny fraction of what was needed to meet their needs. It was always a matter of suffering to some degree the burden of guilt that is felt whenever any of us are forced by circumstances to engage in a token performance. To me, the occupational therapist is a veteran of many battles fought to win respect for the individual.

### EXPANSION INTO THE COMMUNITY

The advent of community psychiatry during these years of intensive industrialization and urbanization is a signal that veterans of state hospital occupational therapy also belong in the community, and that the profession of occupational therapy is coming into its own for the first time. Never before has the opportunity presented itself for the occupational therapist to prepare the groundwork for a comprehensive occupational development service that can begin to meet the needs of patients and community alike.

For the first time, the occupational therapist can explore the value of acquiring the occupational and cultural histories of patients' families. For the first time, he can think in terms of having accurate up-to-date knowledge of the occupational life and resources of the community in which his patients live. And, also for the first time, the occupational therapist can begin to take responsibility, alongside the businessman, the city planner, and the economist, for community occupational development.

At this point it may be helpful to backtrack somewhat and remind ourselves that the efforts of occupational therapy as a hospital service department have never gone far enough to effect a breakthrough. For one thing, due to insufficient personnel and facilities, it could not demonstrate the full extent of the contribution it was capable of making to human growth and development in particular illnesses—or in complete health, for that matter.

Let us also recall how frequently the occupational therapy craft rooms of mental hospitals were found to be little havens of freedom. They were sanctuaries where patients could escape boredom and the anonymity associated with nothing to do, and find something akin to personal identity through occupation and their concomitant association with occupational therapy personnel. These were the days before tranquilizers and large-scale activity programs appeared on the scene of hospital life to greatly increase discharge rates.

It is tempting to call those days "the good old days," when hospital administration neglected occupational therapy and left it to itself. It is also tempting to speculate a bit and ask if patients did not benefit from this particular medical neglect. What was wrong, of course, was that so few patients could receive such benefits.

We are fully aware of being victims of the monstrous standardization and conformity that characterize man-made objects, scenes, and sounds in industrialized America. American cultural bleakness can be readily traced to our pragmatic, first-things-first approach to living. Mass production to meet mass needs has occupied almost all of our energies until very recently. We are only now beginning to invent ways of social organization that can express the cultural capacity, the individuality, and the identity of individuals, ethnic groups, and communities. We have yet to see the blossoming of America's potential for cutural diversity that lay dormant during the many years when priority was given to the process of industrialization.

The American community is composed of people of many ethnic origins, with a rich diversity of cultural backgrounds. Certainly, there must be the potential in American life for developing ways of stimulating and refreshing our ideomotor behavior and our latent powers of imagination. And, certainly, we must not wait for scientific experiments to prove that the achievement of such creativity would raise the levels of citizen morale and mental health as much as any health measures known to medical or mental science. It is indeed time to discontinue those ill-conceived demands for excessive conformity that were imposed by the unrelenting forces of Americanization and modernization. Then, hopefully, the future can bring a restoration of continuity to disrupted cultural heritages and family folkways.

These considerations may not be as visionary as they appear. There is already public recognition of the need to prepare for old age and retirement. Emphasis is being placed on the acquisition of personalized occupations that can extend beyond the years of paid employment. Journalistic protests have already appeared against the disheartening and demeaning spectacle of retirement villages peopled by elderly folk who are bored with the entertainment and busy work provided them, and who are lonely for authentic community life. There is obviously a need for occupational specialists to cope with these problems of the aging. Their services are probably even more needed in the schools for children of all ages, and especially in those for adolescents. In addition, with the increasing amounts of leisure time that automation is expected to bring, can we leave out adults between the years of schooling and retirement?

I am enthusiastic about the idea of humanizing American occupational life by emancipating it from standardization and conformity. I believe that my occupational therapy colleagues can readily assume effective leadership roles as occupational development specialists and can quickly begin the humanizing process.

## OCCUPATIONAL THERAPY: A LIVING LINK WITH THE MORAL TREATMENT OF THE PAST

Therapeutic nihilism and pessimism dominated the mental health hospital scene almost everywhere in the United States until the second decade of this century, when a few hospitals began to give renewed attention to the emotional and psychological factors of mental illness. Gradually, these factors came to be respected as playing important roles in both the therapy and etiology of mental illness.

It was during this period, when respect for the individuality of the patient and for the role of the emotions in illness was reawakening, that one finds the earliest mention of occupational therapy as a term describing a profession. Within a few decades the new profession was in full bloom—with formalized training, requirements, certification, and academic recognition.

As I see it, the appearance of occupational therapy was not a new thing but rather the resurgence of a belief about patient care that had not completely died out and was not completely lost from memory since the days of moral treatment. After all, when occupational therapy arrived on stage between 1900 and 1920, there were men and women still living who had personally known the leaders of moral treatment in the pre-Civil War period.

In its own mind and in its own memory, however, occupational therapy is only a newcomer on the stage of history, having only 50—at most 60 years—to look back on. In a sense, then, since organizations of any size take longer to reach maturity than individuals, occupational therapy is a rather young adult. It is time for occupational therapists to heed the idea that their profession has been the child of medicine long enough and to consider that its next step toward full maturity and social effectiveness is to go off on its own.

We must remind ourselves that moral treatment was an exceptionally effective means to recovery from mental illness, and that its effectiveness consisted in being a *comprehensive occupational-recreational program.*

It would be most unfortunate for all of society, but especially for the mentally ill, if occupational therapy were to limit itself by continuing to be satisfied with running dinky little sideshows in large medical institutions. It can never make the contributions of which it is capable until it sees its way clear to acquiring and operating comprehensive community occupational-recreational programs on a scale large enough to accommodate every citizen who needs them.

It is my contention that moral treatment will never again be developed by medical men to meet the needs of the times. All of them, including psychiatrists, are too thoroughly possessed by the need to keep up with the latest technical knowledge in their specialized areas of endeavor.

Let me repeat: a new era of moral treatment tailored to our times is sorely needed not only by thousands of persons in our communities who are burdened with chronic residues of psychoses, but also by many thousands of others with emotional and physical limitations.

It is fair to say that modern society has a greater need for comprehensive community occupational-recreational programs than it has for mental health centers. I say this because I know that, when such programs required the services of psychiatrists, the occupational therapists in charge would make arrangements to obtain such services.

To my way of thinking, we urgently need to give top priority to occupational programs. Thousands upon thousands of Americans are drifting about in a state of social disorientation, suffering the lives of displaced persons in their own country. They need concrete, tangible, highly visible activity programs to attract their interest, to help them discover their own values, and to find their way out of demoralization. The need is so extreme that we should be thinking in terms of crash programs even greater than those put into operation to train restoration aides during World War I and occupational therapists during World War II to care for military casualties. But the measures required to cope with the civilian casualties of our current social revolution remain to be put into effect.

It is timely to suggest that the profession of occupational therapy may have reached a point in its growth and development where it can assert leadership in devising and organizing the crash programs needed by so many urban industrial communities currently undergoing social upheaval.

I suggest that there be a *consolation house* (a vocational bureau; a neighborhood workshop) within walking distance of every urban dweller. Similarly, I would like to suggest that occupational therapy be the wellspring for a sorely needed alternative system of education for individuals of all ages for whom the formal public school system, as we know it today, is inadequate.

### THE NEED FOR AGGRESSIVE COMMUNITY OCCUPATION DEVELOPERS FROM WITHIN THE PROFESSION OF OCCUPATIONAL THERAPY

### Items for Consideration

I.   All human beings are plagued with problems that they cannot solve in isolation. It is not until our personal problems become social problems that we can hope for relief. But this does not happen until our problems become severe enough in their disruption of social tranquility to stimulate the adoption of corrective measures.

II.   Human problems can best be understood in organized, goal-directed activity that has emotional and intellectual ego-meaning to the self and to others. Without meaningful, synchronized, productive interchange with others, there tends to be nothing but fanciful, hypothetical, abstract as-if-ism in our preventive, therapeutic, and rehabilitative endeavors. Individual psychotherapy, group psychotherapy, and non-goal-directed milieu activities are, by themselves, not only not enough to do the job; they are *unreal* and humor an unrealistic attitude orientation of participants toward themselves and toward others.

III. Occupational therapists are the only professionals who already understand the nature and value of synchronized, goal-directed, productive interchange in bringing relief to human problems. Hence, occupational therapy is the professional discipline best suited to correct the off-course trend of today's so-called progressive reform movements to meet human needs.

IV.  Occupational therapists have a social obligation to break loose with crash programs where they are entirely free to meet the needs of problem people in their own way.

V.  We should remember the following:

1. Moral treatment broke down because of a narrowly conceived organic brain-disease theory of mental illness and because of racial, religious, and class prejudice.

2. Community psychiatry is similarly breaking down, even as it develops, because of a narrowly conceived intra-psychic psychopathogenesis theory of mental illness and because of academically fostered professional elitism; there is prejudice among those with the most years of higher education against professionals with fewer years of academic preparation and against problem people who come from the less privileged social classes.

### CONCLUSION

There is a tendency among a fairly large minority of Americans, mostly with academic backgrounds, to believe that a body of knowledge already exists that could put into effect a mode of social organization superior to what we now have, and that this would eliminate most of the social evils that plague our lives. It is vital that we become aware that this belief is a fantasy, for it overlooks and fails to respect the degrees of complexity, uniqueness, and essential unknowability of any individual or any groupings of individuals. It is damaging and self-defeating to rest our hopes on this fantasy and to allow it to guide our activism.

Failure to respect the uniqueness and complexity of individuals and their groupings is inevitably accompanied by absence of respect for their very real needs for varieties of experiences and for discussing and thinking out what these experiences mean. Present-day social leadership leans toward activism and reactionism, and demands impatiently that our citizenry change their ways or accept imposed change immediately unless they wish to face disaster.

Obviously, many changes *are* needed to correct defects in our economy and politics, and in the quality of individual and social life. Yet practically no area of leadership clarifies the fact that such changes are cultural processes that depend on loving cultivation and careful attention to supplying such prerequisites as accessible learning experiences and sufficient time for them to be absorbed, integrated, and applied by the population.

If an individual is not given time or help with the arrangements needed to think out proposals with his fellow citizens, does this not show disrespect for him and for the contribution he can make? I contend that it is valid to say that occupational therapists have an inborn respect for the individual that grows out of their work with people suffering all varieties of problems. The occupational therapist's inborn respect for the realities of life, for the real tasks of living, and for the time it takes the individual to develop his own modes of coping with his tasks, leads me to urge that profession to assert its leadership in fashioning the design of human services programs that are on the drawing boards throughout the country or are already in early phases of development.

# XIII

## Exploration in Correcting Neglect:
## Milieu Rehabilitation

During the course of the rehabilitation project at Butler Health Center (see Chapter X), the working concept of the principles applied was known as milieu rehabilitation. The idea of milieu rehabilitation provides a frame of reference within which we can discuss the experience of personnel who participated in this endeavor. The basic principles had their origin in the troublesome and often immobilizing difficulties involved in deciding whether to deal with a client as being sick or not. In either case it was useful to clarify the difference between treatment and rehabilitation, if any, in considering each client. Efforts along these lines were found to be helpful in reducing the inconsistencies, on the part of different members of the rehabilitation team, in dealing with a client. Out of these efforts there came a growing recognition among personnel that they could detect a difference between their feelings, attitudes, and personal aims with respect to clients whom they associated with their rehabilitation efforts and those whom they associated with treatment. As awareness of this difference progressed and became more differentiated, it was possible, in their dealings with clients diagnosed as sick, to identify which of their inner responses and consequent efforts were therapeutic and which were rehabilitative in nature. This added capacity to differentiate among their responses was an important advance in their capacity to differentiate between a sick individual and one who was not sick.

Milieu rehabilitation is a method for rehabilitating handicapped individuals that gives special attention to the obvious fact that each member of the rehabilitation team is a part of the human milieu experienced by the client. Since the physical milieu of the rehabilitation setting is controlled by the rehabilitation team, the client's experience is entirely dependent on the responses to him on the part of the rehabilitators and the other clients, both as individuals and as groups.

Acknowledgment that a client's fate in a rehabilitation program is wholly determined by these responses carries with it an obligation to learn what these responses are in order to determine which ones have an important bearing on his progress. Once a way is provided for learning the "what" of as many responses as can be observed in the time available, the necessity arises to study why they are what they are and how to change them in ways that will come closer to meeting the client's rehabilitation needs.

These considerations led to the adoption of a number of policies and practices by the director of the rehabilitation program under discussion. In retrospect, these appear to have been crucial for the development of a valuable attribute among personnel which, for want of a better name, might be called "milieu sensitivity." (Many of these policies and practices were put into effect to some degree in the administration of the entire milieu therapy program of Butler Health Center. The recognition that milieu rehabilitation is a discernible concept as well as a functional operating entity is, of course, the basis for this presentation.)

Milieu sensitivity might be described as a high degree of perceptiveness to the inner responses and outward actions of the other people making up the human milieu. It includes awareness of the likely effects of one person's outward actions on another. For milieu rehabilitation to exist and progress in any meaningful sense, there should be a continuous development of milieu sensitivity in the handicapped client as a means to discover and develop his particular individual assets.

To achieve a fuller orientation with respect to milieu rehabilitation, it is useful to designate more precisely what the problems are that it attempts to solve. They are, briefly stated, the problems of impaired motivation and damaged morale, which stand in the way of a handicapped person's making full use of either a) discrete rehabilitation aids, such as prosthetic devices or special training courses, or b) his own already existing capacities to give service or secure employment. In a more general way it may be said that the final aims of rehabilitation are to develop substitute, compensatory abilities and supplements for missing or damaged parts of the handicapped person's totality of life-processes.

### PERSONNEL POLICIES

Personnel policies formulated by the superintendent derived from a basic major consideration, namely, that personnel can reasonably be expected to be responsive to the needs of clients or patients only if their supervisors are equally responsive to their needs. On this basis the superintendent, clinical director, and department heads of Butler Health Center assumed the obligation to be accessible to all personnel at all times. Rules and regulations were kept to the bare minimum essential to avoid useless duplication of effort and to spare individuals the frustration of working in opposite directions. Those that were adopted were not put into effect until the individuals concerned had had a full voice in their formulation and recognized their value and workability. Regulations that did not accomplish this purpose, from the point of view of those expected to observe them, were either rescinded or modified.

The position taken by the administration with respect to punctuality, hours worked per week, time allowed for meals, and coffee breaks was that these are not matters which warrant being isolated and made subjects of rules or regulations. They were regarded as matters of no significance in themselves in the context of a group of individuals whose work itself consists in meeting responsibilities to each other in the process of their common endeavor to meet the needs of clients and patients. If an individual did not meet his responsibilities to others, it was to be regarded as a sympton of an underlying problem that needed solving, not as the occasion for outlawing the individual's particular act of nonfeasance.

## SELECTION OF PERSONNEL

Applicants for positions on the rehabilitation staff (or in other clinical departments) were interviewed by as many of the staff members as were available. Applicants were invited and encouraged to spend a full day, or at last a half-day, visiting all areas of the health center and becoming acquainted with personnel. The final decision on whether to employ the applicant was based on the combined appraisals of those who had become acquainted with him. The factor given first consideration was whether or not the applicant was needed by the rehabilitation program for his particular personality make-up as well as for his qualification to fill the particular available position. For example, if an applicant for the position of instructor in carpentry were, say, a fast-talking, practical-joking, quick-to-get-acquainted, comedian sort of young man, the question would be whether there were already enough persons of similar make-up on the staff. The outcome of these deliberations could well be a decision that the clients were more in need of an opportunity to be in contact with a slow-talking, gentle-natured, serious-minded older man.

In addition to a needed type of personality make-up, the other qualities sought in an applicant had to do with a) ability to communicate openly about other people's behavior in a relatively unbiased manner, and b) interest in learning. The amount of an applicant's formal education was not given weight as a determining factor.

## PERSONNEL COUNSELING

Most problems having to do with the relations of personnel to each other were taken to the superintendent, while those having to do with the relations of personnel and clients were taken to the psychiatrist in charge of the day program or to the clinical director. When extraordinarily complex problems came up, impromptu group meetings were held; these included all three of these men along with those personnel closest to the problem.

By and large, the counseling efforts were directed toward demonstrating to personnel that their individual personalities were more important than the position they held. On this basis it was possible for them to recognize the pointlessness of sharply demarcating each person's area of work or authority or of requiring strict adherence to lines of authority.

## PERSONNEL EDUCATION

Recognition of the importance of the personality make-up of the personnel who care for patients is a first step toward the most important factor in the success of milieu rehabilitation—a manifestation by those in authority of genuine respect for human individuality. Respect for the individuality and personality assets of patients is not forthcoming from personnel unless they experience the same respect for their own individuality and personality from the senior staff members.

Open group discussions led by those in authority tend to motivate staff members of different professional training to exchange knowledge and techniques and to pass them on to those who lack professional training. Absence of an opportunity for such a learning experience, on the other hand, tends to foster a tendency among personnel to stress a narrow, status-invested interpretation of their professional and nonprofessional roles. If this tendency is unchecked, barriers to communication arise and often lead to conflict between different professional groups.

Another dimension of respect for the individuality and capacity of personnel is their inclusion as full participants in the scientific aspect of the program by giving them a clear picture of the state of our present knowledge of life-processes, including the fact that it is insufficient at all levels—physiological, psychological, and social. The important point here is that all personnel have a full opportunity to grasp the implications of the simple truth that the professional members of the staff are operating on the same footing of personal ignorance about any newly introduced individual as those who have had no scientific training. Acknowledgment that the actions of the professional staff are also based on personal, subjective inner responses rather than on esoteric scientific knowledge provides a bedrock foundation for a meeting of minds. The desired end of such a meeting of minds is that it be on the common ground of investing energy in learning. On this basis, personnel can come to understand that milieu rehabilitation is not a matter of a professional person applying his knowledge and having orders carried out, but that it is a research enterprise every step of the way with every client. Viewed from this perspective, personnel are in no way providing ancillary services in the usual sense. On the contrary, they are research workers whose powers of observation, thoughts, and communications are vitally important to the rehabilitation of every handicapped client.

It is evident from the above that the education and development of the assets of workers constitute an indispensable element of milieu rehabilitation. Indeed, it may be worth stating, as an axiom of rehabilitation, that development of the assets of the handicapped is dependent on simultaneous investment in the development of the assets of their immediate rehabilitators. Provisions to be made for education and development of personnel include: enlistment of their participation in all professional staff conferences; access to the medical library; arrangement for time off to attend lectures and to take courses in nearby universities, and financial assistance for payment of tuition.

## CLINICAL ADMINISTRATION

The task the clinical director assigned himself in the administration of milieu rehabilitation was to accomplish two intimately related goals with each client. The method was to elicit from the personnel acquainted with the client as full a picture of their inner responses to the client as he could draw out of them.

These efforts were made in one-to-one interviews and in group
discussions with members of the rehabilitation team. They took
place both in informal contacts and in scheduled staff conferences. The purpose of these efforts was to achieve the first of the
two goals, namely, to formulate the role actually being played by
each member in the client's life, a role that could be acknowledged by the individual member himself and the group as a
whole to be a meaningful, subjectively satisfying, and adequately
accurate representation of the facts insofar as they could be
ascertained. The phenomenon of arriving at a common conception in this manner will be referred to, for convenience, as Group-
Gestalt Closure. Achievement of such closure on the part of the
client's direct-contact helpers was regarded as a prerequisite to
the client's achieving a similar closure—the second of the two
goals. The client's achievement of Group-Gestalt Closure with
respect both to his group of helpers and other clients was
regarded as indicative that he had attained sufficient emotional mobility to adopt new self-concepts and new perspectives
of other people. In other words, he had reached the point where
milieu rehabilitation had accomplished its major purpose of
starting him on the path of developing his own assets and making
use of available resources in the community at large.

The occurrences of Group-Gestalt Closure in the personnel
and in the client represented two end-points that were the
results of daily effort and thought invested by many staff members. The role of the clinical director in this process was to bring
these efforts to a head at a timely juncture.

Having placed the cart before the horse, so to speak, in discussing the goals of the clinical program first, we will now turn
to a discussion of what the client experienced on his first contact
with the rehabilitation team, i.e., diagnosis and evaluation.

## INITIAL DIAGNOSIS AND EVALUATION

The evaluation-diagnosis of new patients leads to classifying
statements about what is wrong with him. In one sense, the
evaluating and diagnostic processes are so complex that no
adequate accounting can be given of them; in another sense,

they are so self-evident that no accounting need be given of them. This is the case because the so-called processes are the responses of the individuals who make up the diagnosing-evaluating team. These responses are a conglomeration of emotional reactions, intellectual efforts, and recollections from past experience. When the team meets and compares its responses ("findings," as we prefer to call them) and discusses them, a consensus is arrived at which is summarized by the senior staff members in appropriate terminology. This becomes the diagnosis; another statement presents the needs of the client. This is followed by a third statement—the recommendation as to what is to be done to meet the needs of the client.

## CONTINUOUS EVALUATION AND PROGRAM ADAPTATION

Since the diagnosis is a summing up in a few words of the responses of the staff to the client, it is not a fixed entity and may change either as a result of a change in the client or in the staff's responses to him. In view of the fluidity of this situation, personnel in direct contact with clients need orientation to the idea of *continuous evaluation* and program adaptation. This is implemented by charging them with the responsibility of calling impromptu on-the-spot conferences of all available staff members for review of a client's case whenever they observed significant changes in him. In this manner, timely and precise clarification of the nature of the various problems confronting the client was facilitated.

A client was rarely given a rehabilitation prescription, but was encouraged to follow his own interests or to choose among various activities to learn which ones suited him best. The important thing was to have a wide range of learning experiences accessible to the client and that he came to recognize that he and the rehabilitation staff had a common task in learning what his assets, liabilities, and needs were and how they might be most effectively met. If the client's emotional problem or stage of psychological development was such that he was incapable of this recognition, and if he repeatedly made choices that were clearly self-defeating, it might be necessary to require him to accept direction from a staff member or to accept group therapy or individual psychotherapy.

## PRESCRIPTION AND RECOMMENDATIONS

It was stated previously that a client was rarely given a rehabilitation prescription. By "rehabilitation prescription" we mean an order to carry out a specific standardized procedure designated by name, such as training in a particular craft, education in a particular course, or engaging in a particular recreational activity. The reason for such infrequent use of prescriptions was based on the realistic consideration that it was exceedingly rare that a client was well enough known for anyone to say what the indications were for a particular prescription. It made a considerable moral impact on the client if the staff adhered faithfully to a policy of trying to put across to him that none of them could do more than engage in a fact-finding mission, in conjunction with him, on his behalf. To put this across successfully required that his helpers not yield to the temptation of appearing to know what was best for him by telling him what to think or by making his decisions for him.

If, due to the pain a client suffered from his emotional illness, he was clearly unable to think or decide in his own behalf, then an approach aimed at relieving the pain was indicated. This is the province of therapy as distinguished from rehabilitation. Therapeutic measures included affectionate, comforting, protecting relationships with those staff members best able to provide them. Here it might be essential for appropriate staff members "to take over" and do the patient's thinking for him whenever he was at a loss to think for himself. It might also be necessary to prescribe appropriate pharmacological agents.

## INFORMAL (LAISSEZ-FAIRE)
## MILIEU REHABILITATION

In the daily practice of a rehabilitation program with a steady influx of new clients, it is useful to adopt the local idiom for the concepts used. The concept of informal or *laissez-faire* milieu rehabilitation was never referred to as such in this project. Terms such as "free-choice," "free-lance," or "self-selected program" were generally preferred to convey the idea that the client was free to work out his own destiny and make use of the accessibility of facilities and personnel as he saw fit. In like manner, personnel were also defined as free of any particular responsibility to the client other than the general expectation of being receptive and responsive to him. A number of clients discovered personnel and activities, and made effective use of them in their own self-rehabilitation. In some instances, the selections made by clients were surprising to the staff and would not have been recommended on the basis of the initial diagnosis and evaluation.

### ORGANIZED MILIEU REHABILITATION

The first word of the concept, "organized milieu rehabilitation," refers to personnel rather than to the client in that it has to do with the selection of personnel who are to be responsible for exploring the development of particular kinds of relationships with the client. The selection of both personnel and the kind of relationships was made in staff conferences and came about as the result of consensus of the staff.

### PERSONALITY MATCHING

Personality matching is an essential component of all aspects of milieu rehabilitation. It is, however, an exploratory endeavor and has not reached the point where a matching could be prescribed prior to an actual meeting of the two personalities in question. The most that can be done at present is to maximize the opportunities for personality combination to occur and to facilitate their continuation when they are accompanied by constructive motivational change.

The policy adopted in this regard by the directors of this project may be summed up by stating that every effort was made to interest all personnel, whatever their educational background

or professional training, in becoming well acquainted with clients
in an informal manner. The hoped-for sequence of events was
that acquaintance would lead to meaningful affective involvement, which would in turn progress to a well-understood working
engagement with the client. The method adopted for providing
guidance of personnel-client relationships was threefold: 1)
scheduling frequent meetings of personnel to discuss their dealings with clients; 2) encouraging informal group discussions; and
3) individual consultations with the psychiatric staff. Personnel
were encouraged not only to have one-to-one acquaintanceship
with patients, but to have group meetings as well. Some personnel were urged or even requested to have scheduled group
discussions with clients, focusing on the personnel's special areas
of knowledge and experience.

On the basis of these efforts we have made some progress in
learning how to match the personality qualities of personnel with
those of patients in order to obtain rehabilitative or therapeutic
results. For example, the sprightly, alert, quick-thinking, fast-
talking members of the staff, if they are also warm, friendly and
cheerful, are often able to establish constructive relationships
with patients in acute turmoil. On the other hand, the blunt,
forthright, challenging person who is at home with cynicism
can frequently relate with paranoid patients. The slow-moving,
docile, placid individuals with infinite patience, who are thoughtful and reflective, can establish relationships with patients with
anxiety reactions; if they are also thick-skinned and able to take
considerable punishment, they can meet the needs of nagging,
agitated, depressed patients. Individuals who are sullen, mulish,
defiant, arrogant, and gifted with great tenacity are especially
valuable in meeting the manic patient in head-on collisions, which
builds a relationship endowed with much-needed consistency.

These generalizations are, of course, still in the impressionistic
stage of development. As has been observed, the matter of
individual personality make-up transcends the individual's particular professional background.

There is another fruitful area of personality matching that
has been but little explored, namely, its use in selecting con-

sultants to assist personnel in their work with patients. An example is the vocational counselor who, by virtue of his personality and background, is able to give both a faithful representation of the outside employer's point of view and the precise reasons for a client's unacceptablity for employment. These reasons are often revealing to other staff members and can lead them to bend their efforts with the client in a more realistic direction.

### GROUP THERAPY

It has been briefly mentioned that personnel were urged and even requested to conduct regularly scheduled group discussions with clients. These discussions were probably the most representative example of an application of the guiding principle adopted in directing the rehabilitation project—the principle of facilitating open, unexpurgated expression of inner responses on the part of personnel and clients in order to come to grips with the emotional (and hence motivational) center of gravity of all who have dealings with one another.

The significance of persuading personnel to engage in group therapy is that it was applied to wholly inexperienced and untutored personnel as well as to the psychiatrically sophisticated. An advantage of placing an inexperienced person in the role of group therapist is that both he and the client members of the group are in the same boat of having a new and unfamiliar role to fill. This relationship fosters a "*we* have a job to do together—let's do it" attitude rather than an "I am here to help you" attitude. The latter is a difficult one for a psychiatrist to escape.

In the course of the three years' funding period of the project, group therapy was conducted by two vocational counselors, two registered nurses, a rehabilitation counselor, a physical therapist, a social worker, and four psychiatrists. The group conducted by the rehabilitation counselor is one of particular importance, partly because he was wholly inexperienced and partly because his success suggests the value of the group therapy method for rehabilitation counselors in general. His group was, from the outset, topic-centered: it dealt primarily with the occupational sector of the clients' lives. An account of a typical group meeting, written by the counselor, is presented below:

"Rehabilitation people present at today's meeting, 10:00 A.M. to 11:15 A.M. are: Mr. R., Mr. N., Mrs. N., Mr. B., Mr. Y., Mr. Q., Mrs. C., Mr. O. and Miss U.

"The aim of this morning's meeting was to educate the group in preparing and conducting themselves for a job interview with a prospective employer. I first explained how a person's physical appearance must be kept in mind when being seen for a job interview. Also, how a person goes about selling himself to an employer and how one must bring out the good points in oneself and discuss one's assets, not liabilities. One should never tell an employer that he was fired, or was found too slow on the job, etc.

"A socio-drama was put on and Mr. R. was picked by me to act as the personnel manager who interviewed prospective employees. The whole thing was taken very seriously by the entire group, which was quite happy to cooperate. Mr. O. volunteered first and applied for a job, "breaking off" (slang for a production-line procedure). He handled the job interview very poorly. During the interview he acted quite silly and laughed inappropriately. Mr. O. was corrected and was told how he had handled the interview.

"Mrs. C. was the second person to volunteer, and applied for work as a hotel or restaurant working manager. Mrs. C. did a remarkable job during the interview, and not only handled herself well, but really knew what she was talking about regarding the duties of a working manager. Mrs. C. was hired for the position by Mr. R.

"Mr. B. was next to volunteer, and he applied for a waiter's or cook's job. He did not handle the job interview very well and talked about being slow on former jobs and also mentioned that he had been fired. He was warned by Mr. R. not to talk about one's bad points during an employment interview, and was told that he should talk only about his good points. Mr. R. pointed out that a prospective employee should always talk about his assets, not his liabilities. Mr. R. tried to learn how much Mr. B. knew about waiter's work. When asked about various procedures to follow in waiting on people, it was learned that he did not know too much about that.

"Miss U. was asked if she would like to be interviewed and she flatly refused. She wanted no part of it. It was brought out by me at this time that this socio-drama was quite serious and should not be taken lightly since they would all have to go through this realistically some day. I made a point that this had educational value, and that it was not put on to make fun of anyone, etc. The group realized this, and enjoyed this socio-drama very much, as I learned from the various people after the meeting.

"Mr. B., Miss U., and Mr. O. were not too attentive during the meeting. Miss U. looked flatly into space and seemed unaware about what was going on.

"Mr. N. was the last to vounteer and be interviewed. He applied for a job in precision plating. He handled the job interview beautifully, and when asked what the difference was between first plating and precision plating, he displayed a remarkable knowledge. The group enjoyed his dissertation and explanation, and thought it was quite educational. He impressed the employer (Mr. R.) favorably and was hired for the job.

"The people who were not interested today will be asked to participate in the job interview at next Thursday's meeting."

This sample of a group session suggests the extent to which a realistic pinpointing of problems can be carried.

Another noteworthy feature of the group therapy program was that clients were welcome to become members of more than one group. In general, the majority of clients in the rehabilitation counselor's group were at one time or another members of both a psychiatrist's group and a psychiatric social worker's group. In both of these groups the therapists were highly active both as participants and in giving direct psychodynamic interpretations in the midst of emotionally charged interactions. By and large, the psychiatrists focused on the clients' relations within the group, and the social workers focused on the clients' relations with their families, but there was considerable overlap between the two groups in these respects, as well as with the rehabilitation counselor's group.

### PSYCHOTHERAPY

Since each member of the rehabilitation team is a part of the human milieu experienced by the handicapped client, and since the client's fate is determined by the responses to him on the part of personnel, we have an obligation to learn what these responses are and to discover how to change them in ways that will better meet the client's needs. The effectiveness of the rehabilitation effort, therefore, obviously depends on there being a psychotherapeutic orientation behind the staff's everyday dealings with clients.

Our concept of individual psychotherapy has developed within the context of this philosophy of rehabilitation. An important aspect of this philosophy with respect to the use of individual psychotherapy is the view that its effectiveness with a great many clients depends on the extent to which it contributes to the effectiveness of other members of the rehabilitation team. In other words, individual psychotherapy was looked upon as being a label for *one* of the relationships a client might have with one part of the human milieu of the rehabilitation program. As such, the chief effort was to assign psychotherapy to its appropriate position in the Gestalt of the client's total program. An important part of this effort was to match the personality of the therapist with that of the client. By selecting the therapist best suited to conduct a search for those facets of the client's make-up and motivational pattern that could be articulated with corresponding traits of other people on the program, a productive, coordinated endeavor was achieved. It should be mentioned in passing that the selection of therapists is best made in conference with the staff as a whole rather than by any one individual.

A number of therapists who were staff members of the rehabilitation program developed a mode of psychotherapy that differed in a number of respects from conventional psychoanalytically oriented psychotherapy. In this mode of psychotherapy, the therapists functioned in a role resembling at times that of the coach and sparring-partner, and at times that of the guidance counselor. The goal of therapy was to reveal to the client more effective ways of handling his relations with others. The therapist used the one-to-one therapeutic relationship as an on-the-spot demonstration of the client's self-defeating behavior and accompanied it with a demonstration of self-fulfilling behavior accessible to the client. An example of this would be for the therapist to point out to the client, at a timely moment, his overt display of capacity to deal effectively with the therapist in the very area he represents as being his weakness in dealing with other people.

This type of therapeutic intervention was sometimes reinforced by enlisting the assistance of one or more co-therapists from members of the rehabilitation team who had a relationship with the client in work and recreational activities. From the perspective of present-day psychodynamics it is perhaps accurate to define the above-described psychotherapeutic endeavor as one that seeks to provide psychological aids to ego development.

As an example of this method, let us consider the case of a woman in her late 50's, who steadfastly refused to participate in any activity offered her. She spent day after day pacing the corridors, wringing her hands, whimpering, wailing, and moaning. Individual psychotherapy was of symptomatic value only in that there was cessation of this behavior during the therapeutic hour. However, her thoughts continually reverted back to the sources of her anguish. Two members of the staff were enlisted as co-therapists—a nurse and the homemaking instructor. It was pointed out to them that there was every indication that she was at a crucial point with respect to regaining control of herself. Continued failure to gain control would very likely result in commitment to a state hospital and a life of pacing the floor and wringing her hands.

The nurse and the instructor responded wholeheartedly in the affirmative when asked if they thought they would have the patience both to hear her out when she wished to talk with them and to persuade her to engage in activities in the homemaking department. The patient was told by her therapist that, if she wished to avoid the fate of lifelong hospitalization, it was crucially necessary for her to use her last vestige of self-control to force herself to engage in activities. The patient responded, in pleading desperation, "What should I do?"

The patient was then instructed to seek out the nurse and ask her what she could do to begin the process of making herself useful to herself and her family. The patient responded to this realistic account of her situation by ceasing to whimper and wring her hands and asking, "Where is the nurse?" The immediate outcome of this arrangement was that she spent the next day with the homemaking instructor and baked a cake. From that point on she took part in the homemaking activities and assisted nurses on the ward. She also began to discuss plans for the future in her psychotherapy appointments. She progressed steadily and, in time, took her place in her own home with her daughter and granddaughter.

The rather large proportion of clients on the program who presented exceptionally difficult problems, and the fact that the program was located in a psychiatric setting, were factors which led rehabilitation personnel to exert considerable pressure in efforts to persuade the administrators that clients were in need of individual psychotherapy.

In general, the point of view of the clinical administrators was that individual psychotherapy should be used to accomplish a specific, sharply defined goal. They frequently took the stand that, when personnel requested psychotherapy for a client, it was either an expression of their rejection of the client or a symptom of disagreement among personnel as to the client's needs. Many a staff conference was held for the purpose of clarifying a client's situation in the program. The outcome of a number of these conferences was a clear depiction of the effectiveness of a group of workers in bringing about personality and behavior changes in clients for whom individual psychotherapy had been a source of immobilizing puzzlement.

One type of client who would be considered a likely candidate for individual psychotherapy was the isolated patient who was unable to accept group therapy and who withstood the efforts of personnel to break through his pattern of alienation. Here a therapist-member of the rehabilitation staff would be chosen.

A number of individual psychotherapists conducted their therapeutic relationships with clients in a manner consistent with their training in psychoanalytically oriented psychotherapy. There were variations in the degree to which they sought to maintain an impersonal relationship with the client or followed a policy of noncommunication with the client's relatives, family, physician, teachers, etc., or the staff of the rehabilitation program. The desires of a therapist in this regard were fully respected by the rehabilitation staff and utilized as a basis for selecting therapists.

A number of clients who suffered from anxiety arising from unconscious conflicts needed therapists who were, to a varying degree, dissociated from the rehabilitation program. For some of these clients, rehabilitation and treatment had to be completely dissociated for either to be effective. Rehabilitation efforts in their behalf often had to be entirely centered on the development of assets, since treatment of psychopathology was being taken care of elsewhere. For still other clients in psychotherapy, the rehabilitation program served as a *laissez-faire* sheltered workshop or recreational center in that the organized thought and rehabilitation efforts of personnel were unplanned and left to come about spontaneously.

Milieu rehabilitation, as the reader may already have surmised, is practically a synonym for moral treatment and its inner working.

# XIV

## Community Psychiatry: A Growing Source of Social Confusion

The federal government and the 50 states are presently embarking on a bold experiment to bring relief from the distress of mental illness. The experiment consists of establishing partnerships between community-based mental health programs and community leaders in more than 1,000 localities throughout the country.

In localities that plan to acquire mental health programs, community leadership is especially pleased with the prospect of having troublesome people taken care of without delay. Mental health professionals, on the other hand, are especially pleased with the prospect of community resources being made immediately available to their convalescing patients. In short, each partner has the expectation that the other is ready to take on the problems he sends him. Each partner, furthermore, bases his expectation on his own criteria for distinguishing between problems arising from the inequities, dissatisfactions, and disagreements normal to everyday life and those due to mental illness.

### DEFINITION AND DIVISION OF RESPONSIBILITY

The indefinability of mental illness and the absence of objective tests for it are inescapable realities. They are realities that place

246

insoluble difficulties in the way of those who attempt to draw up agreements assigning specific and fixed divisions of labor between those responsible for the citizen affairs of the community and those responsible for the mentally ill.

The intangibility, tentativeness, and subjective nature of psychiatric judgments are perhaps partially responsible for the tendency of the psychiatric profession to include all human mishaps and vicissitudes within its boundaries. The obligation to prevent mental illness is an added force that fosters extension of this tendency to the point of including all aspects of human behavior. After all, it does not require a great deal of imagination to identify a given bit of behavior    either    as    an early form of a psychiatric symptom or as injurious to someone else's future mental health—especially if the someone else is a child.

It would appear that, *to be successful, a mental health program must first win acceptance of the view that the members of a community are to be regarded as patients (or potential patients) first and as citizens second, and that the mental health professional should occupy the key position of coordinating community functions.* Psychiatric guidance of community life would presumably be expected to bring about a greater sensitivity in the interpersonal relations of the community, a greater sympathy for the emotional needs of individuals, and a reduction in the occurrence of mental illness. This preventive success would also, presumably, be matched by a corresponding increase in the effectiveness of community contributions to the rehabilitation of patients discharged from hospital care.

The rapid evolution of psychiatry as a social force since World War II is a phenomenon of American history that is worthy of considerable respect. It is a matter of particular cogency, moreover, that psychiatry has been linked primarily with the emotions and hence considered as a means of transformation from unhappiness to happiness. For Americans, this would place psychiatry in a position of prominence as a major partner of government in fostering the citizen's pursuit of happiness.

The alacrity and eagerness with which Americans are currently supporting the community mental health center movement is strongly indicative of a considerable unmet need of some kind in American community life today. We must, however, scrutinize more thoroughly just what the nature of this unmet need may be. Might it not be a need that can be met by provisions other than psychiatric services? Might it not be that some other provision would be more socially wholesome than widespread stimulation of public alarm over sickness and prevention of sickness of the mind, and the morbid preoccupation, self-doubt, and passivity such propaganda tends to engender?

### CONSTRUCTIVE ATTITUDES TOWARD INDIVIDUALITY: THE UNDERLYING CONSIDERATIONS

It is critically important that mental health workers and their volunteer helpers recognize the extent to which the stigma of mental illness springs from the total inability of legal, medical, philosophical, or other minds to define mental illness. This inability underlies the present demoralizing state of affairs, where every individual senses not only the mysteriousness of the indefinable but also the ominous fact that he is vulnerable to being labeled as mentally ill by anyone of influence who sees fit to do so. In view of this, mental health workers may have to seek as their primary goal means of establishing an attitude, within their own group and within the community, that is based on affectionate respect for all troubled people, including the mentally ill. The attitude we seek suggests that mental health professionals could benefit the community by acknowledging two errors of the past that tend to persist even now: 1) the error of professional oversell, and 2) the error of professional overcontrol.

The attitude we seek also suggests that we mental health professionals could benefit from acknowledging that we have had a goal-defeating tendency to underestimate the capacities of others:

- We tend to underestimate the patient's capacity for spontaneous recovery.
- We tend to underestimate the patient's capacity to expedite the recovery of other patients.

- We tend to underestimate the capacity of individual citizens and citizen groups to expedite the recovery of mentally ill patients.

- We tend to underestimate the capacity of individual citizens and citizen groups to prevent mental illness by early action to help people in trouble.

- We tend to underestimate the capacity of individuals and groups to expedite the rehabilitation of persons handicapped by the effects of past mental illness.

Acknowledgment, by the staff of a mental health center, of these elements can lead to facing the fact that the greatest need of our communities is for *settings* in which citizens and citizen groups can learn helpful attitudes and ways to help one another. Specifically, our communities are in great need of *multipurpose activity centers for all age groups* and for all conditions of ability and disability. These centers, to be effective, should be operated by citizens fully representative of all the people of the community rather than by professional people. They should be designed to provide maximum opportunities for people to meet and mingle in a diversity of settings and activities. They should, furthermore, be under guidance that favors the development of conditions that will foster the emergence and growth of affectionate respect for the individual.

Perhaps we should call a spade a spade and make it clear that, as mental health professionals, we feel we have but few lessons to teach. We have, on the other hand, the obligation to try to describe the helping attitudes we seek in ourselves and others in regard to troubled individuals in the community.

Talking about troubled people as patients and generalizing about abstract considerations does not get us very far. Our greatest hope for progress is in working together to help specific individuals. We need concrete examples of ways of relating to troubled persons, such as:

- If we feel like pitying a person, we should exercise forebearance and restrain our impulse to express our pity lest we make him feel more humiliated and demeaned.

- If we feel patronizing toward a person, the same considerations should be borne in mind.
- If we feel like criticizing a person or admonishing him on how to behave, we should consult with our colleagues. By discussion with others we can better ascertain whether we really can understand the person we would help better than he understands himself.

### PARTICIPANT CITIZENSHIP AND
### COMMUNITY DEVELOPMENT

The above considerations lead us to a topic that is very likely to be a fruitful source of answers. It is the topic of community management and the individual citizen's role in it, a topic that has come to the fore quite rapidly since the post-World War II social revolution, with its attendant increases in social and geographic mobility, with its affluent majority, with its ethnic minorities in poverty, and with its varying degrees of social dislocation.

The shapers of public policy should remind themselves that we have been living in an epoch of social reform for several decades, and that the present day is notable for a marked acceleration in the pace of that reform. They should be aware that reforms are taking place in several areas simultaneously, and that some of these reforms may unwittingly interfere with or duplicate the efforts of others. Concern over the harmful effects on the individual of mechanistic, standardized, impersonal methods of mass management have been voiced repeatedly in Anglo-American literature ever since Charles Dickens portrayed the sordid consequences of industrialization over 125 years ago.

It is also pertinent to note that American industry and American education have long been hosts to applied psychology and that a new growth in attention to the needs of the individual is developing.

### COMMUNITY MANAGEMENT AND
### COMMUNITY PSYCHIATRY

More pertinent still to the present issue are the parallel changes in recent history in community management, on the one hand, and in management of the mentally ill on the other. Both areas were designated as objects of shame by telling critiques of the American social scene: Lincoln Steffens' *The Shame of the Cities* (1904) and Albert Deutsch's *The Shame of the States* (1948). The latter described the deplorable snake-pit level of care in state hospitals in America. The historical antecedent of Deutsch's book—*A Mind That Found Itself* by Clifford Beers— could just as well have had Deutsch's title, although it appeared in 1909, a few years after Steffens' book.

The reform movements in community management and in mental health management have both been gaining momentum for over 60 years, but lately their development has greatly accelerated. These historical considerations are helpful in understanding how the two separate phenomena of community management and community psychiatry impinge on each other.

The activities of community management take place in the domain of political decisions affecting socioeconomic concerns. The activities of community psychiatry, on the other hand, take place in the domain of medical scientific decisions affecting human health. Community psychiatry is in principle ethically constrained to apply the exacting demands of the scientific method. In practice, however, its generalizations are highly speculative, and its effectiveness depends almost wholly on personal experience and very little on application of scientific rules or formulae. Community management, on the other hand, insofar as its activity is sociopolitical in nature, is concerned with the desires of individual citizens and of citizen groups. As a descendant of the American political tradition, community management has inherited the task of securing the rights of all men to life, liberty and the pursuit of happiness in the locale in which they live. Leaders of the community clearly seem to have a responsibility to determine the goals of community development and advancement, on the one hand, and of participant citizenship development and advancement on the other.

American idealists of the extreme right and the extreme left have recoiled from the dehumanizing excesses of Hitlerism and Stalinism. One might wonder if they, and with them many less doctrinaire voters, have lost faith in political processes due to the shock of observing such dehumanization being directed by *political* leaders. One might wonder further if this has *resulted in a tendency for faith to be transferred to scientific authorities and especially those who concern themselves with human health.* Such a transfer of faith would not be at all likely in America, however, if Americans were paying adequate attention to the historical fact that the American political tradition is based on entirely different values and has an entirely different structure from those of Germany and Russia. Indeed we all need to recall that respect for individuality and sensitivity was the reason for its original founding. It has, furthermore, been political endeavor—and not science—which has led the reforms of modern history to correct the dehumanizing effects of both the old and the new industrial revolution. Can we now be entering a period when political leadership is abdicating? Or are its powers being usurped by the technocrat?

In connection with the above considerations, it is relevant to call attention to the marked extent to which community psychiatry, in its planning at least, seems to find it necessary to elaborate its endeavors, both in breadth of scope and refinement of detail, to exercise influence on every community function that may conceivably affect the destinies of the individual citizen, and to be the coordinator of such functions.

This planning would seem to be based on an assumption that community psychiatry alone has the proper background and values to show respect for human individuality and sensitivity to the individual's right to be a fully participant citizen. It is at this precise point that one must ask if either the community psychiatrist or the social scientist has firm evidence that sociopolitical leadership *at the local community level* is incapable of bringing about further advances in the development and maturation of the American community. It would seem highly unlikely that such evidence exists.

It would appear more likely, however, that certain consequences have resulted from the great increase in the number of scientific specialists appointed to positions in the constantly expanding federal and state agencies. The most important of these consequences are those which result in the creation of climates of opinion and images that encourage views favorable to placing professional specialists in charge of public affairs rather than individuals chosen on the basis of their being representatives of the electorate. The loyalties of specialists, like those of other people, tend to rest with those of their own kind. The problem and danger is that specialists may deceive themselves and other people that they are not vulnerable to vested interests or to playing favorites. The professional political leader, on the other hand, has less tendency to be self-deluded in this regard and is far more aware of the nature of political ethics as it has evolved in safeguarding the authority of the American electorate.

It may well be the better part of wisdom for proponents of community psychiatry and for community leaders to reexamine their position vis-à-vis one another. Community psychiatry faces the predicament of an acute shortage of trained manpower at the same time that it makes plans for programs for prevention of mental illness which are largely based on speculative considerations and, possibly, wishful thinking. Community leaders, for their part, are faced with the necessity of embarking on programs of community development which have psychosocial aspects that could very well have as much effect in preventing mental illness as those contemplated by mental health professionals. It is, furthermore, entirely likely that these programs could be more effective in preventing mental illness *precisely because* they would be part of creative endeavors with positive progressive goals and would be free of morbid, hypochondriacal connotations.

It is a social curiosity of our times that community psychiatry and the community mental health center movement receive little in the way of genuine active support from the majority of psychiatrists, just as the Medicare movement had little support from the medical profession in general. Indeed, it would appear that medical people, including psychiatrists, who give direct care to patients, and "old time" private practitioners with little time for extra-professional activities have little political influence, and that "old-time" politicians are listening to the new breed of salaried professionals who can spend more time propagandizing in favor of health care reforms directed by themselves.

## PUBLIC POLICY AND THE PURSUIT OF HAPPINESS

The American way of life is currently undergoing a revolutionary change. Deliberate effort must be made to avoid loss of familiarity with even the most permanent-seeming features of one's immediate environment. Serious study is required to keep abreast of developments outside one's private world. Without it there is a growing risk of losing awareness of the community of which one is a part and of becoming socially disoriented as a functioning citizen.

Periods characterized by an accelerating tempo of change would be expected to be accompanied by more widespread social disorientation of the citizenry than periods with little change. Scientific and technologic advances are currently contributing to further social disorientation by producing increasing numbers of specialized disciplines, with attendant uncoordinated compartmentalization.

This may well be the most hazardous period yet faced in the history of American sociopolitical development. It is characterized, on the one hand, by an extraordinary network of efficient industrial and financial organization and communications technology. In marked contrast to this effectiveness of American organization for great mechanical accomplishments is the abovementioned social disorientation and absence of meaningful organization in American community life and in the lives of private citizens.

The greatest American accomplishments of modern times have resulted from standardization of technologic procedures and the development of generalizable abstractions from scientific endeavor. Both of these accomplishments pursue the value of commonality at the expense of individuality. The American mentality has been strongly conditioned by these accomplishments to seek solutions of widespread social problems by standardized techniques and production line methods.

The confusions and anxieties associated with modern social disorientation, and their appearance of having kinship with psychiatric ills, have greatly contributed to the rapid growth of the mental health movement in America today. As newly established community mental health centers begin responding to applicants for services, they find themselves promptly confronted with the problems that attend the assignment of priorities to mental ills rather than to social problems.

The inescapable necessity to assign priorities, and the resulting selection of persons to receive immediate services and those to be refused services—to cite the extremes—are attended by the highlighting of a major unmet and unrecognized need in the community. This need is in the long run probably *greater* than the need for mental health service. It is the need of the present-day citizen for access to means of social orientation to the community life of which he is a part. This need cannot be met by any agency other than responsible community leadership.

It is a matter of major importance, however, to awaken to the fact that community leadership gives evidence of laboring under the impression that this basic social need will be met by the introduction of community psychiatry and community mental health programs. It is even more important to recognize that an unspoken mutual misunderstanding exists between psychiatry and civil leadership. The source of this misunderstanding is perhaps more or less readily and adequately explained by the observation that psychiatry has permitted itself to be oversold and extended beyond its competence and outside the domain in which its application is socially relevant and appropriate. The consequence of this misunderstanding is the adverse effect it could well have in retarding the adoption of civil programs for development of relevant citizen participation in community life.

### THE POVERTY OF MEDICAL SCIENTISM
### AS A GUIDE TO PUBLIC POLICY

For many decades there has been a trend in American politics in the direction of relieving, at public expense, all human suffering and hardships resulting from disease and injury. In recent years this trend has acquired sufficient strength and persistence to effect the provision of hospital and medical care for most of the ills of large segments of the population. The involvement of political leaders and governmental administrators in the organization and provision of medical services has been accompanied by a gradual and almost unwitting adoption of what amounts to a *medical outlook* as the determining component of what appears to be a newly emerging political philosophy. Indeed, it is no exaggeration to point out that at times government seems to indicate that its primary function is that of keeping citizens healthy. In more and more instances it seeks to train the citizen in the ways of health, whether he likes it or not, and sometimes it seems to act as if the citizen is automatically expected to give up his political rights and individual liberties where matters of health are concerned. There is little doubt either that Americans are encouraged, almost to the point of morbidity, by both government and private agencies to be preoccupied with health concerns. It is not far-fetched to portray America as seeming to strive for the establishment of a Health Utopia as the acme of human accomplishment. As might be expected, however, preoccupation with health has had the inevitable result of calling more attention to disease than ever before. In other words, health-mindedness and disease-consciousness appear to be inseparable. It would seem self-evident that emphasis on health matters is not an appropriate basis for fostering citizen development. It would seem equally self-evident that citizens should not be encouraged to invoke "sickness in the head" as the explanation of personal discontent or of troublesome behavior in others. For community leadership to do so amounts to subversion of the self-respect and self-reliance of the individual citizen.

*DIVIDING-LINE BETWEEN SOCIAL*
*PROBLEMS AND MENTAL ILLNESS AND THE*
*DIVISION OF LABOR BETWEEN COMMUNITY*
*LEADERSHIP AND MENTAL HEALTH CENTER*

Plans for the establishment of mental health centers have for the most part been based on assumptions that mental health and psychiatric practices are to be extended into every conceivable trouble spot in the community. Little or no attention has been given to the possibility of undesirable social consequences of the application of psychiatric methods to social problems *as if they also* were matters of mental illness.

Such overextension of psychiatric effort with its concomitant over-applications of concepts of psychopathology, would seem, on the basis of past experience, to have the inevitable result of greatly increasing the numbers of people categorized as afflicted with mental illness and thereby compromised in the area of their rights. Such great increases in the apparent magnitude of the problem could not conceivably be matched by a corresponding increase in psychiatric services. It would seem that such an outcome would be accompanied by a reaction of rather considerable disappointment on the part of the community and with it a rather complete disenchantment with mental health services.

Another adverse consequence of overextension of efforts in the area of community psychiatry is the effect it could well have in diverting effort away from development of community organization to meet the very large unmet needs resulting from social problems.

The fact that mental illness and social problems may both arise from an interplay of psychological needs of individuals with social situations is rather obviously a major source of the dilemma that must be faced in making decisions of public policy regarding mental health.

Almost everyone is probably aware of the fact that, or assumes that, relief from gross socioeconomic stress and deprivation can, by itself, be expected to result in some lessening of the problems of mental illness.

What may be equally apparent to many, but is accorded very little in the way of official recognition or support, is the fact that socially transmitted attitudes toward human individuality *as such* have a great deal to do with the precipitation and cessation of attacks of mental illness. This fact is a matter of telling importance to everyone interested in advancing the values of democratic, open societies. Indeed, the importance of socially transmitted attitudes brings us face to face with the consideration that the most effective measure of modern psychiatry turns out to be sociopolitical in nature rather than of purely medical origin. Demonstration of respect for the individuality of hospitalized patients on the part of mental hospital personnel is accompanied by a very considerable shortening of the duration of attacks of mental illness—from a matter of years to a matter of weeks. Indeed it is fair to state that the greatest gains made in the treatment of the mentally ill were those which resulted from unlocking the doors of mental hospitals and recruiting volunteers from the community to take part in resocializing patients.

It is worthwhile to place particular emphasis on the importance of the political component of these sociopolitical measures. The term "political" is applied here in its basic sense of having to do with the exercise of individual preference and influence in everyday life in accordance with the propensities of human nature to help friends and hinder enemies.

The above considerations can be profitably regarded as strong indications that both the mental illnesses and the social problems of individuals are but different forms of failure of morale and competence which vary in frequency, severity and duration *in correlation with the level of sociopolitical maturity of the society to which the individuals belong.* In short, the higher the level of socio-political maturity a people reaches, the more it respects the individuality of its members, and the more it applies tolerance, forbearance, and helpfulness in reaction to discordant, deviant, idiosyncratic, or indigent behavior.

## HISTORICAL PERSPECTIVE

From the perspectives of history there are more than a few indications that physicians did not acquire responsibility for deviant behavior because the latter was demonstrably due to illness. Indeed, historical evidence suggests that physicians acquired such responsibility because they were the only authoritative group in the Western world endowed with a humanistic value system, uncomplicated by theological confusion. This happened to be the case because the medical tradition traced its origin back to the pre-Christian social teachings of Hippocrates and the philosophers of classical Greece. Christian churchmen and jurists had their own reasons for being more than willing to turn such problems over to physicians. At least, this finally became true when they came to their senses and looked back in shame and horror at the witchcraft madness they had so vigorously supported. It would appear, then, that medicine became responsible for deviant individuals by permitting itself to be used as an expedient means for administering a more humane and nonpunitive social control of these persons than had existed previously.

Thus it happened that physicians—become psychiatrists—were placed in a position to be the earliest to discover the critical importance of sensitivity and respect for individuality to the destinies of those who suffer dislocation from the mainstream of community life.

It must be fairly apparent that this country is rapidly reaching a point in its history which will require community management to assume responsibility for programs to raise the level of the community's sociopolitical maturity by increasing its sensitivity to the individuality of its citizens and by making judicious provisions to meet their social needs as persons.

These matters have a bearing of the utmost importance on the judgment used in reaching a decision as to where to draw the line in the division of labor between the sociopolitical leadership of the community and the mental health center. Our discussion thus far indicates that it is imperative that far more investment be made to develop a full spectrum of appropriately coordinated educational, occupational, recreational, and psychological services as well as welfare and family service agencies. In the long run, such an investment would be effective and economical as a first line of recourse immediately available to citizens who have suffered setbacks of any kind. The very existence of such recourse would in itself lead to considerable reduction in the number of problem people presently thought of as requiring the psychiatric services of a mental health center. The mental health center would accordingly receive as patients only those individuals who had not responded to the community's efforts and who were incapacitated by a degree of psychopathology actually requiring study by psychiatric specialists.

## SPECULATIONS ON THE FUTURE

Looking to the future, it does not appear unreasonable to expect that community developments will meet more or even most of the needs now thought to require the services of specialists in mental diseases. Psychiatric practitioners can be expected to decrease in number and to concentrate their efforts on patients with severe, intractable mental disease. Nonpsychiatric physicians, on the other hand, can be expected to receive greater numbers of patients referred to them by community agencies since the increased contact of the latter with the public will result in discovering more people with milder emotional states amenable to readily available medicinal treatment.

The need for direct psychiatric services on a large scale is likely to pass out of the picture rather rapidly as soon as the sociopolitical leadership of the community takes active measures to develop social sensitivity to individuality and social attitudes of respect for individuality at the same time that it undertakes programs to extend community services at appropriate levels of quality and quantity.

Future historians may some day designate recent modern history as a period of *cultural lag* between the time when early nineteenth century mental hospital physicians discovered the relationship between social attitudes toward individuality and the destinies of individuals and the late twentieth century's application of that discovery to community life in general.

Psychiatry should in no way attempt to increase the size of the domain under its authority, for by so doing it not only misleads the community but also spares it from making the moral effort that must be made to develop participant citizenship and social respect for individuality, which are sorely needed to achieve social solidarity in community life today.

To quote from Shakespeare—"the time is out of joint," and care must be taken not to choose means for rearticulation which establishes a new order at the cost of the old liberties. If community leadership falters too long, *it is conceivable that matters will be taken in hand by the federal government in combination with the great industrial corporations.*

# XV

## Community Mental Health:
## A New Search for Social Orientation

### AMERICAN PSYCHIATRY:
### INSPIRED HUMANISM

The most unique of medical specialties (and perhaps medicine's black sheep) is psychiatry. It was the first to form an organization of its own, which, from the beginning, was completely independent of the American Medical Association. Psychiatry is also unique on two other scores: 1) it cannot legitimately export specific practices developed in America because it deals with the problems of individualities in relation to the cultural attitudes of Americans; and 2) it did not originate in response to the demands of society for its own protection (in view of this, it is significant that American psychiatry, according to Dr. Gregory Zilboor [52], was from its very origin characterized by its inspired humanism).

### INSPIRED HUMANISM:
### INITIAL SUCCESS AND THEN FAILURE

Thus, in the early decades of its moral treatment phase, the American mental hospital was most effective in bringing relief to the mentally ill. Indeed, the discharge rates of the 1820's, 30's, 40's and 50's were fully on a par with those of our most advanced mental hospitals today. After the Civil War these hospitals deteriorated in their humanistic aspects to a degree that actually impeded the healing powers of nature and almost eliminated recovery as a possibility.

Something may have been lacking in the perspective of the leaders of the moral treatment movement of our early psychiatric history. And, of course, unforeseen social changes of a destructive nature took place that helped bring the moral treatment movement to a halt. Studies which have been made of the entire history of the periods in question indicate that both explanations have some validity. It would seem reasonable to suggest that whatever it was that was missing in relation to the fate of the mentally ill must have had a close relationship to shortcomings in that period's social leadership, which failed to prevent the Civil War and its accompanying damage to American society.

More detailed study of that period suggests that one short-coming in the social attitude was the failure of the dominant ethnic group to extend its great respect for human individuality to members of other groups. Immigrants from Europe of different races and religions and black Americans were not accorded in-dividualized treatment in mental hospitals. It is not likely that they were given greater consideration by other social institutions. Another shortcoming appears to have been a marked tendency to ignore the very existence of interdependence among social insti-tutions and human groupings of all kinds.

### HISTORICAL PARALLELS

The relevance of the foregoing to present concerns lies in the degree of similarity between today's community mental health center movement and the moral treatment movement of the early nineteenth century. There are other similarities. For example, the progressive liberal spirit of the Jacksonian Era is credited his-torically with the rise of the common man and is in other respects similar to the past two or three decades of increasing social welfare and civil rights legislation. Both eras are likewise similar in regard to the presence of widespread social unrest and the occurrence of an unpopular war; namely, the Mexican War of the 1840's and the Vietnam War of our 1960's and 1970's.

To point out the likenesses of these two periods of history is to suggest that there is a possibility that our present mental health endeavors could undergo deterioration and end in much the same kind of failure that overtook the moral treatment movement after the Civil War.

### SOCIAL ORIENTATION: A STRIVING OF DEMOCRATIC PEOPLES—NOT A MATTER OF HEALTH

Public support for mental health movements, including that of moral treatment, can be seen as an expression of an unarticulated but fundamental striving of democratic peoples for social orientation which asserts itself most forcibly when the pace of social change is such that relative disorientation results. Democratic peoples cannot survive without social orientation, which is indispensable if they are to govern themselves successfully. The kinship between the anxiety of disorientation and the idea of mental illness in the public mind may be proposed as one reason underlying the emergence of public support for mental health movements during times of rapid social change. The difficulty lies in the fact that social orientation is not something that mental health services can provide. They should not, moreover, be expected to provide it, since it is not a matter of sickness and health but a matter of social leadership. Indeed, mental health agencies are in search of social orientation themselves.

Perhaps it is not too rash to suggest that this may be the first time in the history of our great American experiment that the entire populace in all walks of life have come to believe that their troubles and miseries are the result of problems which can be solved by applying scientific knowledge already at hand or which scientific research will make available in the near future. This belief is also quite naturally accompanied by expectations, and then by demands, for rapid solutions to problems in varying fields. Federally sponsored programs have done much to foster such beliefs, expectations, and demands. These programs have also included efforts to bring about the direct participation of citizens in the planning of programs in their capacity as consumers of social, health and other public services.

We live in an era in which large scale remedial action is set in motion by big government and private philanthropy to correct social evils as rapidly as they can be brought to light. However, our best intentioned efforts must somehow be going askew, for this selfsame era is even more conspicuous for its mounting volume of open conflict, contentiousness, protestation, and dissension. However, there are signs in practically all groups of a desire for rapport and collaboration.

### THE MENTAL HEALTH ENDEAVOR AND
### AVOIDANCE OF FALSE HOPE

The observation that our quickened pace of social progress is accompanied by even greater social unrest is a matter of some interest, especially when placed alongside the observation that the mental health movement has for several years now enjoyed strong support and relative tranquility. One may speculate that this is so because the mental health agency may occupy a special position in public fantasy as being neutral territory, free of prejudice, where humanistic acceptance prevails and where something called empathy is offered to desperate and troubled people. Thus, the most important task facing the mental health establishment may be that of reassessing its position both as a symbol and as a basis of new hope for resolution of conflicts threatening social solidarity.

There is much work to be done in gathering and interpreting vast amounts of data. One thing that can be said at present is that mental health occupies a position of great potential for truly enormous embarrassment if more groups feel encouraged to believe that it can provide social orientation at about the same time that mental health itself is becoming aware of its pressing need to become socially oriented in its own behalf. To avoid the disaster of such embarrassment, it behooves the mental health forces to acknowledge that they are in the same boat with other groups, and to seek to join forces with them in making a common inventory of the social realities of American life today.

It is suggested that the crucial problems of our time for the individual, for the group, for the community, and for the entire society, may be fruitfully explored as being a problem of social orientation. This problem is of relatively recent origin and has insidiously crept into the American social scene. Its existence is largely due to the preposterous situation that new knowledge and new techniques are being produced much, much faster than they can be absorbed.

## MISPLACED PRIORITIES: A SOURCE OF SOCIAL DISORIENTATION

We must consider what the priorities may be that we hold to and which may be related to social disorientation. It is probably fair to say that the highest priorities in American life are granted, in terms of both time and money, to activities related to 1) formal education, 2) transportation, and 3) entertainment. Relatively very little time or money is spent on small group activities in which sufficient continuity of relationship is sustained long enough to result in more than a superficial acquaintance. It would appear that modern industrial life has taught us to value ideas more highly than people, and to work harder to acquire knowledge of authoritative facts and scientific abstractions than of the individuality of those whose lives bear a relation of interdependence to our own.

Neglect of the uniqueness of human individuality may well be an important source of the problems we face. In relation to community mental health, this is a crucial issue, for mental health in itself defies definition. This is inescapable, since the uniqueness of the human individual extends to the point of requiring that each person be classified as one of a kind chemically, physiologically, anatomically, and psychologically. We must admit that this uniqueness is a nuisance that denies us the certain knowledge of whether such a thing as mental illness actually exists. There is the ever-present possibility that it is merely a label which one variety of unique people who happen to be in the majority apply to other varieties who happen to be in the minority. We should admit that our knowledge in this area is very limited and that many possibilities remain to be considered.

Considerations such as these could well be borne in mind in developing community mental health programs, especially in regard to preventive efforts based on case finding of incipient mental illness. It may never be possible to distinguish between the latter and a developmental phase of a particular unique individuality.

It may well be that community mental health is most effectively secured by community leadership that assumes responsibility for programs to raise the level of the community's sociopolitical maturity. Such programs would be aimed at increasing sensitivity to the individuality of its citizens and making judicious provisions to meet their social needs as persons.

### A CASE FOR THE ROLE OF
### LOCAL GOVERNMENT

Our concern about social orientation leads us to make a case for the role of local government in meeting the psychosocial needs of citizens for adequate orientation to their society and in meeting the needs of the public servants of organized society to be adequately oriented toward recognition of the uniqueness of the individuality of each citizen. There is much to commend this view, for it may be more realistic and more conducive to social solidarity than permeating the community with mental health programs to seek out early cases of mental illness. The latter course of action might tend to foster a social attitude of suspecting every act of nonconformity to be a tell-tale symptom of sickness of the mind. Such an attitude could be as socially divisive as the witchcraft period of our early history and could in no case be appropriate for sponsorship by government.

Government is always an art irrespective of the ideology behind it, and humanistic government is an art based on the humanist's affection for men and women in all their diversity. It is fair to say that the American people, in their practice of this art at the federal and state levels, have successfully propagated pluralistic solutions to sociopolitical problems in a manner that respects the fact of human diversity. They have also been successful thus far in limiting monistic developments to short-lived experimental application.

The glaring exception to this record of achievement is the American people's neglect of government at the local community level. There is little to be recognized in the modern history of city, town, or county government that would warrant classifying it as an art based on humanistic affection for people. Indeed, the main reason for federal legislation providing community poverty programs, model cities programs, and community mental health centers throughout America is to meet the needs that local governments have not met. These measures, however, do not go much beyond providing temporary symptomatic relief. Relatively few results have become visible from efforts made to identify and correct underlying social defects. Perhaps the origin of some of these defects is to be found in the early history of our local communities. I refer to the fact that in Massachusetts, most, if not all, towns were governed by their local church organizations for many decades. Can it be that a power vacuum developed in our cities and towns with the constitutional separation of church and state and the decline of church influence in later years? Is it not probable, furthermore, that this power vacuum would come to be filled by persons less endowed than their clerical predecessors in regard to sense of duty and stewardship to their community? Whatever the answer to these questions may be, it is plain that local government today is faced with an array of pressing human needs which it is almost wholly unprepared to meet. Local citizens, moreover, do not appear to expect local government to reflect the American political heritage. In fact, those of us who say "You can't fight city hall" will not hesitate to fight the federal government by putting pressure on our congressmen.

### RENEWED LOCAL GOVERNMENT:
### A KEY TO PROGRESS?

None of us can afford to let our courage fail us while learning and facing up to the facts of the social reality of our day. Some of these facts are long-standing truisms that somehow remain outside our field of attention; namely, that poverty, social conflict, civil disorder, delinquency, crime, emotional disturbances and retardation of children, mental breakdowns of adults, and long-term mental disability are all afflictions that have their origin and development in local communities. Is it not incongruous that local government is almost completely devoid of the resources needed to deal with these problems?

The principle we need to invoke is that no authority can reasonably be expected to meet the needs of those for whom it is responsible when that authority itself is half-starved and just barely able to assure its own survival. The urgency of the situation demands that full attention be given to the coincidence, if it is such, that America's state hospital system and its system of local government have both shown themselves to be socially, as well as financially, bankrupt at a time when society as a whole needs each of them for guidance more than ever before.

### NEW OPPORTUNITY AHEAD:
### THREE PROGRAMS NEEDED

There is today a growth of support in favor of fundamental changes both in local government and in state mental health services. Thus, there is reason to look forward to increasing opportunity for vitally important new measures to be instituted in the near future. It is imperative that full use be made of this prospective period of opportunity.

On the basis of our experience thus far, three separate endeavors suggest themselves which require the joint efforts of mental health professionals and local governmental authorities.

*1. Provision of new measures by local government to meet the needs of each citizen for information, guidance, advice, socialization, recreation, training, and education in a way that takes into account his individuality and personal situation so that his personality assets will have all possible opportunity to develop to fullest capacity. This endeavor would be the responsibility of citizen organizations and political leaders, and of educators, lawyers, psychologists, and social scientists.*

*2. Provision by local government of a full range of facilities within the community itself, to meet the needs of citizens afflicted with long-term mental disabilities. These facilities would be designed to provide each disabled citizen with an individualized rehabilitation program that would include the necessary variety of occupational, recreational and residential settings. Other facilities would be designed to provide similar settings on a lifelong basis, and shelter as required, for those individuals for whom rehabilitation goals may be unrealistic. Mental health professionals would serve as consultants to this type of endeavor but would not administer the programs.*

*3. Provision by local government of facilities for prompt treatment of individuals afflicted with acute mental illnesses. These facilities would probably function best as psychiatric units of general hospitals.*

In Chapter X, I discussed our administrative and clinical experiences at Solomon Center. The most impressive of these experiences was observing a large majority of patients undergo marked improvement in but a few weeks with relatively little in the way of formal treatment beyond pharmaceutical prescriptions and with a great deal in the way of informal personal attention and effort provided patients by everyone employed at the center.

This improvement should not, however, be attributed entirely to treatment efforts made at the center. There is much to suggest that ameliorative forces of considerable effectiveness arose spontaneously within the community due to the quality of human interest generated in this particular community by locating the entire treatment of the patient in its midst. At any rate, positive forces must be at work in this community in view of the fact that of some 600 admissions to the Inpatient Service, less than a dozen have required continuous hospitalization since admission.

These experiences raise the important matter of the uniqueness of each community and of the great need each community has for a person, or perhaps a task force of persons, to develop approaches to meaningful comprehension of the inner workings of the community. Study is needed in terms of scheduled formal activities and in terms of spontaneous informal activities as well.

Relative to this, we should be reminded that American psychiatric practices, as they have evolved in recent decades, are not suitable for application in most communities in the United States. Study is needed of each community to determine what the most suitable psychiatric approach might be as one element in the entire spectrum of community services already in existence or to be provided in the future.

## THE NEW PSYCHIATRY: ITS AROUSAL OF OLD SOCIAL PROBLEMS

The observation that marked improvement is the rule following admission to the community mental health center has another side to it that has great public importance. I refer to what may properly be called social relapses, since they may be without recurrence of mental illness, or may be accompanied by mild symptoms only reminiscent of the original illness. The exact number of such ex-patients is not yet known, but there is evidence that a fair proportion undergo loss of morale and personality regression, and settle into varying states of social dependency.

The occurrence of social dependency following mental illness is to be matched by another observation; namely, that it is not at all unlikely that our services as a community mental health center have the effect of arousing socially quiescent individuals and stirring them to greater activity, some of which may add to the diversity of community life but may or may not lead to the patient's filling a satisfactory social role. It would appear that the community mental health center may have the effect of reducing rather than increasing the tranquility of community life and of increasing rather than decreasing its overall social burden.

It would seem equally apparent, moreover, that the community mental health center could never meet the full array of emotional deprivation and personality underdevelopment of any community. This requires a close, ongoing working relationship with those who carry administrative responsibility for the community as a whole. In the absence of a community administrative body adequately staffed and equipped to serve its citizens, it is not likely that the community mental health center will be able to contribute much within the framework of its particular area of competence. It is more likely that the community mental health center will find itself immersed in case finding of social need and protesting the absence of community resources.

# References

1. Allen, N. *The treatment of the insane*. Albany: Joel Munsell, 1876, pp. 5-7, 14, 15.
2. Annual report of the Butler Health Center, 1958.
3. Annual report of the Worcester State Hospital, 1881.
4. Annual report of the Worcester State Hospital, 1882.
5. Annual report of the Worcester State Hospital, 1883.
6. Babinski, J., & Froment, J. *Hysteria or pithiatism*. London: London University Press, 1918, pp. 28-29.
7. Brigham, A. Moral treatment. *American Journal of Insanity, 4,* 1-15, 1847.
8. Bucknill, J. C., & Tuke, D. H. *A manual of psychological medicine*. London: John Churchill, 1858, p. 9.
9. Butler, J. S. *Curability of insanity and the individualized treatment of the insane*. New York: G. P. Putnam's Sons, 1887.
10. *Commonwealth history of Massachusetts*, A. B. Hart (Ed.), five volumes. New York: The States History Company, 1927.
11. Deutsch, A. *Shame of the states*. New York: Harcourt Brace, 1948.
12. Dickens, C. *American notes*. Leipzig: Bernard Tauchnitz, 1842.
13. Earle, P. *Curability of insanity*. Philadelphia: Lippincott, 1887.
14. Earle, P. *History, description and statistics of the Bloomingdale Asylum of the insane*. New York: Egberg, Hovey and King, 1849.
15. *Essays of William Graham Sumner*, Vol. II. New Haven: Yale University Press, 1934, p. 107.
16. *Ibid.*, pp. 27-28.
17. *Ibid.*, p. 100.
18. *Ibid.*, Vol. I, pp. 86-87.
19. *Ibid.*, Vol. II, p. 95.
20 *Ibid.*, Vol. II, p. 100.

21. First annual report of Worcester State Hospital, 1833.

22. Gray, J. P. Insanity: its frequency, and some of its preventable causes. *American Journal of Insanity, 42,* 1-45, 1885-1886.

23. *Ibid.,* p. 277.

24. *Ibid.,* p. 278.

25. Greenblatt, M., York, R. H., Brown, E. L., & Hyde, R. W. *From custodial to therapeutic patient care in mental hospitals: explorations in social treatment.* New York: Russell Sage Foundation, 1955.

26. Hall, J. H., Zilboorg, G., & Bunker, H. A. *One hundred years of American psychiatry.* New York: Columbia University Press, 1944, p. 386.

27. Hammond, W. A. The non-asylum treatment of the insane. Syracuse: *Transactions of the Medical Society of New York,* 1879.

28. James, W. Letter to Clifford Beers. In *A mind that found itself.* New York: Doubleday, Doran, 1939, p. 261.

29. Kelly, H. A., & Burrage, W. L. *American medical biographies.* Baltimore: Norman, Remington, 1920.

30. Mitchell, S. W. Address before the fifteenth annual meeting of the American Medico-Psychological Association. *Transactions of the American Medico-Psychological Association, I,* 1894.

31. Page, C. W. Dr. Eli Todd and the Hartford Retreat. *American Journal of Insanity, 69,* 783, 1912-1913.

32. *Ibid.,* p. 763.

33. *Ibid.,* p. 782.

34. *Ibid.,* p. 779.

35. Page, C. W. & Butler, J. S. The man and his hospital methods. *Amercian Journal of Insanity, 57,* 490, 1901.

36. *Ibid.,* p. 481.

37. *Ibid.,* p. 499.

38. Pinel, P. *A treatise on insanity.* Translated from the French by D. D. Davis. London: Cadell and Davies, 1806.

39. Ray, I. Recoveries from mental illness. *Medical and Surgical Reporter, 41,* 72-74, 1879.

40. Rowland, H. Interaction processes in the state mental hospital. *Psychiatry, 1,* 323-337, 1938.

41. Sanborn, F. B. *Memoirs of Pliny Earl, M.D.* Boston: Damrell and Upham, 1898, p. 306.

42. *Ibid.,* p. 306.

43. *Ibid.,* p. 150.

44. *Ibid.,* p. 263.

45. *Ibid.,* p. 362.

46. *Ibid.,* p. 281.

47. *Ibid.,* p. 151.

48. *Ibid.,* p. 274.

49. *Ibid.*, p. 299.

50. Williams, S. W. *American medical biography.* Greenfield, Mass.: S. Merriam and Company, Printers, 1845.

51. Woodward, S. B. Annual report of the Worcester Lunatic Hospital, 1842.

52. Zilboorg, G., The unwritten history of an inspiration. *Centennial Papers, St. Elizabeths Hospital.* Baltimore: Waverly Press, 1956, p. 251.

# Bibliography

## BOOKS

A Late Inmate of the Glasgow Royal Asylum for Lunatics at Gartnavel. *The philosophy of insanity*. Edinburgh: Maclachlan & Stewart, 1860.

Ashburn, F. M. *The ranks of death: A medical history of the conquest of America*. New York: Coward-McCann, 1947.

Beard, C. A., & Beard, Mary R. *A basic history of the United States*. New York: Doubleday, Doran, 1944.

Beard, G. M. *American nervousness*. New York: G. P. Putnam's Sons, 1881.

Becker, C. L. *Freedom and responsibility in the American way of life*. New York: Vintage Books, 1955. (First published in 1945 by Alfred A. Knopf.)

Beers, C. W. *A mind that found itself*. New York: Longmans, Green, 1908.

Berger, P. L., & Luckman, T. *The social construction of reality*. New York: Anchor Books, 1967. (First published by Doubleday, 1966.)

Bond, E. D. *Thomas Salmon: psychiatrist*. New York: W. W. Norton, 1950.

Boring, E. G. *History, psychology and science*. New York and London: John Wiley and Sons, 1963.

Brinton, C. *The shaping of the modern mind*. New York: Mentor Books, 1953.

Bromberg, W. *Man above humanity*. Philadelphia: Lippincott, 1954.

Brown, N. O. *Life against death*. New York: Vintage Books, 1961.

*Bulletin of the Isaac Ray Medical Library*, Vols. 1-3, 1953-1955.

Cassirer, E. *An essay on man: An introduction to a philosophy of human culture.* Garden City, New York: Doubleday, 1953.

Centennial Commission, St. Elizabeth's Hospital, *Centennial Papers.* Washington: Centennial Commission, Saint Elizabeth's Hospital, 1956.

Charcot, J. M. *Lectures on diseases of the nervous system* (1881). New York: Hafner Publishing Company, 1962.

Clouston, T. S. *Clinical lectures on mental diseases.* Philadelphia: Lea Brothers & Co., 1897.

Collingwood, R. G. *The idea of history.* London: Oxford University Press, 1946.

Commager, H. S. *The American thought and character since the 1880's.* New Haven: Yale University Press, 1950.

Croce, B. *History as the story of liberty.* New York: Meridian Books, 1955. (First published in English by George Allen and Unwin, 1941.)

Cullen, T. S. *Henry Mills Hurd: The first superintendent of the Johns Hopkins Hospital.* Baltimore: Johns Hopkins Press, 1920.

Dain, N. *Concepts of insanity in the United States, 1789-1865.* New Brunswick: Rutgers University Press, 1964.

Dewey, J. *Reconstruction in philosophy.* New York: Mentor Books, 1950. (First published in 1920 by Henry Holt & Co.)

Feuchtersleben, E. von. *The principles of medical psychology.* London: The Sydenham Society, 1847.

Fish, C. R. *The rise of the common man, 1830-1850.* New York: Macmillan, 1950. (Volume 6 of *A history of American Life* in twelve volumes edited by Arthur M. Schlesinger, Sr., and Dixon Ryan Fox.)

Flugel, J. C. *A hundred years of psychology.* London: Gerald Duckworth and Co., Ltd., 1953.

Francis, W. W. et al (Eds.) *A way of life, and selected writings of Sir William Osler.* New York: Dover Publications, 1958.

Galdston, I. (Ed.) *Historic derivations of psychiatry.* New York: McGraw-Hill, 1967.

Garrison, F. H. *An introduction to the history of medicine.* Philadelphia: Saunders, 1929.

Glass, A. J., & Bernucci, R. J. *Neuropsychiatry in World War Two.* Volume One: *Zone of the Interior.* Washington: Office of the Surgeon General Department of the Army, 1966.

Goldhamer, H., & Marshall, A. M. *Psychosis and civilization: Two studies in the frequency of mental disease.* New York: The Free Press, 1953.

Goshen, C. E. *Documentary history of psychiatry.* New York: Philosophical Library, 1967.

Greenblatt, M., York, R. H., Brown, E. L., Hyde, R. W. *From custodial to therapeutic care in mental hospitals: explorations in social treatment.* New York: Russell Sage Foundation, 1955.

Greenblatt, M., Levinson, D. J., & Williams, R. H. (Eds.). *The patient and the mental hospital: contributions of research in the science of social behavior.* Glencoe, Ill.: Free Press, 1957.

Grob, G. N. *The state and the mentally ill: A history of Worcester State Hospital in Massachusetts 1830-1920.* Chapel Hill: University of North Carolina Press, 1966.

Haggard, H. W. *Devils, drugs, and doctors.* New York: Blue Ribbon Books, 1929.

Haggard, H. W. *The lame, the halt, and the blind.* New York: Blue Ribbon Books, 1932.

Hall, J. K., Zilboorg, G., & Bunker, H. A. (Eds.) *One hundred years of American psychiatry.* New York: Columbia University Press, 1944.

Handlin, O. *Race and nationality in American life.* New York: Doubleday Anchor Books, 1957. (First published by Little, Brown, 1950.)

Handlin, O., & Handlin, M. *The dimensions of liberty.* Cambridge: The Belknap Press of Harvard University Press, 1961.

Haymaker, W. (Ed.) *The founders of neurology.* Springfield, Ill.: Charles C Thomas, 1953.

Heilbroner, R. L. *The wordly philosophers.* New York: Simon & Schuster, 1953.

Hendrick, I. *The birth of an institute: Twenty-fifth anniversary: the Boston psychoanalytic institute.* Freeport, Maine: Bond Wheelwright, 1961.

Hertzler, A. E. *The horse and buggy doctor.* New York: Harper and Brothers, 1938.

Hoffer, E. *Ordeal of change.* New York: Perennial Library, Harper and Row, 1967. (First published by Harper & Row, 1963.)

Hofstadter, R. *The age of reform.* New York: Vintage Books, 1955.

Hofstadter, R. *The American political tradition.* New York: Vintage Books, 1955.

Hofstadter, R. *Social darwinism in American thought.* Boston: Beacon Press, 1955.

Hunter, F. *Community power structure: A study of decision makers.* New York: Anchor Books, 1963. (First published by the University of North Carolina Press, 1953.)

Jarvis, E. *Insanity and idiocy in Massachusetts: Report of the commission on lunacy, 1855* (with a critical introduction by Gerald N. Grob). Cambridge: Harvard University Press, 1971.

Joint Commission on Mental Illness and Health. *Action for mental health.* New York: Basic Books, 1961.

Jones, M. *Social psychiatry.* London: Travistock Publications, Ltd., 1952.

Kastenbaum, R. (Ed.) *New thoughts on old age.* New York: Springer, 1964.

Kastenbaum, R. (Ed.) *Contributions to the psychology of aging.* New York: Springer, 1965.

Kraepelin, E. *One hundred years of psychiatry.* New York: Citadel Press, 1962.

Laski, H. *The American democracy: A commentary and interpretation,* New York: Viking Press, 1948.

Lasswell, H. D. *Psychopathology and politics, 1960.* (First published by the University of Chicago, 1930.)

Ling, T. M. *Mental health and human relations in industry.* New York: Paul B. Hoeber, 1955.

Mahan, A. *The system of mental philosophy.* Chicago: G. C. Griggs, 1883.

Meade, M. (Ed.) *Cultural patterns and technical change.* New York: Mentor Books, 1955. (Copyright 1955 by the United Nations Educational Scientific and Cultural Organization.)

Menninger, K. *Man against himself.* New York: Harcourt, Brace, 1938.

Menninger, K., Mayman, M., & Pruyser, P. *The vital balance.* New York: Viking Press, 1963.

Menninger, K. *The human mind.* New York: Alfred A. Knopf, 1930.

Milbank Memorial Fund. *The biology of mental health and disease.* New York: Paul B. Hoeber, 1952.

Misiak, H., & Sexton, V. S. *History of psychology: An overview.* New York: Grune and Stratton, 1966.

Mumford, L. *The human prospect* (Harry T. Moore and Karl W. Deutsch, Eds.) Beacon Press, 1955.

Munro, H. S. *Suggestive therapeutics.* St. Louis: C. V. Mosby, 1911.

Murphy, G. *Historical introduction to modern psychology.* New York: Harcourt, Brace, 1950.

Oberndorf, C. P. *A history of psychoanalysis in America.* New York: Grune and Stratton, 1953.

Otto, M. C. *Science and the moral life.* New York: Mentor Books, 1949.

Page, C. W. *The care of the insane and hospital management.* Boston: W. M. Leonard, 1912.

Paine, T. *Basic writings of Thomas Paine: Common sense, rights of man, age of reason.* New York: Wiley, 1942.

Persons, S. (Ed.) *Evolutionary thought in America.* New Haven: Yale University Press, 1950.

Pollak, O. *Integrating sociological and psychoanalytic concepts: An exploration in child psychotherapy.* New York: Russel Sage Foundation, 1956.

Pollock, F. *An introduction to the history of the science of politics.* Boston: Beacon Press, 1960. (First published by Macmillan and Co., Ltd. in 1890.)

Popper, K. R. *The poverty of historicism.* New York: Harper Torchbooks, 1964.

Psychopathic Hospital and Board of Insanity, Commonwealth of Massachusetts. *Collected contributions.* Boston. 1916.

Pugh, T. F., & MacMahon, B. *Epidemiologic findings in United States hospital data.* Boston: Little, Brown, 1962.

Ray, I. *A treatise on the medical jurisprudence of insanity* (1838). Winfred Overholser (Ed.), Cambridge: The Belknap Press of Harvard University Press, 1962.

Ridenour, N. *Mental health in the United States: A fifty year history.* Cambridge: Harvard University Press, 1961.

Riesman, D. *The lonely crowd: A study of the changing American character.* Garden City, New York: Doubleday, 1953.

Roback, A. A. *History of American psychology.* New York: Library Publishers, 1952.

Roback, A. A. *History of psychology and psychiatry.* New York: Philosophical Library, 1961.

Robinson, V. *The story of medicine.* New York: New Home Library, 1943.

Runes, D. *The selected writings of Benjamin Rush.* New York: Philosophical Library, 1947.

Rush, B. *Medical inquiries and observations upon diseases of the mind* (1812). New York: Hafner Publishing Company, 1962.

Russel, B. *The conquest of happiness.* New York: Signet Books, 1951. (First published in 1930 by Horace Liveright, Inc.)

Savelle, M. *Seeds of liberty: The genesis of the American mind.* Seattle: University of Washington Press, 1965.

Schlesinger, A. M., Jr. *The age of Jackson.* Boston: Little, Brown, 1946.

Schneck, J. M. *A history of psychiatry.* Springfield, Ill.: Charles C Thomas, 1960.

Shryock, R. H. *The development of modern medicine.* New York: Alfred A. Knopf, 1947.

Sigerist, H. E. *American medicine.* New York: W. W. Norton, 1934.

Spurzheim, J. S. *Observation on the deranged manifestation of the mind, or insanity.* Boston: Marsh, Capen and Lyon, 1833.

Starkey, M. L. *The devil in Massachusetts: A modern enquiry into the Salem witch trials.* Garden City: Dolphin Books, 1961.

State Board of Insanity, Commonwealth of Massachusetts. *Collected Contributions.* Boston: Wright and Potter Printing Company, State Printers, 1916.

Steffens, L. *The shame of the cities.* New York: Hill and Wang, 1957. (First published in 1904 by McClure, Phillips and Co.)

Sullivan, J. W. N. *The limitations of science.* New York: Mentor Books, 1950. (First published in 1933 by the Viking Press.)

Tawney, R. H. *Religion and the rise of capitalism: A historical study.* New York: Mentor Books. 1950. (First published in 1926 by Harcourt, Brace.)

Tiffany, F. *Life of Dorothea Lynde Dix.* Boston: Houghton, Mifflin, 1890.

Tuke, J. B. *The insanity of overexertion of the brain.* Edinburgh: Oliver and Boyd, 1894.

Veblen, T. *The theory of the leisure class.* New York: Mentor Books, 1953. (Published in 1899 and 1912 by Macmillan.)

Waelder, R. *Progress and revolution.* New York: International Universities Press, 1967.

White, M., & White, L. *Intellectual versus the city.* New York: Mentor Books, 1964. (First published in 1962 by Harvard University Press.)

White, W. A. *William Alanson White: The autobiography of a purpose.* New York: Doubleday, Doran, 1938.

Whyte, L. L. *The next development in man.* New York: Mentor Books, 1950.

Worcester, E., McComb, S., & Coriat, L. H. *Religion and medicine.* New York: Moffat, Yard and Company, 1908.

Wydenbruck, N. *Doctor Mesmer.* London: John Westhouse, 1947.

Zilboorg, G., & Henry G. W. *A history of medical psychology.* New York: W. W. Norton, 1941.

## PAPERS

Burnham, J. C. The beginnings of psychoanalysis in the United States. *American Imago*, Vol. *13*, No. 1.

Burnham, J. C., Freud, S., & Hall, G. S. Exchange of letters. *The Psychoanalytic Quarterly, XXIX*: 307-316, 1960.

Carlson, E. T., Amariah Brigham: I. Life and works. *American Journal of Psychiatry, 112*, No. 10, April, 1956.

Carlson, E. T., & Chale, M. F., Dr. Rufus Wyman of the McLean Asylum. *American Journal of Psychiatry, 116,* No. 11, May, 1960.

Carlson, E. T., & McFadden, R. B. Dr. William Cullen on mania. *American Journal of Psychiatry, 117,* No. 5, November, 1960.

Carlson, E. T., & Dain, N. The meaning of moral insanity. *Bulletin of the History of Medicine, XXXVI,* No. 2 March-April, 1962.

Carlson, E. T., & Simpson, M. M. Benjamin Rush on the importance of psychiatry. *American Journal of Psychiatry, 119,* No. 9, March, 1963.

Carlson, E. T., & Simpson, M. M. Opium as tranquilizer. *American Journal of Psychiatry, 120,* No. 2, August, 1963.

Carlson, E. T., & Simpson, M. M. The definition of mental illness: Benjamin Rush (1745-1813). *American Journal of Psychiatry, 121,* No. 3, September, 1964.

Carlson, E. T., & Simpson, M. M. Moral persuasion as therapy. *Current Psychiatric Therapies, IV,* 13-24, Grune and Stratton, 1964.

Carlson, E. T., & Simpson, M. M. Benjamin Rush's medical use of the moral faculty, *Bulletin of the History of Medicine, XXXIX,* No. 1, January-February, 1965.

Dain, N. & Carlson, E. T., Moral insanity in the United States 1835-1866. *American Journal of Psychiatry, 118,* No. 9, March, 1962.

Galdston, I. Trade routes and medicine. *Bulletin of the New York Academy of Medicine.* Second Series, Vol. 37, No. 5, 342-358, May, 1961.

Galdston, I. Doctor and patient in medical history. *Journal of Medical Education, 37,* March, 1962.

Galdston, I. The pathogenicity of progress: An essay on medical historiography. *Medical History, IX,* No. 2, April, 1965.

Garber, R. S. Two Philadelphia psychiatrists and a theory of American psychiatry. *Mental Hygiene, 53,* No. 1, January, 1969.

Grob, G. N. Samuel B. Woodward and the practice of psychiatry in early nineteenth century America. *Bulletin of the History of Medicine, XXXVI,* No. 5, Sept.-Oct., 1962.

Grob, G. N. Adolph Meyer on American psychiatry in 1895. *American Journal of Psychiatry, 119,* No. 12, June, 1963.

Grob, G. N. Origins of the state mental hospital: A case study. *Bulletin of the Menninger Clinic, 29,* No. 2, March, 1965.

Lebensohn, Z. M. American psychiatry—retrospect and prospect. *Medical Annals of the District of Columbia, 31,* No. 7, July, 1962.

Marx, O. M. Freud and aphasia: An historical analysis. *American Journal of Psychiatry 124,* 6, December, 1967.

Marx, O. M. American psychiatry without William James. *Bulletin of the History of Medicine, XLII,* No. 1, Jan.-Feb., 1968.

Marx, O. M. J. C. A. Heinroth (1773-1843) on psychiatry and law. *Journal of the History of the Behavioral Sciences, IV,* No. 2, 163-179, April, 1968.

Marx, O. M. Diet in European psychiatric hospitals, jails, and general hospitals in the first half of the 19th century according to travellers' reports. *Journal of the History of Medicine:* July, 1968.

Marx, O. M. Morton Prince and the dissociation of a personality. *History of the Behavioral Sciences, VI,* No. 2, 120-130, April, 1970.

Marx, O. M. What is the history of psychiatry? *American Journal of Orthopsychiatry, 40,* 4, July, 1970.

Mora, G. Biagio Miraglia and the development of psychiatry in Naples in the eighteenth and nineteenth centuries. *Journal of the History of Medicine and the Allied Sciences, XIII,* No. 4, 1958.

Mora, G. Pietro Pisani and the mental hospital of Palermo in the early 19th century. *Bulletin of the History of Medicine, XXXIII,* No. 3, May-June, 1959.

Mora, G. Bi-centenary of the birth of Vincenzo Chiarugi (1759-1820): A pioneer of the modern mental hospital treatment. *American Journal of Psychiatry, 116,* No. 3, Sept., 1959.

Mora, G. Vincenzo Chiarugi (1759-1820) and his psychiatric reform in Florence in the late 18th century. *Journal of the History of Medicine and the Allied Sciences, XIV,* No. 4, 1959.

Mora, G. Historiographic and cultural trends in psychiatry: A survey. *Bulletin of the History of Medicine, XXXV,* No. 1, Jan.-Feb., 1961.

Mora, G. On the 400th anniversary of Johann Weyer's "De Praestigus Daemonum"—Its significance for today's psychiatry. *American Journal of Psychiatry, 120,* No. 5, November, 1963.

Mora, G. One hundred years from Lombroso's first essay on genius and insanity. *American Journal of Insanity, 121,* No. 6, December, 1964.

Mora, G. The historiography of psychiatry and its development: A re-evaluation. *Journal of the History of the Behavioral Sciences, I,* No. 1, 43-52, January, 1965.

Overholser, W. An historical sketch of psychiatry. *Journal of Clinical Psychopathology, 10,* No. 2, April, 1949.

Overholser, W. Pioneers in Criminology III. Isaac Ray (1807-1881). *Journal of Criminal Law, Criminology and Police Science, 45,* No. 3, September-October, 1954.

Stearns, A. W. Isaac Ray, psychiatrist and pioneer in forensic psychiatry. *American Journal of Psychiatry, 101,* No. 5, March, 1945.

Veith, I. Glimpses into the history of psychotherapy. *Progress in Psychotherapy,* Vol. III.

Veith, I. Freud's place in the history of medicine. *Behavioral Science, II,* No. 1, January, 1957.

Veith, I. Benjamin Rush, M.D., social and political reformer, psychiatrist, physician. *Modern Medicine,* February 20, pp. 198-208, March 6, pp. 186-198, March 20, pp. 220-232, 1961.

Veith, I. Galen's psychology. *Perspectives in Biology and Medicine, IV,* No. 3, Spring, 1961.

Woods, E. A., & Carlson, E. T. The psychiatry of Philippe Pinel. *Bulletin of the History of Medicine, XXXV,* No. 1, Jan.-Feb., 1961.

# Index

287

Impersonal dealings, 87
Impersonality, 85
Incipient mental illness indistin-
guishable from develop-
mental phase of unique individuality, 267
Incurability
belief in, 66
Earles stress on, 50
myth of, 31
Indignity, 6
Individuality
constructive attitudes toward,
248
respect for, 139
Individualized attention, 92
Individual psychotherapy, 36
Industrial idealism, 166
legacy of its breakdown, 167
Industrial organization in contrast
with social disorganization,
254
Industrial urban communities, 89
Inner response of personnel to
clients, 233
Inpatient days, at 6 to 8½ months
follow-up, 174
Inpatient service of mental health
center—question of its indis-
pensibility, 173
Insane asylum, 1
Insane foreign pauper, 22
Insanity, 17, 34, 41, 42, 45, 75
"Insanity is no disease," 42
Insensibility attributed to patients,
88
*Insistent and Fixed Ideas*, 92
Inspired humanism, 262, 263
Inspired leadership, 20
Institutional psychiatry, 3
pertinence of social science to,
103
Intellectual indolence, 39
Intellectual work, 76
Intemperance, 10

Interaction processes in mental hos-
pital wards, 98
Interpersonal relationships, 15
Interpretations, anthropomorphic,
94
Intractable prisoners, patients han-
dled as, 32
Intrigue, semi-political, mental hos-
pitals as centers of, 39
Introspection, meditative specula-
tion approach, 205
Irish immigrants, 23, 24
Irish potato famine, 166
Isaac Ray Library, 145

Jackson, Hughlings, 93, 98
Jacksonian Era, 263
Jails, 38, 39, 43
James, William, 91, 93
Jarvis, Edward, 21, 25
Jefferson, Thomas, 83, 200
Joint Commission for Mental
Health and Illness, 115
Johns Hopkins University, 92
Jung, Karl, 93, 95

Kerr-Mills Act, 158
Kindness, 18, 35, 36, 70, 76
forebearance and, in face of ab-
normal behavior, 77
Kirkbride, Thomas, 21, 22, 36, 43
Kleptomania, 40
Knives and forks provided patients
in moral treatment hos-
pitals, 19
Knowledge and health, means, not
ends, 217
Kraepelin, Emil, 94
Kraepelinian psychiatry, 213

Laboratory facilities, 54
Labor strife, 166
Large hospitals, 22
Law of love in moral treatment,
19, 24

Research, psychiatric, 91
Research, retardation of in mental
hospitals, noted by neurologists, 28
Resistance
in rehabilitation and therapy,
140
to giving service, 141
Respect, 35
for individuality, 82, 139
for patients, 109
Responsible care: moral treatment,
the first practical effort to pro-
vide, 13
Responsibility for relationships, 100
Rest, 40–43
Restraint, 37, 69, 70
abolition of, 42
all forms eliminated at Boston
Psychopathic Hospital, 128
Revolutionary War, 89, 201
Rhode Island Division of Voca-
tional Rehabilitation, 136
Rights, 6, 31, 69, 168
*Rise of the Common Man, The,
1820–1850,* 16
Rockefeller, John D., 209
Romantic movement, 16
Roots of personality, 82
Rothschild, David, 121
Rum and tobacco, Irish castigated
for use of, 24
Rural to urban life, 21
Rush, Benjamin, 13, 200

St. Lawrence Hospital, New York,
92
Sakel, Manfred, insulin treatment
and, 98
Salmon, Thomas, 96
Salpetriere, The, 44
Sanborn, Franklin B., 30, 39, 49
Sanctuary provided by sovereign
state, 201
*Scholar, The,* 16

School
in Bloomingdale Asylum, 72
exercises, 71, 74
School teacher, 45
Science, 10, 11
the final reality, 84
no longer humanistic, 86
priority of, in German universities, 209
Scientific authority, 9
transfer of faith to, 252
Scientific detachment, 85
Scientific experiments, demonstra-
tion of to patients by Earle,
45
Scientific method, 68
Scientific psychiatry, 43, 90
"Scientific Society, The: A Social
Psychosis?," 196
Scientifically proven psychoses, 68
Scientist-politician communication
breakdown, 203
Seclusion
abolition of, 42
reduced greatly at Boston Psy-
chopathic Hospital, 128
Seclusion rooms, convince patients
of futility, 107
Sedative drugs, discontinued at
Boston Psychopathic Hos-
pital, 128
Self-defeating behavior, 243
Self-respect, 19, 36
Sense of responsibility, 82
Sensibilities, 6, 24
Sequestration, 29
Sewing circle, 19
*Shame of the Cities, The,* 251
*Shame of the States, The,* 100, 251
Sharp instruments, patients' use of,
19, 78
Sheltered workshop, 180
Sherrington, Sir Charles, 93, 98
Shopping trips, 7
Sidis, Boris, 92, 93